Major Canadian Authors

DAVID STOUCK

Major Canadian Authors

A Critical Introduction

University of Nebraska Press: Lincoln & London

The paper in this book
meets the guidelines for
permanence and durability of
the Committee on Production
Guidelines for Book
Longevity of the Council
on Library Resources.

Library of Congress Cataloging
in Publication Data

Stouck, David, 1940–
Major Canadian authors.

Bibliography: p.
Includes index.
1. Canadian literature –
History and criticism –
Addresses, essays,
lectures.   I. Title.
PR9184.3.S84   1984
810'.9'971   83-10216
ISBN 0-8032-4119-4

For my mother, Winnifred Stouck

Contents

Preface

This collection of essays is designed to introduce to a wide audience Canada's most important authors writing in English and to give information and critical assessments concerning their work. The essays treat writers of both sexes, from the nineteenth and twentieth centuries, and from east and west, but are confined to the genres of belles lettres—short stories, novels, poetry, and occasionally drama. Several histories and thematic studies of Canadian literature have been published (see the Bibliography), but this is the first book to focus exclusively on major authors and their works.

The essays, arranged chronologically, situate the authors in their historical context and thereby provide a brief outline of the development of Canadian literature. Some of the elements that have shaped Canadian culture (the vast northern wilderness, the long colonial history, the Calvinist strain of religion) are described when an author's work offers a particularly striking illustration, but there is no one thesis underlying this book as a whole. The richness and diversity of a national literature invariably elude a systematized, thematic approach; the full story is best told in terms of the country's most accomplished artists and their finest works. The aim here is to provide the fullest possible access to the individual writers. Each commentary, after situating the author historically, attempts some insight into that author's imagination and offers a description of works that includes mode, structure, and style, as well as moral or social vision.

The selection of major authors, particularly those writing since World War II, is inevitably a matter for some disagreement in a literary tradition that is relatively young and does not number several authors of international renown. I have used two principal criteria for choosing important writers: either they have produced a body of work of consistently high quality, or they have written at least one major piece regarded as an indisputable classic in the canon of Canadian literature. For example, neither Archibald Lampman nor Ethel Wilson could be said to have produced a single work that stands out as one of the country's literary masterpieces, yet the overall quality of their work is very high. Conversely, Sinclair Ross and Earle Birney have published inferior works, but in any overview of Canadian literature Ross's *As for Me and My House* and Birney's poem "David" stand out as undisputed landmarks. This book does not include a study of French Canadian literature; however, there is an essay here on Gabrielle Roy because her novels have appeared quickly in English translations and have constituted a central chapter in the development of Canadian fiction. I have not included discussions of talented younger writers such as Michael Ondaatje, Patrick Lane, Margaret Atwood, or Richard B. Wright, because they are in mid-career and perhaps have not yet published their most significant and lasting works.

Editions of works cited in these essays are those most available to the general reader as well as the scholar. Notes in the first two essays dealing with nineteenth-century prose writers are keyed to abridged, unscholarly editions published in McClelland and Stewart's New Canadian Library series. It seems wholly impractical to give references to original editions that are unavailable to the reader and may remain so for some time. General availability has determined the choice of editions cited for subsequent authors as well.

A book of this kind is an amalgam of information and critical opinion, and I am indebted to the tradition of Canadian literary criticism which informs my interpretations. Sources are too numerous to cite throughout the book but the pervasive influence of certain scholars and teachers must be acknowledged. They include Archibald MacMechan, Desmond Pacey, Carl F. Klinck, Northrop Frye, Roy Daniells, Malcom Ross, Sandra Djwa, George Bowering, and W. H. New.

Acknowledgments

My first debt of gratitude is to the late Virginia Faulkner of the University of Nebraska Press, who suggested this volume and whose initial editorship was a creative force behind the book.

I wish to thank Kathleen and George Quick and Estella Howey, who for several years have faithfully provided me with articles and reviews about Canadian literature; Professor Blanche Gelfant, Dartmouth College, Professor John J. Murphy, Merrimack College, and Professor Warren French, Indiana University and Purdue University, who have been reading Canadian books and encouraging me to write a critical introduction; Pearl and Christopher Kilpatrick and Phyllis and Thomas Swan, who have helped to create for me the space and time in which to write. And once again I acknowledge the influence of my wife, Mary-Ann, whose literary values have provided sure guideposts through the wide range of genres and modes encountered in examining a national literature.

Sections of this work have appeared in different form in the following periodicals: "'Secrets of the Prison-House': Mrs. Moodie and the Canadian Imagination," *Dalhousie Review* 54, no. 3 (Autumn 1974): 463–72, published by Dalhousie University; "The Mirror and the Lamp in Sinclair Ross's *As for Me and My House*," *Mosaic: A Journal for the Comparative Study of Literature and Ideas* 7, no. 2 (Winter 1974): 141–50, published by the University of Manitoba; and "Ethel Wilson's Novels," *Canadian Literature* 74 (Autumn 1977): 74–88, published by the University of British Columbia. I am grateful to the editors of these journals for their encouragement and for their permission to revise and reprint.

The following acknowledgments are made for permission to reproduce the portraits in the book: *Thomas Haliburton*, engraved by D. J. Pound from a photograph by Mayall. Picture Collection, Public Archives of Nova Scotia. *Susanna Moodie*, from the collection of the family of J. F. Killough, Castlegar, British Columbia, descendants of Samuel Strickland, Ontario. *Archibald Lampman*, photo by W. J. Topley, Ottawa. Public Archives Canada, C-68850. *Frederick Philip Grove*, Public Archives Canada, C-36086. *E. J. Pratt*, photo by Ashley and Crippen, Toronto. *Ethel Wilson*, photo by Stanley Read. Special Collections, University of British Columbia Library, Vancouver. *Earle Birney*, photo by Bruce Cole, Plum Studios, Toronto. *Sinclair Ross*, Schiffer Photography, Vancouver, British Columbia. *Ernest Buckler*, from the photograph collection of McClelland and Stewart, Toronto. *Gabrielle Roy*, photo by Annette and Basil Zarov. From the photograph collection of McClelland and Stewart, Toronto. *A. M. Klein*, photo by Garces Studios, Montreal. From the photograph collection of McClelland and Stewart, Toronto. *Irving Layton*, photo by Studio Lausanne, Montreal. From the photograph collection of McClelland and Stewart, Toronto. *Robertson Davies*, photo by Ashley and Crippen, Toronto. *Margaret Avison*, photo by Newsome Photography. From the photograph collection of McClelland and Stewart, Toronto. *Al Purdy*, photo by William Toye, Toronto. Courtesy of Oxford University Press. *Margaret Laurence*, from the photograph collection of McClelland and Stewart, Toronto. *Alice Munro*, photo by Dennis Roberts, Simon Fraser University News Service, Burnaby, British Columbia.

Thomas Haliburton

The first writings about Canada are narratives by the explorers
and missionaries who visited the country in the seventeenth and
eighteenth centuries and left awesome accounts of the country's
vastness, its intemperate climate, and strange inhabitants. These
works belong essentially to a tradition of English travel writing.
The first indigenous literary activity in English Canada appeared
in the Maritime colony of Nova Scotia in the 1830s. The area
was settled in the 1780s after the American Revolution by the
United Empire Loyalists, a large number of whom were educated, professional men, graduates from Harvard and Yale. In the
early part of the nineteenth century the Maritime colonies enjoyed
an economic prosperity that allowed the American and English
settlers to maintain the relatively high standard of living to which
they had been accustomed. But the good European markets for
timber and agricultural products were largely stimulated by the
upheaval of the Napoleonic Wars, and when peace came to Europe, the Maritime economy went into decline. The deflation
of the economy and its attendant political turmoil, however,
brought about the flowering of early Maritime culture in the form
of satirical prose fiction.

In the 1820s Thomas McCulloch, a Scottish emigrant and
Presbyterian minister in Nova Scotia, began publishing a series of
fictional letters in the *Acadian Recorder* in which the thriftlessness and unstable character of a rural Maritime community are
held up for laughter and scorn. McCulloch was genuinely dis-
mayed at the demoralizing effects of the depression, especially the
threat to religious values, and in the fictional person of one
Mephibosheth Stepsure, a shrewd, successful farmer, he instructs
Maritimers that economic depression can be surmounted through
those long cherished Scottish values of hard work and thrift. Step-

sure, who was an orphan and lame from birth, has prospered through hard work, while most of the community has sunk into debt and debauchery. Although *The Letters of Mephibosheth Stepsure* were not published as a book until 1860,[1] they had an important influence in serial form on Thomas Haliburton, author of *The Clockmaker* and the man generally regarded as Canada's first important writer.

Haliburton was born in 1796 in Windsor, Nova Scotia, to a leading Tory family which had migrated north from New England before the outbreak of the American Revolution. He was educated at King's College, Windsor, the seat of Anglicanism and social privilege, and, following his father's footsteps, was called to the bar of Nova Scotia in 1820. He practiced law in Annapolis, and when he was thirty, he was elected to the provincial House of Assembly, the legislative body of the colonial government, where he served as a member for three years. On his father's death in 1829 he succeeded him as a judge of the Court of Common Pleas and in 1841 was made a judge of the Supreme Court of Nova Scotia. When he retired in 1856, he moved to England, where he was elected to the House of Commons, retaining his seat until his death in 1865.

From the time he was a young man, Haliburton was strongly conservative in politics. On certain issues such as education he supported liberal policies (he wanted, for example, to see education taken out of the hands of the Church of England), but he could not support the growing reform movement in the 1830s that called for responsible government in the colonies. Although he thought reasoned protest against Britain's mismanagement of her colonies was justified, he feared that the agitation for reform would end in complete independence, after which the colonies would eventually become part of the United States. Politically, he argued for even closer ties with Britain. However, he contended that the economic situation of Nova Scotians could be improved if they exercised some of the energy and enterprise of the Americans to develop the country's natural resources.

[1] Thomas McCulloch's work is available in the New Canadian Library under the title *The Stepsure Letters* (Toronto: McClelland and Stewart, 1960).

To create an outlet for his political and social opinions, Haliburton followed McCulloch and began in 1835 writing a series of sketches for the *Novascotian*, a Halifax newspaper, in which he traced the ills of his province to the fact that Nova Scotians were lacking in initiative and too dependent on government patronage. He wanted his countrymen to emulate the hard work and ingenuity of the Americans, and so he created the character of Sam Slick, a shrewd outspoken Yankee who travels about the province selling clocks and openly criticizes the people of Nova Scotia, the "Bluenoses," for their dullness and lack of industry. The fact that Sam was an American, an outsider, made the people take note and listen. Sam proclaims to an English squire, who travels with him and serves as narrator for the sketches, that Americans "reckon hours and minutes to be dollars and cents," but that Nova Scotians do nothing but waste their time:

They do nothing in these parts but eat, drink, smoke, sleep, ride about, lounge at taverns, make speeches at temperance meetings, and talk about "House of Assembly." If a man don't hoe his corn, and he don't get a crop, he says it is owing to the bank; and if he runs into debt and is sued, why, he says the lawyers are a curse to the country. They are a most idle set of folks, I tell you.[2]

Sam outlines the American formula for success: "We rise early, live frugally, and work late; what we get, we take care of." He insists that the province is rich in resources, but observes that with the Nova Scotians "it's all talk and no work." Says Sam, "If we had this country, you couldn't see the harbours for the shipping." Sam focuses squarely on what Haliburton thought was the chief failing of the Nova Scotians, their preference for political complaint rather than economic enterprise.

The satire in Haliburton's *Clockmaker* sketches is complicated by the fact that Sam, as a Yankee, is not held up as an ideal. Haliburton admires his self-confidence, his vigour, and his ambition, but decidedly disapproves of his crudeness, his corruptibility, and his love of violence. Sam displays those qualities that make up the American stereotype—he is loud and boastful, a

[2]The most readily available text of *The Clockmaker* is the New Canadian Library edition of the first series (Toronto: McClelland and Stewart, 1958).

manipulator, an opportunist—and in this way Haliburton sati-
rizes the American way of life as well as that of the Nova Scotians. (As Sam is made to say in an introductory letter to the series: "It wipes up the Bluenoses considerable hard, and don't let
off the Yankees so very easy neither.")

Sam's boastful chauvinism is voiced in almost every sketch. He
says to the squire that the stars in the heavens remind him of the
American flag, which is generally considered "the first flag in the
univarse now," and comments on the appropriateness of the eagle
as the American emblem: "afeared of nothin' of its kind, and
president of all it surveys." He outrages the squire's and the
reader's sense of proprieties when he discusses at length the profit
to be made from building churches. He says if a "crack" preacher
can be found and pews let and sold quickly, then it turns out "a
real good investment." Sam is depicted as an energetic entrepreneur who grasps business opportunities that the Bluenoses fail
to see, but he is also revealed to be at times unscrupulous and
unethical. Haliburton wanted Nova Scotians to emulate the
American virtues while avoiding the vices.

The squire is also presented as a national type. Being very
much the correct gentleman, he serves largely as a foil for Sam,
but he has characteristics which are identified as peculiarly English, namely tenacity and pride. In the first sketch the squire
modestly states that he has "made no great progress in the world,"
but takes pride in believing that he owns the fastest horse in the
province. (It is Sam's first achievement, as an American, to pass
him on the road.) In another sketch he confesses that he plays a
game that caresses his vanity; by traveling incognito he hopes to
be taken for an important English lord. One of Haliburton's purposes in these sketches of national types was to make Canadians
(specifically Nova Scotians) try to reach some comparable picture
or definition of themselves.

Haliburton had a simple propagandistic motive for publishing
the *Clockmaker* sketches: he wanted to arouse his countrymen to
the need for agricultural and commercial reforms. He wanted to
see farms enlarged, harbors developed, and railways and canals
built across his province. But this didactic purpose does not stand
in the way of our contemporary enjoyment of his writing. For

Haliburton was a satirist with a broad vision, and the most important and most durable part of his writing in the *Clockmaker* series is his commentary on human nature in general. Much of the humor in the sketches derives from Sam's application of "soft sawder [cider] and human natur'" in order to sell his clocks in a market that is already glutted. Sam's formula combines the use of flattery with a knowledge of human weaknesses. In "Gulling a Bluenose" Sam tells a skeptical client named Zeb Allen that he was wise not to buy one of his clocks, because of late they have been inferior articles. But then Sam mentions an older type of clock of superior make that an important man in the community has commissioned him to find. Believing that the clock is highly valued by this neighbor, Allen insists on buying it, and Sam finally accedes to the sale. But Sam admits to the squire afterward that "he got the most inferior article I had, and I just doubled the price on him." Although Sam is dishonest in his business, we laugh because he has exposed the gullibility and pretensions of a close-fisted farmer who also has a reputation for shady dealings.

Another difficult customer is Deacon Flint, an honest, industrious man, but whose name points to a hardhearted, stingy nature. The sketch in which Sam sells the Flints a clock, titled simply, "The Clockmaker," is one of the best in the series, revealing several facets of Haliburton's humor. Sam stops at the Flint farm on the pretext of saying good-bye to Mrs. Flint before leaving the area, but he is no sooner in the door than he begins to praise extravagantly the deacon's farm. The effect is not lost, although when the conversation turns to the subject of clocks, Deacon Flint says he has a watch and no need for a clock. Sam says he has only one clock left and that it is promised to "neighbour Steel." But then he suddenly notes the lateness of the hour and his promise to be in River Philip by nightfall, whereupon he asks if the Flints would look after the clock for him until his return trip from the States. The Flints comply; and when they are on the road again, Sam tells the squire that the clock is sold, for "we can do without any article of luxury we have never had, but when once obtained, it is not in 'human natur' to surrender it voluntarily."

Much of the humor in this sketch is verbal, with a racy edge that makes fun of the pious, straight-living Flints. Haliburton was especially fond of what is now called anal humor, as is evident in the following exchange where Sam praises the fertility and depth of one of the deacon's fields:

"Why, there ain't such a location in all New England. The Deacon has a hundred acres of dyke—"

"Seventy," said the Deacon, "only seventy."

"Well, seventy; but then there is your fine deep bottom, why I could run a ramrod into it—"

"Interval, we call it," said the Deacon, who though evidently pleased at this eulogium, seemed to wish the experiment of the ramrod to be tried in the right place.

The joke is carried further when Sam tells the deacon he is "in the wrong furrow" and when he tells the squire that it is indeed done with "soft sawder." Some of the jokes are purely verbal as when the squire refers to the Yankee pedlar who sells polyglot Bibles all in English, while others involve more complex literary references. One of the best of these literary jokes alludes to Tristram Shandy and the circumstances of his conception. When Sam leaves the clock for the Flints to look after until his return, we are told that "he delivered the key to the Deacon with a sort of serio-comic injunction to wind up the clock every Saturday night," and that "Mrs. Flint said she would take care it should be done, and promised to remind her husband, in case he should chance to forget it." Mr. Shandy performed his marital duties on the same night of the month that he wound his clock. The Flints are not aware of this sexual joke being made at their expense.

A broader form of comedy lies in Sam's depiction of women. Haliburton himself was happily married twice and is reputed to have always acted as a gentleman towards women, but Sam does not take women seriously and usually refers to them in the same terms as cattle or furniture. When he gives an account of the innkeeper's wife at Amherst, he says she has a "good eye—good foot —neat pastern—fine chest—a clear set of limbs, and carries a good ———" (the expurgating dash is one of Haliburton's favorite comic techniques). The basic joke running throughout the sketches is of women getting the upper hand, becoming fractious and overbearing with their husbands. Sam makes it clear that he has no trouble managing women, because they are as receptive to his "soft sawder" as are his clock customers. When Marm Pugwash, the temperamental innkeeper at Amherst, threatens to raise a storm because Sam and the squire have arrived very late, Sam praises the beauty of her child at great length and observes in a calculated afterthought that the child looks just like its mother. And of course Sam and the squire are treated handsomely that night. In "Taming of a Shrew" Sam tells of a man who has not been successful in managing his domestic affairs, how John Porter was accustomed "to fret and take on dreadful oneasy" because his wife had such a terrible temper. One night Sam shows his friend how to deal with such a woman. In the dark he imitates Porter's voice, and when the woman comes after him, he gives her a sound beating until she is groveling for mercy. When the two men go into the house together, Sam says: "She was all docility now. As we returned we saw a light in the keepin' room, the fire was blazin' up cheerfulsome, and Marm Porter moved about brisk as a parched pea, though silent as dumb, and our supper was ready in no time." Porter, however, does not follow Sam's example, and she soon gets the upper hand again. Sam concludes breezily with a saying of his grandfather's: "A woman, a dog, and a walnut tree. The more you lick them the better they be."

The real humor in these sequences dealing with women lies not so much in the sexist attitudes as in the language and lively dialogue that these situations call forth. In a sketch titled "The Blowin' Time" Sam compares women before and after marriage. Before marriage, says Sam, a woman is pretty and sweet, and so distracting that on a sleigh ride a man is likely to forget the road and capsize the sleigh into a snowdrift. The woman laughs and chatters as she gets up and enjoys herself thoroughly. But after the wedding a man learns, says Sam, that vinegar is made "with plenty of sugar in the water aforehand." And should they go sleighing and upset, says Sam, "it's no longer a funny matter; he catches it right and left."

Her eyes don't look right up to his'n any more, nor her little tongue ring, ring, ring, like a bell any longer; but a great big hood covers her head, and a whappin' great muff covers her face, and she looks like a bag of soiled clothes a-goin' to the brook to be washed.

The joke is crude, but the aptness and lively originality of the similes Sam uses makes these descriptions genuinely funny and memorable.

As a writer of humorous sketches for newspaper serialization, Haliburton was most often making lighthearted fun of human weaknesses, but at the same time there was a breadth to his vision as a satirist that encompassed both an ideal order of existence and a vision of human depravity. The norm by which Haliburton measures the failings of his fellow Nova Scotians is embodied in the life and philosophy of Reverend Hopewell. This minister, who spends much of his time in his garden and who makes, according to Sam, the best cider in Connecticut, holds that farming is the best life for any man or woman. When asked for advice regarding an uncertain youth, he says, "Put him to the PLOUGH, the most nateral, the most happy, the most innocent, and the most healthy employment on the world." This accords with Haliburton's firm conviction that Nova Scotians needed to develop the agricultural resources of their province. Reverend Hopewell describes his pastoral picture of the good life in a little sermon to Sam:

These are the pleasures . . . of a country life. A man's own labour provides him with food, and an appetite to enjoy it. Let him look which way he will, and he sees the goodness and bounty of his Creator, his wisdom, his power, and his majesty. There never was anything so true, as that 'ere old sayin' "Man made the town, but God made the country," and both bespeak their architects in terms too plain to be misunderstood. The one is filled with virtue, and the other with vice. One is the abode of plenty, and the other of want; one is a ware-duck of nice pure water, and t'other one a cess-pool. . . . No, *make a farmer of a man, and you will have the satisfaction of seeing him an honest, an independent, and a respectable member of society.*

The minister's picture of the good life carries weight because he is neither foolishly sentimental nor naïve regarding the nature of society. He recognizes that factories are necessary to produce many of the goods people use and enjoy, and as a minister he acknowledges the value of the professions, whether law, medicine, or the ministry. But the most important life, he insists, though not the most fashionable, is the farm. "That is an innocent and happy vocation. Agriculture was ordained by Him as made us, for our chief occupation." Haliburton allies himself with the conservative values of the eighteenth-century English squire.

Haliburton knows, however, that people seldom choose the good life on their own, that they are more often persuaded by laziness, greed, and the herd instinct to follow in the well-beaten path of the majority. Satire is usually grounded in a basic cynicism regarding human nature, and through Sam's father we are given a glimpse of life's uglier side. In "The Dancing Master Abroad" (the title of the sketch referring to the antics of the political candidate at election time), Sam's father, enjoying praise and monetary success on winning a horse race, cautions his son that a crowd is always fickle and that popularity soon won is soon lost. In a cynical mood he tells Sam that it is the very same in politics: "Serve the public nine hundred and ninety-nine times, and the thousandth, if they don't agree with you, they desart and abuse you." He gives examples: "See how they sarved old John Adams; see how they let Jefferson starve in his old age; see how good old Munroe like to have got right into jail, after the term of President was up." With anarchistic fervor he advises Sam never to have anything to do with elections. As for the independence much prized by Americans, Sam's father says its true source and mainstay is, not ideals, but a well-lined pocket. The old man's skepticism is rooted, not in a churlish, cynical nature, but in his experience as a soldier in the Revolutionary War. His conscience is still troubled by the fact that during the battle at Bunker's Hill he was forced to kill a man: "A rael handsum man: I can see him now with his white breeches and black gaiters, and red coat." He says that he still dreams about the man: "I see him as plain as if he was afore me; and I go over it all ag'in till I come to that 'ere shot, and then I leap right up in bed and scream like all vengeance." Sam's father is a mouthpiece for Haliburton, for the old man questions the wisdom and justice of the revolution and calls American democracy rule by a mob. In a strikingly prophetic note (the sketch was written in 1835) Sam's father states that "the blood we shed in our Revolution will be atoned for in the blood and suffering of our fellow citizens. The murders of the civil war will be expiated by a political suicide of the state."

There are several such observations on the political and economic turmoils of the nineteenth century, but the lasting pleasure in reading the *Clockmaker* sketches lies, not in what is said, but in how it is said, in the humor and the vitality of Haliburton's oral style. Although the squire generally introduces each sketch in his formal English speech, it is long-winded Sam who does most of the talking in a dialect that imitates New England country speech. Sam's speech is exaggerated (although the essence of satirical humor lies in exaggeration and distortion), and he characteristically speaks at great length, but there is a vividness and an audacity of expression to everything he says which delights the reader by its very energy. Sam's language is filled with similes and metaphors constructed from everyday experiences.[3] His description of a man belonging to a vegetarian religious sect provides a good example of the richness and inventiveness of Sam's comparisons:

I once travelled all through the State of Maine with one of them 'ere chaps. He was as thin as a whippin' post. His skin looked like a blown bladder arter some of the air had leaked out, kinder wrinkled and rumpled like, and his eye as dim as a lamp that's livin' on a short allowance of ile. He put me in mind of a pair of kitchen tongs, all legs, shaft, and head, and no belly; a real gander-gutted lookin' critter, as holler as a bamboo walkin' cane, and twice as yaller. He actilly looked as if he had been picked off a rack at sea, and dragged through a gimlethole. He was a lawyer. Thinks I, the Lord a massy on your clients, you hungry, half-starved lookin' critter you, you'll eat 'em up alive as sure as the Lord made Moses. You are just the chap to strain at a gnat and swallow a camel, tank, shank, and flank, all at a gulp.

There is a freshness and originality in Haliburton's use of literary dialect, and he is credited as the author of such familiar phrases as "stick-in-the-mud" and "quick as a wink" and with aphoristic statements like:

---

[3] There is a good discussion of Haliburton's style in L. A. A. Harding's "Folk Language in Haliburton's Humour," *Canadian Literature* 24 (Spring 1965): 47–51. Harding describes Haliburton's homely similes and earthy, colloquial language, which he says comes from the farms, the workshops, the kitchens, and the wharves of Nova Scotia.

The early bird gets the worm.

An ounce of prevention is worth a pound of cure.[4]

Sam also delights in constructing his own words such as *wamble-cropt* ("feeling nauseated") and in using archaic ones like *meeching* ("pale, skulking") and *transmogrify* ("alter, change"). The verbal fun in these sketches is inexhaustible.

H. L. Mencken gives Haliburton a place beside Seba Smith and James Russell Lowell as one of the "pioneers of a really indigenous humour." V. L. O. Chittick, who has written a book and several articles on Haliburton, points to Seba Smith as an important influence on Haliburton.[5] Seba Smith, a Maine journalist, created Jack Downey, a peddler of ax-handles, hoop-poles, and so forth, who is a country bumpkin but is shrewd in business matters and comments on the political stupidity evident at the local legislative hall. He writes letters back home filled with his observations on life and politics in town. Downey's fictional letters were published by Smith in the *Portland* (Maine) *Daily Courier* beginning in 1830 and were immensely popular and frequently imitated throughout the country. In both style and content they would have provided Haliburton with an obvious model. Chittick suggests that Haliburton in turn inspired Artemus Ward and therefore played an important role in a tradition of humorous writing which in the United States culminated in the work of Mark Twain.[6]

The popularity of Sam Slick on both sides of the Atlantic resulted in eleven volumes of his sayings and doings: *The Clockmaker*, in three volumes; *The Attaché*, in four volumes; *Sam Slick's Wise Saws* and its sequel, *Nature and Human Nature*, in two volumes each. Sam changes his occupation in the various volumes; from being a peddler of clocks he becomes an attaché

[4] See R. E. Watters's introduction to *The Sam Slick Anthology*, by Thomas C. Haliburton (Toronto: Clarke, Irwin, 1969), p. xvii.

[5] See Walter S. Avis, "A Note on the Speech of Sam Slick," in *The Sam Slick Anthology* (Toronto: Clarke, Irwin, 1969), p. xxi; V. L. O. Chittick, "The Hybrid Comic: Origins of Sam Slick," *Canadian Literature* 14 (Autumn 1962): pp. 35–42.

[6] V. L. O. Chittick, *Thomas Chandler Haliburton* (New York: Columbia University Press, 1924), pp. 358–84.

to the American embassy in England and eventually a special American commissioner studying the fisheries of the Maritime provinces. As so often with sequels, the first pieces are the best. As the series continued, Haliburton addressed his sketches more frequently to the political and economic ills of his day; although Sam retains his boisterous high spirits, his outrageous sense of humor, and colorful speech, his opinions are more focused on specific issues that Haliburton felt needed immediate attention. The first series, published in Joseph Howe's *Novascotian* still holds the broadest universal appeal.

Artemus Ward is said to have called Haliburton "the father of American humour,"[7] ignoring, ironically enough, Haliburton's prized identity as a Canadian. The confusion arises because Sam Slick so much embodies the American national type. But in fact Haliburton could be said to be the father of Canadian literature, for on many levels he anticipates the concerns of subsequent Canadian writers. We find voiced in an early sketch, "The American Eagle," the perennial Canadian fear that someday the country will be taken over by the United States. Sam says that Nova Scotians "must recede before our free and enlightened citizens, like the Indians . . . they must give place to a more intelligent and active people." In a speech filled with Manifest Destiny convictions, Sam tells the squire that Nova Scotians will eventually have to move to Labrador, until another wave of American civilization reaches them: "I hear the bugle of destiny a-soundin' of their retreat, as plain as anything." As Sam and the squire ponder the future of the Nova Scotians, Haliburton raises another perennial question: Just what is a Canadian? How does he differ from the braggart American and the supercilious squire? What traits can he call his own? Haliburton wants his Canadian readers to take stock of themselves. Perhaps he intends one idea: that Canadians have a different way of laughing at things. Where British humor is class-structured, one group laughing at the eccentricities of another, and where American humor involves deflating society's most cherished assumptions, Canadian humor stems from an ironic perspective on both society and self. As Sam

---

[7] *Ibid.*, p. 358.

laughs at the Nova Scotians for their want of shrewdness and enterprise, his creator takes a clear-eyed look at both his society and himself. In this way Haliburton stands at the wellsprings of a society and a literature wherein self-scrutiny is one of the prevailing modes.

Selected Writings

An Historical and Statistical Account of Nova Scotia. 2 vols. Halifax: Joseph Howe, 1829.

The Clockmaker; or, The Sayings and Doings of Samuel Slick, of Slickville. First Series. Halifax: Joseph Howe, 1836. Published anonymously. Second and Third Series in 1838 and 1840. Many later editions, including McClelland and Stewart's New Canadian Library Series, no. 6, (Toronto, 1958).

The Attaché; or, Sam Slick in England. First Series. 2 vols. London: Bentley, 1843. Published anonymously. Second Series, 1844.

The Old Judge; or, Life in a Colony. 2 vols. London: Colburn, 1849. Published anonymously. Reprint, edited by R. E. Watters (Toronto: Clarke, Irwin, 1968).

Sam Slick's Wise Saws and Modern Instances; or, What He Said, Did, or Invented. 2 vols. London: Hurst and Blackett, 1853.

Nature and Human Nature. 2 vols. London: Hurst and Blackett, 1855. Published anonymously.

Susanna Moodie

Unlike their counterparts in the Maritimes, the Loyalists who settled in Upper Canada (later Ontario) were for the most part farmers concerned with clearing the land and were not engaged in literary activities. But between 1825 and 1840, as a result of economic depression in Britain, large numbers of English-speaking immigrants entered the province. In their number were many educated men and women, some of whom were published authors. The latter continued to produce verse and fiction for an English audience, but the experience of coming to Canada itself produced a new literary form, the emigration book, which has an important place in the history of Canadian literature. Books about emigration describe for the prospective settler the trip to the New World and the difficulties encountered during the first years and give much practical information on such topics as food, clothing, weather, and recreation. The style of such narratives is heavily realistic, the tone counseling. Between 1815 and 1840 there were no less than one hundred such books published in Britain, many of which found their way to Canada with the immigrants' belongings. The emigration book was used for a variety of literary purposes: the Scottish-born novelist John Galt adapted it to fiction in *Bogle Corbet* (1831), the realistic story of a middle-aged pioneer in Upper Canada; William "Tiger" Dunlop burlesqued the genre in *Statistical Sketches of Upper Canada* (1832), while feminist Anna Jameson in *Winter Studies and Summer Rambles* (1838) used it as a vehicle for travel writing and for giving an account of the position of women in both frontier and savage life.

The writers in this genre who left the most lasting imprint on Canadian literature were two sisters, Catharine Parr Traill and Susanna Moodie, who emigrated to Canada with their husbands

in 1832. Both women pioneered with their families in the bush country near Peterborough, Ontario, and the books they published give a realistic and sometimes harrowing account of the early settler's life. Mrs. Traill and Mrs. Moodie, however, wrote books which were vastly different from each other, reflecting the flexibility of the genre. Mrs. Traill, who approached emigration not just as a necessity but as an adventure, wrote a series of letters home to her mother describing in detail the difficulties and pleasures of settling in the new country. Mrs. Traill's letters were published as *The Backwoods of Canada* in 1836 and proved so popular that she subsequently published *The Canadian Settler's Guide* in 1855, a storehouse of information and wisdom about life in Canada. Whether she is describing in loving detail the plant life in the new country or giving recipes and useful hints for homemaking in a log cabin, Mrs. Traill is exhilarated by her subject and makes emigration an attractive prospect. In the very opposite vein Mrs. Moodie sets out in *Roughing It in the Bush*, published in 1852, to warn prospective emigrants against coming to Canada unless they are willing to work exceedingly hard and endure privations of every kind. Although Mrs. Moodie casts herself as a survivor, the tone of her narrative is grimly antiheroic as she recounts her failure to adapt to the life of the backwoods.

Mrs. Moodie was born Susanna Strickland in Suffolk, England, in 1803, to an upper-middle-class family that numbered several accomplished authors among its members. Before emigrating to Canada, Susanna had published a book of verse, *Enthusiasm and Other Poems* (1831), and looked forward to a career as a writer in England. The Strickland family, however, fell victim to the severe depression that settled over Britain after the Napoleonic Wars; and Susanna and her husband, J. W. D. Moodie, a half-pay officer in the British army, like many genteel poor in England and Scotland, took up a land grant in the colony of Upper Canada as a way of salvaging their dwindling circumstances. Mrs. Moodie was comforted by the proximity of her sister Catharine and a brother Samuel (who in *Twenty-seven Years in Canada West*, published in 1853, also gave an account of pioneering), but she lived nonetheless with the hope of returning home to England and becoming a celebrated writer like two of her sisters who remained there.[1] The Moodies, however, were not successful pioneers, and with each passing year the chances of being able to return to England grew more remote. As a refined gentlewoman accustomed to keeping servants and enjoying literary society, Mrs. Moodie was not prepared for the hardships she experienced during her early years in Canada or for the disrespectful treatment she received from the other settlers in the area, who made fun of her attempts to preserve her English customs. Her only cultural tie with the larger world during the years she lived in the backwoods trying to raise a large family was her affiliation with the Montreal journal, the *Literary Garland*, to which she contributed poetry, sketches, and serialized fiction. The loneliness and frustration of those years are poignantly distilled in the sketches which make up *Roughing It in the Bush*, some of which were first printed in the *Garland*.

Mrs. Moodie was not unfamiliar with the sketch as a literary form when she undertook to describe her life in the woods. In England she had written a number of prose sketches for a London journal entitled *La Belle Assemblée*, using Suffolk legends as told to her by elderly natives of the region. She was attempting in her early compositions to emulate the work of a popular local colorist, Mary Russell Mitford, who did sketches of Berkshire life and published them in five volumes as *Our Village: Sketches of Rural Character and Scenery* (1824–37). Mitford in turn had been an admirer of Washington Irving's *Sketch Book of Geoffrey Crayon* (1818).[2]

A collection of sketches (Thoreau's *Walden* is a good example of this form developed to its highest literary and philosophical end) achieves its unity and interest from the personality of the writer. What is fascinating in *Roughing It in the Bush* is the way

[1] The story of the Strickland family is told by Audrey Y. Morris in *Gentle Pioneers* (Toronto: Hodder and Stoughton, 1968). For a shorter account, see Clara Thomas's "The Strickland Sisters," in *The Clear Spirit*, ed. Mary Innis (Toronto: University of Toronto Press, 1966).

[2] See Carl Ballstadt, "Susanna Moodie and the English Sketch," *Canadian Literature* 51 (Winter 1972): 32–38. *Roughing It in the Bush* can also be viewed in the context of travel writing. See Janet Giltrow's "'Painful Experience in a Distant Land': Mrs. Moodie in Canada and Mrs. Trollope in America," *Mosaic* 14, no. 2 (Spring 1981): 131–44.

Mrs. Moodie's public statements continually belie the drift of her unconscious feelings. As Margaret Atwood has put it in the preface to her poems about this writer, Mrs. Moodie speaks with two voices: with one, her public voice, she attempts to affirm the myths of the pioneer experience and lauds Canada as the land of future promise; but with the other, her private voice, she inadvertently expresses negative, inadmissable feelings which invalidate her patriotic rhetoric.[3] The fundamental opposition between these voices (between what is socially acceptable and what is privately felt) reveals a dichotomy in the author's personality and gives the book an imaginative dimension which other accounts of life in the Canadian backwoods do not have.

Mrs. Moodie's imaginative conflict is most strikingly apparent in the book's style—in the contrast between the Wordsworthian and sentimental response to the landscape and the writer's realistic day-to-day observations. She asserts in rhapsodic fashion that the mountains along the Saint Lawrence form a "stupendous background to a sublime view":

As the clouds rolled away from their grey, bald brows . . . they loomed out like mighty giants—Titans of the earth, in all their rugged beauty— a thrill of wonder and delight pervaded my mind. The spectacle floated dimly on my sight—my eyes were blinded with tears—blinded by the excess of beauty. I turned to the right and to the left, I looked up and down the glorious river, never had I beheld so many striking objects blended into one mighty whole! Nature had lavished all her noblest features in producing that enchanting scene.[4]

The landscape in this passage is scarcely described; the distant panorama yields to an idea and correspondent emotion which blinds the narrator to the actual scene. The idea of nature as an unfailing source of inspiration persists throughout the book, and in her public-spirited, affirmative mood, Mrs. Moodie asserts that "Nature ever did, and I hope ever will, continue: *'To shoot marvellous strength into my heart.'*" But that very passage is followed

---

[3] Margaret Atwood, *The Journals of Susanna Moodie* (Toronto: Oxford University Press, 1970), p. 42.

[4] All references are to the abridged New Canadian Library text of *Roughing It in the Bush* (Toronto: McClelland and Stewart, 1964), pp. 22–23.

by a confession that her feeling for Canada was like the feeling of a condemned criminal whose only hope for escape from prison is through the grave. In the accounts of day-to-day life there are descriptions of nature which, far from Wordsworthian rapture, direct us to an undercurrent of negative feelings about the country and the conditions of pioneer life:

A thaw in the middle of winter is the most disagreeable change that can be imagined. After several weeks of clear, bright, bracing, frosty weather, . . . you awake one morning surprised at the change in the temperature; and, upon looking out of the window, behold the woods obscured by a murky haze—not so dense as an English November fog, but more black and lowering—and the heavens shrouded in a uniform covering of leaden-coloured clouds, deepening into a livid indigo at the edge of the horizon. The snow, no longer hard and glittering, has become soft and spongy, and the foot slips into a wet and insidiously-yielding mass at every step. From the roof pours down a continuous stream of water, and the branches of the trees, collecting the moisture of the reeking atmosphere, shower it upon the earth from every dripping twig. [p. 151]

In this mood the author describes not just the horizon but also the details in the foreground in a realistic, documentary style which is closer to the style of Frederick Philip Grove than to her contemporaries. This is the mood in which Mrs. Moodie explores her genuinely imaginative feelings about Canada, though at the same time never allowing herself to abandon the nineteenth-century myths of nature, mother country, and pioneer.

The conflict of styles, however, involves much more than simply a literary manner unevenly executed. The Wordsworthian stance was for Mrs. Moodie not just a learned set of attitudes or an affected literary pose, but involved a definition of self fundamental to survival in the backwoods. The Moodies were repeatedly exploited and victimized in all their transactions with their neighbors. John Moodie lacked force and practical wisdom, and Susanna lived with a physical fear of her neighbors. Both had an inordinate dread of being laughed at. In her account of her life in the woods, we see Mrs. Moodie clinging desperately to her role as a gentlewoman and a woman of letters in order to evade relationships with the other settlers. Frequently the reader's first opinion of Mrs. Moodie is that she is an intolerable prude, proud and affected beyond endurance. She defines her Canadian neighbors as her inferiors both socially and intellectually and thus explains her reluctance to participate in their society. At times we may feel like her nearest neighbor, "Mrs. Joe," who one day finds Mrs. Moodie scrubbing a tubful of clothes and says: "Well! I am glad to see you brought to work at last. I hope you may have to work as hard as I have. I don't see, not I, why you, who are no better than me, should sit still all day, like a lady!" (p. 101). But some forms of pride have their source in feelings of self-doubt, and in order to read Mrs. Moodie's book with any sympathy, one must recognize that her role-playing throughout is a bulwark against a profound sense of inadequacy. Indeed, at the time of Mrs. Joe's sneering remarks, the author is trying to wash out the baby's things and has rubbed the skin off her wrists. In all her efforts at pioneer house-keeping—baking bread, milking cows, making maple sugar—she is remarkably unsuccessful.

But Mrs. Moodie's role as a gentlewoman in the backwoods is an uneasy one because her sister Catharine took cheerfully to pioneer tasks and published domestic guides for female settlers coming to Canada. Mrs. Moodie's sense of failure and inadequacy in fact extends further than ineptitude in the backwoods; it is rooted deeply in her nature and is given direct expression when she reflects on her separation from England. In outbursts of homesickness she upbraids herself as a guilty, unworthy creature whose exile in Canada is a form of punishment for an unspecified crime:

Dear, dear England! why was I forced by stern necessity to leave you? What heinous crime had I committed that I, who adored you, should be torn from your sacred bosom, to pine out my joyless existence in a foreign clime? Oh that I might be permitted to return and die upon your wave-encircled shores, and rest my weary head and heart beneath your daisy-covered sod at last! [p. 56]

Death is the price the writer is willing to pay in order to be re-united with the maternal land. The same bargain is metaphorically struck at least twice again in the narrative. When taking up her first residence in the backwoods, Mrs. Moodie's thoughts are full of England: "One simple word dwelt forever in my heart, and swelled it to bursting—'Home!' I repeated it waking a thousand times a day, and my last prayer before I sank to sleep was still

'Home! Oh, that I could return, if only to die at home!'"(p.67). Later the sound of the stream near the log cabin makes her thoughts journey back to England, and she concludes that her only escape from Canada will be "through the portals of the grave." Although Mrs. Moodie nostalgically romanticizes the past ("the daisied meadows of England . . . the fragrant shade of her green hedgerows"), a conviction of guilt and failure is her actual legacy from the mother country, which did not provide her family with a livelihood and forced her to emigrate.

When she first reaches Canada, she looks upon the new country as a possible refuge, a "second Eden." As she and her husband step ashore at Grosse Isle, they instinctively draw away from "the noisy, riotous crowd" to a little secluded copse by a river. The scene inspires Mrs. Moodie with content at having found a haven from "the cold, sneering world," but the idyllic Canadian scene is quickly spoiled by "the profane sounds" and "discordant yells" of her fellow emigrants, whom she bitterly designates as "filthy beings." In spite of her Wordsworthian faith in nature and the ennobling effects of poverty, Mrs. Moodie soon finds Canada no second Eden. Her sense of failure is reinforced by her anomalous presence in the backwoods, and she retreats into her role as a gentlewoman in exile. Only through her writing can Mrs. Moodie salvage something of her self-respect, and here she significantly evades self-knowledge and dramatizes herself in her public voice as a martyr figure—first as a victim of unjust social conditions in England, and second as a self-sacrificing pioneer, forgoing personal happiness so that a new country can be formed.

Roughing It in the Bush is no affecting creation story with Mrs. Moodie a figure of fertility. The author remains emotionally fixated on the past ("Dear, dear England"), and her creative instincts are immobilized by feelings of rejection and inadequacy. In lieu of personal achievements her narrative focuses on an impersonal image of growth—the idea of Canada, "a noble, free, and rising country," and the idea of humanity slowly but surely moving toward the fulfillment of a sublime and mysterious destiny—a sentimental vision accommodating both Victorian Christianity and Social Darwinism. Such statements throughout the book project an idealized and dramatic sense of self in relation to society, but one which is inadequate as a total self-image. More revealing and suggestive is the way random vignettes in the narrative—the vivid character sketches and the anecdotes—fall together to form a pattern of social aversion and a preoccupation with failure and death.

All the characters that Mrs. Moodie describes at any length are, like herself, totally out of place in the backwoods. The pattern is begun with the description of the Moodies' friend in England, Tom Wilson. Scarcely a promising pioneer, he is described as "a man in a mist, who seemed afraid of moving about for fear of knocking his head against a tree, and finding a halter suspended to its branches—a man as helpless and as indolent as a baby." The tone here is deliberately comic, and yet there is a note of concern in the narrator's voice which suggests a sympathetic identification with her friend. In the same vein she writes: "Tom would have been a treasure to an undertaker. He would have been celebrated as a mute; he looked as if he had been born in a shroud, and rocked in a coffin" (pp. 49–50). Tom has already failed as an emigrant to Australia and soon matches that adventure with a similar experience in Canada. The Moodies look after him for a while (characters like Tom Wilson are the only society they ever do seem to entertain), but he eventually returns to England, having lost everything he started out with.

Tom Wilson belongs to a remarkable gallery of characters who are failures and who are associated with death in some form. After Wilson leaves, the Moodies hire an Irish boy, John Monaghan, who is seeking refuge from a harsh master. He is a spirited youth, but dogged by misfortune which he attributes to the fact that he is an orphan. We hear an echo of the narrator's own preoccupation—she calls herself an "orphan of civilization"—which is underscored by Monaghan's obsession that he is actually of gentle birth. Brian, the Still-Hunter, another emigrant from Britain, is a man of genuine despair. He appears at the log house one day without speaking and follows this visit with several more, doing little kindnesses for Mrs. Moodie. Once a man of much promise, he began drinking, and as he grew more incontinent, he became disgusted at having betrayed his family's hopes. A first attempt at suicide (he slashed his own throat) failed, but Mrs.

Moodie tells us that some years after she left the bush, she heard that he finally succeeded in taking his own life. Brian's sense of guilt and his suicidal despair seem to touch something at the quick of the narrator. The story of Phoebe R——, the sensitive and gentle child born to the uncouth family of "Uncle Joe," is a paradigm of the author's own feeling of being unappreciated and unjustly treated by the world. That girl's early death moves the narrator to an outburst of grief that is colored by self-pity: "Gentle child of coarse, unfeeling parents, few shed more sincerely a tear for thy early fate than the stranger whom they hated and despised" (p. 120).

Perhaps the most vivid of the character sketches is the portrait of Malcolm, "the Little Stumpy Man," who, uninvited, stays with the Moodies for nine months. Mrs. Moodie's unyielding social manner is nowhere as omnipresent and oppressive. One critic has suggested that Mrs. Moodie's fear of Malcolm and his ill temper is sexual in origin, that she is at a fundamental level attracted to him physically.[5] Typically, Mrs. Moodie deflects the reader's attention from herself to the unscrupulous character of her visitor and thereby covers her true feelings. She was writing, of course, in a prohibitive, genteel tradition, so that sex is limited to such innocent vignettes as the courtship of the servants, Jacob and Mary. But when sex does appear, violence and death are its corollary. When Malcolm, left alone one day with Mrs. Moodie, tells his story, he reveals that he is a murderer (he once shot a man in South America) and is haunted by guilt. The same unrecognized equation is more blatantly operative in the charivari stories, where sex is invariably a cause for violence and, in the case of the black who marries a white woman, the occasion for death.

We do not know the exact process by which *Roughing It in the Bush* took final shape, whether extracted from diaries or written as sketches entirely from memory. In the reshaping of the original experience Mrs. Moodie selects and omits details in response to the unconscious drift of her feelings and in accord with a dra-

[5] See R. D. MacDonald, "Design and Purpose," *Canadian Literature* 51 (Winter 1972): pp. 20–31.

matic sense of self. *Roughing It* accordingly has a definite shape in both the structure of its events and its patterns of imagery. The picture of Canada as a land of failure and death is present from the beginning with the ship of immigrants journeying into a country laid waste by cholera. The first paragraphs of the book describe the inspection and warning by the health officers when the boat reaches Montreal, and one of the doctors is described as "no bad representative of him who sat upon the pale horse." Mrs. Moodie emotionally seeks a second Eden, but when she looks at the new land, she says, "The lofty groves of pine frowned down in hearse-like gloom upon the mighty river." Montreal is a city of death, and among the first people that the Moodies meet and talk with are a middle-aged couple who have just lost their son in the plague—their son who was their only child and their reason for coming to a new land. Mrs. Moodie later tells the reader that after staying in Canada for a long time, "it is as if the grave has closed over you."

Her sense of expiating some unnamed guilt, however, brings her to love her prison, her grave in the backwoods, and when her husband finally arranges their move to Belleville, she is reluctant to leave her "dear forest home . . . consecrated by the memory of a thousand sorrows." Mrs. Moodie's final stance in the book is not unlike that of the Ancient Mariner, who tells of his voyage through guilt, despair, and death and who reemerges to warn those who might follow in his path.

Mrs. Moodie concludes *Roughing It in the Bush* by asserting that for the gentleman without money emigration to Canada presents no advantages. She summarizes the value of her experience for the reader in images of disaster. "If these sketches," she writes, "should prove the means of deterring one family from sinking their property, and shipwrecking all their hopes, by going to reside in the backwoods of Canada, I shall consider myself amply paid for revealing the secrets of the prison-house, and feel that I have not toiled and suffered in the wilderness in vain" (p. 237). The Moodies' situation improved somewhat in the 1840s when John Moodie was appointed sheriff for Hastings County and the family moved to the town of Belleville on Lake Ontario, and we know that Mrs. Moodie before her death in

1885 did find some happiness in the land she was forced to adopt. But in a sequel, *Life in the Clearings* (1853), her praise for the country's democratic spirit and its economic prospects is again undercut by her preoccupation with failure and defeat.

Life in the Clearings, structured around a pleasure trip to Niagara Falls, is an interesting picture of life in the young towns and cities along Lake Ontario. Its purpose is to analyze the social scene, but the real interest of the book lies in the series of narratives that the author relates about the people she meets or hears about on the way. Once again her curiosity is stirred by "odd characters," as she titles one of her chapters, and she finds them in the places she chooses to visit—a religious camp meeting, a village funeral, a traveling circus, a prison, and the insane asylum in Toronto. The characters she describes remind us of those bizarre and desperate figures in *Roughing It*. There is Michael McBride, an Irish boy who dies after being cruelly misused by his uncle in Canada, and Jeanie Burns, a pathetic Scottish girl who dies after traveling to Canada and finding that her fiancé has married another. There is the tale of two children lost in the forest, and the remarkable story of the murderess, Grace Marks, whom Mrs. Moodie finds years later in the Toronto asylum. The bereaved, abandoned, and crazed appear on almost every page, and their stories are told with genuine sympathy.

Roughing It in the Bush is a classic in the Canadian literary heritage, yet it is a book which has resisted definition and critical assimilation. Part of the reason for this is the sketch form, which admits all manner of literary expression; Mrs. Moodie accordingly lets the Crusoe-like interest of her book (her account of survival in the backwoods) be diverted for long stretches by landscape descriptions, character portraits, and so forth.[6] But the greater reason for the confused and dislocated responses to this book lies in our learned cultural expectations. As North Americans we have been conditioned to view the pioneer experience as the he-

[6] In "Crusoe in the Backwoods: A Canadian Fable?," *Mosaic* 9, no. 2 (Winter 1976): 115–26, T. D. MacLulich argues that the Crusoe dimension to Mrs. Moodie's story is also undercut by her failure to adapt and change. Her tale of exile and deliverance, says MacLulich, lacks the repentance and alteration of character which Robinson Crusoe undergoes.

roic period of our history, as a simpler and more affirmative era in which our ancestors made creative sacrifices to ensure and enhance the lives of future generations. But *Roughing It* is no splendid celebration of pioneer life such as one finds in the classic texts of American literature, no Franklinesque account of how to rise in the world; rather, it is a tale of hardship and misery which culminates in withdrawal and defeat. Above all it is a book which denies the myths of renaissance and individual power in a new land. But if one relinquishes what might have ideally been a heroic account of pioneer life, one is rewarded in turn with a book much richer than expected, one which comments directly on the imaginative life of Canada.

At least three definable aspects of Mrs. Moodie's experience seem to be continuous in Canadian writing. First, the Moodies came to Canada, not with a dream of forging their own empire, but with the modest hope of salvaging a way of life threatened at home; they accordingly viewed Canada as a temporary refuge rather than a land of future opportunities. But when it was impossible to return home, they began to feel the country was a prison, a place of exile in a hostile wilderness, negative sentiments which have left an indelible imprint on the Canadian psyche.[7] Second, the image of the settler as a self-pitying failure rather than a buoyant pioneer characterizes a literary tradition peopled with victims and failures.[8] In nineteenth-century American fiction, the hero or heroine risks property, sanity, and life itself, but will never surrender the dream of improvement or the sure sense of life's wonder and promise. In contrast, Canadian heroes and heroines of the same period brood on inevitable failure and defeat. Third, the curious affection Mrs. Moodie feels for her forest home at the time of leaving is an ascetic pleasure which recurs with significant frequency in Canadian art. Through suffering and self-denial Mrs. Moodie has become attached to her life in the backwoods

---

[7] Northrop Frye refers to Canada's "garrison mentality"—a beleaguered quality in its citizens that originated in the small, isolated communities surrounded by a vast and menacing wilderness. See Frye's conclusion to the *Literary History of Canada*, 2d ed. (Toronto: University of Toronto Press, 1976), 2:342.

[8] See Margaret Atwood's *Survival: A Thematic Guide to Canadian Literature* (Toronto: Anansi Press, 1972).

and to her rough home, which she describes as "consecrated by the memory of a thousand sorrows."

In a literature dominated by women writers, Mrs. Moodie stands at its beginnings, a figure struggling against formidable odds, knowing the certainty of defeat. The image of one of Canada's first writers in a log house working far into the night by the light of sluts (twisted rags soaked in lard) is powerfully suggestive and recurs, probably without coincidence, in the picture Frederick Philip Grove gives in his autobiography of his wearing mittens against the cold of a Manitoba winter while trying to write a novel. Ben Franklin, of course, submitted himself to similarly astringent circumstances in order to realize his ambitions both literary and political, but what a difference there is in his recounting of those sacrifices! His confidence as a youth and his self-satisfaction as an old man telling his story of success are in sharp contrast to Mrs. Moodie's and to Grove's underlying conviction that life has been a failure. Susanna Moodie's cautionary tale, *Roughing It in the Bush*, is not a polished work of art, but the narrator's personal drama of rejection and exile, and her search for a refuge from an uncaring world is very central to what is imaginative in the Canadian experience.

Selected Writings

Roughing It in the Bush; or, Life in Canada. London, Bentley, 1852. Several later editions including an abridged version (London: Nelson, 1932). Reprint, abridged, in McClelland and Stewart's New Canadian Library, no. 31 (Toronto, 1962).

Life in the Clearings versus the Bush. London: Bentley, 1853. Reprint, edited by R. L. McDougall (Toronto: Macmillan, 1959).

Archibald Lampman

In the late nineteenth century Toronto was the cultural center of English Canada and the center of publishing, but the creative force which resulted in some of Canada's finest lyric poetry originated in the small Loyalist city of Fredericton, New Brunswick. There Charles G. D. Roberts, a clergyman's son, at the age of twenty published a collection of verse titled *Orion and Other Poems* (1880) and went on to earn the reputation of Canada's first man of letters. Roberts's immediate influence was on his cousin and close companion, Bliss Carman, who became the distinguished author of a number of love poems, most notably "Low Tide at Grand Pré." But the influence of *Orion* reached further. Archibald Lampman, who was a student at Trinity College, Toronto, tells us how the book affected him:

Like most of the young fellows about me, I had been under the depressing conviction that we were hopelessly situated on the outskirts of civilization, where no art and no literature could be, and that it was useless to expect that we could do it ourselves. I sat up most of the night reading and re-reading *Orion* in a state of the wildest excitement and when I went to bed I could not sleep. It seemed to me a wonderful thing that such work could be done by a Canadian, by a young man, one of ourselves. It was like a voice from some new paradise of art, calling us to be up and doing.[1]

Orion in retrospect is not a very distinguished book, but it roused for the first time a national feeling in a group of aspiring young writers. In literary history Charles G. D. Roberts, Bliss Carman, Archibald Lampman, and Duncan Campbell Scott are known as the Confederation poets. All four can be described as late Romantics, indebted to Wordsworth, Keats, and Tennyson. They

[1]Quoted by D. C. Scott in his introduction to Lampman's *Lyrics of Earth* (Toronto: Musson, 1925), pp. 8–9.

were not technical innovators or philosophers; nonetheless, they achieved integrity as poets from their personal interpretations of the Canadian countryside and gave rise to a national literature.

Although Roberts wrote some fine landscape poems focused on rural life and Scott produced memorable narratives about Indians, the outstanding poet from this group is Archibald Lampman, a young clerk in the Federal Post Office Department who died in Ottawa at the age of thirty-seven. Lampman was born in an Anglican rectory in the village of Morpeth, Ontario, in 1861. His parents, both lovers of the arts, were descended from United Empire Loyalists that had settled in the Niagara Peninsula. In 1867 the family moved to Gore's Landing on Rice Lake, near Peterborough, Ontario, a locale of woods and lakes and fields ideally suited to the temperament of a nascent poet. Here Lampman established that habit of intimacy with nature which was to be the trademark of his finest verse; here too he enjoyed a friendship with the elderly writer and botanist Catharine Parr Traill. But Rice Lake was also where Lampman as a boy contracted rheumatic fever, which left him physically weakened the rest of his life.

The poet was educated at private Anglican boys' schools and entered Trinity College in Toronto as a scholarship student in 1879. During his three years at Trinity, probably the happiest period of his life, he was less serious and studious than he had been as a child. In addition to studying classics, he took part in debates and concerts, contributed to the college magazine, and enjoyed the beer, tobacco, and lively conversation of several good friendships. The result, however, was a second-class standing when he graduated in 1882, which cost him his chances for a professorship and university career. Briefly he turned to teaching high school in Orangeville; but finding the work incompatible with his gentle, idealistic nature, he secured a post with the Federal Civil Service in the Post Office Department, where he worked until his premature death in February 1899.

In the history of Canadian letters Lampman has long been regarded as the type of suffering poet and unrecognized genius. Certainly his life in Ottawa was marked by hardships and a series of personal misfortunes. His work in the civil service, while not taxing, was not a source of personal satisfaction and provided him with only a meager income. His marriage to a young Ottawa girl also failed to provide personal fulfillment, and, though he remained faithful to his wife, he loved for several years a woman working in the Post Office Department with whom he felt a deep spiritual bond. In letters Lampman refers frequently to the bouts of melancholy and periods of inertia that he experienced. In retrospect it is hard not to relate Lampman's nervous despondency to the heart disease he unknowingly lived with and which eventually claimed his life. Moreover, within his family circle there were several occasions for grief and depression: there was the suffering and slow death of the poet's father from cancer and the death of a much-beloved infant son. But perhaps the greatest source of frustration in the poet's life was his inability to find a responsive public for his poetry or publishers who would bring his work before a wider audience. During his lifetime only two volumes of verse appeared. The first collection, *Among the Millet and Other Poems*, was published in 1888 at the author's own expense. It received favorable notices—indeed, it contains some of the poet's best pieces—but it did not draw wide enough attention or praise to guarantee the poet future publication. Over the years individual poems were printed in prestigious magazines such as *Harper's*, *Scribner's*, and the *Atlantic Monthly* and earned the commendation of notable literary figures such as W. D. Howells. But when Lampman put together a second collection, *Lyrics of Earth*, it was three years before he placed it in 1895 with a small publishing house, Copeland and Day of Boston. A collection of sonnets that made the rounds of publishers was finally abandoned. At the time of his death he had arranged to publish a third collection, *Alcyone*, at his own expense again. Duncan Campbell Scott, Lampman's close friend and the literary executor for his estate, canceled publication of *Alcyone* (except for twelve copies given as mementoes to the poet's family and friends) and in the following year brought out a major collection of his friend's work, *The Poems of Archibald Lampman*.[2]

There is no denying the fact that Lampman's life in Ottawa

[2] The most recent available edition of Lampman's work is *The Poems of Archibald Lampman (Including "At the Long Sault")*, introd. M. C. Whitridge (Toronto: University of Toronto Press, 1974). Poems quoted in this chapter are taken from this edition.

was far from happy or satisfying, but it is also probably true that Lampman's best poems were nurtured by the frustrations and discontents that hung over his life. In despair of making a significant place for himself in the world of human affairs, he retreated to nature, to what he called "the comfort of the fields," where his senses and imagination came fully alive to the shapes, textures, and sounds of the natural world and where its abiding truths gave him a philosophical perspective on the vanity of human wishes. Lampman's greatest pleasure was in going for long walks in the countryside, in escaping the cares of his life in the city. On several occasions he went on canoeing and hiking trips into the northern Ontario wilderness with Scott and with his brothers-in-law. His best poems embody in precise, concrete images the intense love he experienced for the world out-of-doors. A consideration of Lampman's lasting contribution to Canadian literature must invariably focus on a small body of poems about nature.

First, however, it should be shown that although Lampman's output was relatively small, there was considerable range to his poetic interests. Politically, Lampman was a socialist, a member of the Fabian Society, and it could be said that he was the first Canadian poet of a middle-class intellectual background to write of his disaffection with the social system for which he labored. In the sonnet "To a Millionaire" he laments the fate of "the vain multitudes that plod on . . . / And serve the curse that pins them down" and addresses open contempt for their master who lives only for his "one grim misgotten pile." His despair at unregulated capitalism extended to the age in which he lived. Although Lampman, like many of his Victorian contemporaries, apparently believed in the evolution of a world soul towards some sublime yet unrevealed end, in poems like "The Modern Politician" and "To Chaucer" he expressed grave doubts about the progress of modern history. He describes himself living in an age of brass where petty politicians, "clowns," assume power and mimic the strength of vanished kings. In a long utopian poem titled "The Land of Pallas" Lampman describes an ideal society where no one has great wealth or power, where there is no army or judiciary or marriage, and where honor is reserved for the masters of language and philosophy. He did not believe he would see such a society realized during his lifetime, but he believed that peace and harmony in human life would ultimately prevail. Lampman was also sympathetic to the feminist movement of his time and wrote in an essay in the *Globe* that women must be given equal responsibility with men in human affairs "if the race is to reach its noblest and fullest development."[3] In "The Land of Pallas" the source of utopian harmony rests with a philosopher queen as head of state, and in two long narrative poems, "The Story of an Affinity" and "David and Abigail," the dignity and wisdom of the heroines have redemptive powers. While Lampman admired courage and wisdom in women, he was also a love poet who celebrated feminine beauty and the progress of passion in the tradition of courtly love. He wrote a series of sonnets when he was courting his wife, published as "The Growth of Love," and another group published as "Portrait in Six Sonnets" written to Katherine Waddell, the woman he loved later in his life. Love in these poems is deeply and sincerely felt, but its expression is abstract and conventional. Sketching in the range of Lampman's poetic interests, one should also mention his abiding interest in classical subjects in poems like "An Athenian Reverie" and "David and Abigail," which are set in ancient and biblical times.

But to view Lampman in the light of late twentieth-century concerns—in terms of socialism, feminism, or even the more timeless theme of love—leads the reader away from the real center of his poetic achievement. For his distinction rests almost wholly with those poems whose subject is nature. Wearied by the corrupt and vain expediencies of both political and social life in Ottawa, Lampman invariably turned to nature for both an escape and a source of inspiration. His attitude is like Wordsworth's in "Tintern Abbey" where, oppressed by "the fretful stir / Unprofitable, and the fever of the world," the English poet turns to the green pastoral landscape of the Wye to be restored in spirit. The function of nature as a refuge from the city and from social ills is voiced or implied in most of Lampman's best poems.[4] In one of

[3] *Globe*, 27 August 1892. Reprinted in *Archibald Lampman: Selected Prose*, ed. Barrie Davies (Ottawa: Tecumseh, 1975), p. 65.

[4] The opposite view is sometimes put forward. In "Lampman: The Radical Poet," *English Quarterly* 4, no. 1 (Spring 1971): 33–43, Barrie Davies argues that Lampman did not escape into nature, but strove to bring to society the organic values of the natural world.

his finest pieces, "Among the Timothy," the poet retreats to a field on a fair day in summer because he is "weary of the drifting hours, / The echoing city towers, / The blind gray streets, the jingle of the throng." The English poet asserts that "mid the din / Of towns and cities" he owes his sense of tranquil restoration to the meadows and woods that he has roamed. Lampman describes in the poem "April" a similar renewal:

> and once more
> The city smites me with its dissonant roar.
> To its hot heart I pass, untroubled yet,
> Fed with calm hope, without desire or fret.

One idea, whether stated explicitly or not, dominates Lampman's poetry: that in nature there is harmony and a source of happiness, while in the city there is conflict and discord. The idea is a threadbare cliché in late nineteenth-century poetry, and it is a measure of Lampman's talent that he gave the theme renewed substance and value. No doubt this was in part because nature was for the poet a very real form of salvation, not simply a literary pose. In a letter to his friend E. W. Thomson, a magazine editor and short story writer, he writes in June 1895:

I was so far gone in hypochondria on Saturday last that I had not the spirit to go to the office at all. I went straggling up the Gatineau Road and spent the whole day and most of the next under the blue sky and the eager sun—and then I began to perceive that there were actually earth and grass and beautifully trailing clouds in the tender fields of heaven. I got to see at last that it was really fine and that perhaps I was alive after all.[5]

This solitary drama is recreated in several of Lampman's best poems. What makes it fresh is that Lampman recorded his vision of nature in images taken directly from the Canadian landscape. The sonnet "Late November" demonstrates Lampman's skill in observing and describing landscape in a manner true to the Canadian experience.

> The hills and leafless forests slowly yield
> To the thick-driving snow. A little while

[5] Arthur S. Bourinot, ed. *Archibald Lampman's Letters to Edward William Thomson* (Ottawa: The Editor, 1956), p. 29. Hereafter cited as *Letters*.

And night shall darken down. In shouting file
The woodsmen's carts go by me homeward-wheeled,
Past the thin fading stubbles, half-concealed,
  Now the golden-gray, sowed softly through with snow,
  Where the last ploughman follows still his row,
Turning black furrows through the whitening field.
Far off the village lamps begin to gleam,
  Fast drives the snow, and no man comes this way;
    The hills grow wintry white, and bleak winds moan
    About the naked uplands. I alone
  Am neither sad, nor shelterless, nor gray,
Wrapped round with thought, content to watch and dream.

One is struck by the precision with which detail is recorded, by
the colors and contours of particular objects. But more important, one feels the essence of this scene in all its particularity as
the driving snow storm gradually obliterates the visible world. The
clue to the unique sensibility revealed in the poem comes in the
last line, where the poet states that he is "content to watch and
dream." Lampman's poems are indeed the highly visual records
of a man who *watches* with a very keen eye and who is able to
render in poetry the essence of that thing which he has observed.

The word *dream*, with which the poem ends and which recurs
in much of Lampman's verse, has vexed critics and resulted in
some elaborate philosophical accounts of his use of the term.[6] He
used the word rather loosely, so that in one poem it might simply
mean idling away the time, while in another it might involve a
utopian vision of a better world. But in most of the nature poems
the term usually indicates a time of heightened awareness for the
poet, a time when, as E. K. Brown phrases it, he "feels the essence of the scene in which he finds himself."[7] When he says in
"Among the Timothy" that it is sweet to watch the grass and the
clouds and "nor think but only dream," he is close to Keats who
asks "for a life full of sensations rather than of thought." (Lampman had a great passion for the poetry of Keats and in a letter to

[6] For example, in "Lampman and Nelligan: Dream Landscapes," *Canadian Review of Comparative Literature* (Spring 1979), pp. 151–65, Kathy Mezei views
dreaming as the "state of poetic creation."
[7] E. K. Brown, *On Canadian Poetry* (Ottawa: Tecumseh, 1973), p. 97.

Thomson writes, "Keats has always had such a fascination for me and so permeated my whole mental outfit that I have an idea that he has found a sort of faint reincarnation in me.")[8] Dreaming for Lampman meant meditating on the physical essence of things, which is why he renders the details of the natural scene with such immediacy and with such felt presence.

The poem "Heat," often regarded as Lampman's most perfect piece, is the exquisite rendering of an Ontario landscape as perceived under the full sun of a summer day. In the first stanza the intensity of the heat is caught by images of motion that render the landscape liquid:

> From plains that reel to southward, dim,
> The road runs by me white and bare;
> Up the steep hill it seems to swim
> Beyond, and meet into the glare.
> Upward half-way, or it may be
> Nearer the summit, slowly steals
> A hay-cart, moving dustily
> With idly clacking wheels.

Further on the poet suggests that it is the dream state which allows him to experience so intimately the details of the scene.

> In intervals of dream I hear
> The cricket from the droughty ground;
> The grasshoppers spin into mine ear
> A small innumerable sound.

The poem concludes, not with a philosophical reflection on nature's power to heal or inspire, but with the simple statement, "In the full furnace of this hour/My thoughts grow keen and clear." The poet does not say what those thoughts are. This omission is an important feature of Lampman's style and in the context of Victorian poetics makes him something more than a mannerist poet.

Lampman's refusal to make his nature poems didactic or discursive especially characterizes his sonnets. In Canadian literature Lampman is the leading exponent of the sonnet form. Ac-

[8] *Letters*, p. 26.

cording to Duncan Campbell Scott, the poet said of his own sonnets: "Here after all is my best work."[9] The form is particularly congenial to Lampman's talent. Its brevity and its intricate, polished structure are well adapted to a poetry of essences; moreover, the sonnet is intensely personal while remaining a very stylized form, thus suited to the poet's nature, which was both passionate and reticent. Traditionally the sonnet is associated with the theme of loneliness (unfulfilled love) and with the tragic awareness of life's brevity. These associations in Lampman's verse assume a particular poignancy in the light of his short career. His nature sonnets are quietly informed by the same haunting paradox that lies at the heart of Keats's verse—that perceptions and pleasures on earth are fleeting, that only in the stiff, formalized structures of art do they survive.

The great care that Lampman brought to his craft is reflected in the subtle variations he made in his use of the sonnet. A favorite form was the Shakespearean sonnet, but he did not restrict himself to the quatrain sequence; sometimes he set the couplet between the second and third quatrain. Similarly, when using the octave and sestet, he sometimes introduced the sestet with a couplet. There are more than fifty variations that can be distinguished, which include subtle variations in line length when it suited the subject. In a letter to Thomson he says he has "no very profound respect for rules and regulations."[10]

The sonnets suggest several groupings. Some are so completely visual that they can be compared to paintings. Lampman was inspired by his canoe trip to Lake Temagami in the autumn of 1896 to write several sonnets of this kind. Pieces like "Temagami" and "On Lake Temiscamingue" look forward to paintings by members of the Group of Seven who also found inspiration for their art by exploring northern Ontario. In the "Temiscamingue" sonnet everything except for the sound of water is visual; the poem is composed of color, lines, planes of distance. Even the water, described as "a roar of foam," acquires a visual dimension by the suggestion of whiteness in foam.

In a somewhat larger group of sonnets which includes "Eve-

[9] Duncan Campbell Scott, ed., in *The Poems of Archibald Lampman* (Toronto: George N. Morang & Co. Ltd., 1900), p. xxiv.

[10] *Letters*, pp. 32–33.

ning" and "After Mist," the poet records the mood of a season as illuminated by a change in the time of day. One sonnet in this group, "Winter Uplands," was written only eleven days before the poet's death.

> The frost that stings like fire upon my cheek,
> The loneliness of this forsaken ground,
> The long white drift upon whose powdered peak
> I sit in the great silence as one bound;
> The rippled sheet of snow where the wind blew
> Across the open fields for miles ahead;
> The far-off city towered and roofed in blue
> A tender line upon the western red;
> The stars that singly, then in flocks appear,
> Like jets of silver from the violet dome,
> So wonderful, so many and so near,
> And then the golden moon to light me home—
> The crunching snowshoes and the stinging air,
> And silence, frost and beauty everywhere.

The poem holds a special interest not only as Lampman's last piece of writing but also because the manuscript reveals the tightly imposed restrictions within which the poet worked. In the first draft the last two lines ran thus:

> Though the heart plays us false and life lies bare
> The truth of Beauty haunts us everywhere.

But by striking the philosophical generalization, the stock-in-trade of Victorian poetry, Lampman intensifies the effect of the poem's physical immediacy and gives it a satisfying wholeness. This emendation illustrates Lampman's particular genius as a Canadian poet who is being faithful to the scene around him rather than to the conventions of English landscape poetry.

The poet is, nonetheless, a presence in the landscape, there to record the messages of nature. There is a group of sonnets which might be described as Emersonian wherein the poet sees the "natural fact [as] a symbol of some spiritual fact." [11] The sonnet "Goldenrod" concludes:

[11] See Carl F. Klinck's "'The Frogs': An Exercise in Reading Lampman," in *The Lampman Symposium*, ed. Lorraine McMullen (Ottawa: University of Ottawa Press, 1976), pp. 29–37, for a discussion of Lampman's affinities with Emerson. Lamp-

> Mark them well,
> The last and best from summer's empty looms,
> Her benedicte, and dream of dreams,
> The fulness of her soul made visible.

In a sonnet sequence titled "The Frogs" Lampman establishes a correspondence between the sound of the frogs' singing and a principle of harmony in the universe. The frogs are "breathers of wisdom," and their music issues from a land "where beauty hath no change." They assure the listener that "beneath life's change and stir" there is an immutable order and "everlasting rest." Again, it is the poet's ability to dream, or as Wordsworth phrased it, to be "laid asleep/In body, and become a living soul," which allows him to translate the frogs' singing and "see into the life of things." The sequence concludes with the poet's reassurance

> That change and pain are shadows faint and fleet
> And dreams are real, and life is only sweet.

The Emersonian stance is completely absent in another group of sonnets, where nature is revealed as destructive and indifferent to humanity. This theme is subtly deployed in the sonnet "Winter Evening," which describes both the beauty and the terror of the northern winter. After describing the city in a wash of golden light at sunset, the poet warns:

> Soon, soon shall fly
> The glorious vision, and the hours shall feel
> A mightier master; soon from height to height,
> With silence and the sharp unpitying stars,
> Stern creeping frosts, and winds that touch like steel,
> Out of the depth beyond the eastern bars,
> Glittering and still shall come the awful night.

In "A Thunderstorm" he uses the metaphor of a military attack to convey the destructive principle latent in nature. Lampman is not faithful to a philosophy, but writes out of his varied experience of nature.

---

man's enthusiasm for the American Transcendentalists is reflected in his letters from Boston, September 1891. These letters are available in an edition of the Lampman family correspondence by Carol Marie Sommers, "The Letters of Archibald Lampman in the Simon Fraser University Library" (master's thesis, Simon Fraser University, 1979).

Finally, there is a group of landscape sonnets which have a unique place in Lampman's work because of their striking visual effects. The technique the poet uses in these sonnets is to adjust gradually the perspective, the way a cameraman might adjust his lens, so that in the last lines a vague scene is suddenly brought into clear and significant focus. In "A Niagara Landscape" the scene of orchards and fields is blurred by the haze of mid-day heat; as the poem continues, distant towns and villages become even more indistinct, but in the last three lines the poet directs the eye to a city

> far to westward, where yon pointed towers
> Rise faint and ruddy from the vaporous blue,
> Saint Catharines, city of the host of flowers.

The effect achieved is a kind of revelation, like the emergence on the landscape of a heavenly city. Similarly, in "A Sunset at Les Eboulements" the Saint Lawrence River country at evening assumes a magical character in the concluding lines where

> The sun's last shaft beyond the grey sea floor
> Still dreams upon the Kamouraska shore,
> And the long line of golden villages.

The most perfectly wrought sonnet of this kind is "A Dawn on the Lièvre," where the poet's mythic perception of the landscape is developed through a series of shifts of light.

> Up the dark-valleyed river stroke by stroke
>   We drove the water from the rustling blade;
>   And when the night was almost gone we made
> The Oxbow bend; and there the dawn awoke;
> Full on the shrouded night-charged river broke
>   The sun, down the long mountain valley rolled,
>   A sudden swinging avalanche of gold,
> Through mists that sprang and reeled aside like smoke,
> And lo! before us, toward the east upborne,
>   Packed with curled forest, bunched and topped with pine,
> Brow beyond brow, drawn deep with shade and shine,
>   The mount; upon whose golden sunward side,
> Still threaded with the melting mist, the morn
>   Sat like some glowing conqueror satisfied.

The poem moves from semidarkness to the full intensity of daylight, with morning revealed fittingly in the last line as a godlike conqueror.

In stark contrast to these sonnets with their suggestion of something vital and sacred in the landscape, there is a longer poem titled "The City of the End of Things," which presents Lampman's vision of the hell that industrial man is making for his future. In a nightmare landscape that resembles Dante's Inferno, men have become robots following the orders of machines:

> And moving at unheard commands,
> The abysses and vast fires between,
> Flit figures that with clanking hands
> Obey a hideous routine;
> They are not flesh, they are not bone,
> They see not with the human eye,
> And from their iron lips is blown
> A dreadful and monotonous cry.

This city, however, represents the final stage of civilization's self-destruction, and in the concluding stanza the poet foresees a state of entropy where all the machines will have stopped and disintegrated, where no one will be left alive and "over that tremendous town / The silence of eternal night / Shall gather close and settle down." This remarkable poem is cited by critics who see Lampman primarily as a socialist poet warning Canadians of the disastrous consequences of uncontrolled capitalism. But the poem belongs just as significantly to that view which sees the tension between city and country as central to Lampman's art. The city of the end of things is built in a place devoid of vegetation, a "leafless tract," and when it finally crumbles into dust, we are told that no living thing shall grow there again, "nor trunk of tree, nor blade of grass." This apocalyptic city is the culmination of all those images of city living from which the poet is continually fleeing.

Lampman's work did not develop significantly during his brief career. Many of his best poems such as "Heat," "Among the Timothy," and "Late November" appeared in his first volume, *Among the Millet*, and such sonnets as "Winter Evening" and "A Dawn on the Lièvre" are of the same period of composition. Lampman was painfully conscious of this himself. In letters to Thomson in the 1890s he laments that, ten years before, he had been writing better poems.[12] Some critics have argued that a late poem in manuscript titled "At the Long Sault: May 1660" marks a significant development in Lampman's treatment of nature. The poem describes the heroic attempt of a small band of French Canadians to repulse an Iroquois attack on their fort, and the imagery in the poem of hawks and wolves and a bull moose suggests a cruel aspect of nature, "nature red in tooth and claw." The poem is almost unique in employing images of aggressive animals, for nature in Lampman's verse consists generally of woods and fields, birds, plants, and humming insects. But nature as cruel or as an unconscious void appeared in earlier poems such as "Winter Evening" (1888) and "Voices of Earth" (1891) and does not really represent a new departure in the poet's last works.

Lampman's life with its disappointments and suffering is, in retrospect, almost stereotypically romantic. One thinks particularly of Keats. But, to the credit of his verse, his life does not overshadow his work. Lampman judged himself to be not a great poet, "but simply a rather superior minor one who sometimes hits upon a thing which comes uncommonly near to being very excellent."[13] In the context of Canadian poetry that judgment appears now severe. Although he came into full possession of his poetic gift at an early age, there was no diminishment in that talent, and the result for Canadian literature was perhaps its finest body of lyrical verse written in English.

Selected Writings

Among the Millet, and Other Poems. Ottawa: Durie, 1888.

Lyrics of Earth. Boston: Copeland and Day, 1895.

Alcyone. Ottawa: Ogilvy, 1899.

The Poems of Archibald Lampman. Edited with a memoir by Duncan Campbell Scott. Toronto: Morang & Co., 1900.

[12] *Letters,* pp. 30, 38.
[13] *Ibid.,* p. 38.

Lyrics of Earth: Sonnets and Ballads. Introduction by Duncan Campbell Scott. Toronto: Musson, 1925.

At the Long Sault and Other Poems. Foreword by Duncan Campbell Scott, introduction by E. K. Brown. Toronto: Ryerson, 1943.

The Poems of Archibald Lampman (Including "At the Long Sault"), Introduction by M. C. Whitridge. Toronto: University of Toronto Press, 1974.

Lampman's Kate: Late Love Poems of Archibald Lampman. Edited with an introduction by M. C. Whitridge. Ottawa: Borealis Press, 1975.

Frederick Philip Grove

The first two decades of the twentieth century were an era in which a number of popular Canadian writers established international reputations. Robert Service produced his tales of the Klondike, Ralph Connor wrote parables of Christian life on the frontier, Stephen Leacock brought out his annual collection of humorous sketches, and Lucy Maude Montgomery published *Anne of Green Gables*, the first volume in a series of children's classics set on Prince Edward Island. This was also the period in which the Indian poet Pauline Johnson gave dramatic recitals in native costume and Henry Drummond, a Montreal doctor, produced his immensely popular dialect poems about the French Canadian *habitant*. From the works of these best-selling authors came images of Canadian life that persist today: the heroic Northwest Mounted Police, the simple, pleasure-loving *habitant*, romantic tableaux of Indian life, and a picture of the beautiful, unspoiled wilderness. The appeal of these writers was in their celebration of a way of life and a code of values that were quickly disappearing in the rest of the world. With the exception of Sara Jeannette Duncan's *The Imperialist* (1904), a realistic analysis of Ontario's social and political life in the manner of W. D. Howells, Canadian fiction in this period was largely escapist and sentimental.

The first group of realistic novels in Canada is about pioneer farming in the West.[1] Unlike the American experience, there was no tradition of lawless adventure in Canada in either fact or fiction. When the railway was completed in 1884, opening up the West for settlement, the country was surveyed for homesteading

[1] In addition to the works of Grove, this group includes Laura Goodman Salverson's *The Viking Heart* (1923), Martha Ostenso's *Wild Geese* (1925), and Robert J. C. Stead's *Grain* (1926).

and patrolled by the Northwest Mounted Police. The fiction that eventually appeared did not exploit the possibilities of romance and adventure in a new country, but was written in a realistic mode, focusing on the rigors of farm labor and the bleak monotony of the prairie landscape.[2] These novels broke the long tradition of historical romance and represented a shift from English to American literary models.

Frederick Philip Grove, the author of twelve published books, most of which are set in the West, occupies a prominent place in the history of Canadian literature as the first realist to produce a substantial body of fiction. Technically, his novels belong to the Naturalist school: like Zola and Dreiser, Grove viewed the novel as a sociological chronicle in part and asked, as he created characters, whether human destiny was not determined by natural forces indifferent to human purposes. He describes one of his protagonists as "a leaf borne along in the wind . . . a fragment swept away by torrents," epithets which recall Dreiser's *Sister Carrie*, whose heroine is designated "a waif amid forces."

Mystery surrounds Grove's life. Like B. Traven, he took great pains to conceal his identity. His autobiography, *In Search of Myself* (1946), gives a romantic account of his origins and youth. He claims he was of Scottish and Swedish ancestry and was born in 1871 while his parents, wealthy landowners, were traveling in Russia. His childhood, he says, was spent at Castle Thurow, his father's estate in Sweden, but when his parents separated, he traveled extensively with his mother. He describes Castle Thurow as a manor house with twenty-nine main rooms, elegant furnishings, spacious lawns and gardens; and the account of his mother's life is like a tour guide through the most cultured and sophisticated circles of cosmopolitan Europe. When he was sixteen, he says, his mother gave him a yacht, and he sailed to many of the ports of the Mediterranean and North Africa. These travels he claims

---

[2]There are comprehensive studies of western Canadian fiction in Edward A. McCourt's *The Canadian West in Fiction* (Toronto: Ryerson Press, 1949; rev. ed., 1970); in Laurence Ricou's *Vertical Man / Horizontal World: Man and Landscape in Canadian Prairie Fiction* (Vancouver: University of British Columbia Press, 1973); and in Dick Harrison's *Unnamed Country: The Struggle for a Canadian Prairie Fiction* (Edmonton: University of Alberta Press, 1977).

were later supplemented, after his mother's death, by trips to Australia and the South Seas, by a journey across the Sahara desert, and by a research trip with a Scottish uncle, a famous scientist named Rutherford, across the barren wastes of Siberia. Of his education he writes that he was first instructed by private tutors and then attended schools in Berlin, Rome, Munich, and finally the Sorbonne in Paris, where he studied archeology. He claims to have become intimate with José-Maria de Heredia and Mallarmé in Paris, and an acquaintance of Verlaine and Rimbaud. He says he came to North America on a world tour in 1892, but when he was in Toronto learned of his father's death and that the family estate was bankrupt. Thereafter he says he became an itinerant farm laborer in the West for nearly twenty years until he started teaching school in Manitoba in 1912.

In the 1960s Professor Douglas Spettigue of Queen's University questioned the authenticity of this romantic story while he was preparing a monograph on Grove. When he tried to check some of the details in Grove's account, he found there was no place by the name of Castle Thurow, indeed, there were no Groves in Sweden; nor was there any record of Grove's attending European universities. The poets with whom Grove claimed friendships were self-absorbed diarists and letter writers, but they made no mention of Grove in their writings. Furthermore, in his autobiography Grove impossibly fits a term of school, a summer of yachting, the trip across Siberia, and three months in Java into one year. The trip across Siberia before the railway alone would have been an incredible feat. The scientist by the name of Rutherford could not be traced. Eventually, after several years of research, Spettigue was able to prove more or less with certainty that Grove was originally a German by the name of Felix Paul Greve, born in 1879 at Radomno on the Polish-Prussian border. His father was a poor tenant farmer who later became a streetcar conductor in Hamburg. When his parents separated, his mother set up a boarding house in Saint Pauli, a poor and disreputable area of the city. The boy's dreams of wealth and education were partly realized when he attended the University of Bonn, where he lived extravagantly, supported perhaps by a beneficent uncle. From 1902 to 1909 he was a free-lance writer and translator, writing articles on Oscar Wilde and preparing a definitive German translation of the *Arabian Nights*. He lived a decadent life and was imprisoned for debt for several months. Eventually he disappeared, leaving a suicide note for his mistress.[3]

He escaped his debts and emotional entanglements by coming to North America in 1909, but it is not known what he did until 1912, when he took his first teaching position. Likely he traveled through the American and Canadian West, although for a much shorter period than he claimed in his autobiography. From 1912 until 1924 he taught at various schools in Manitoba, marrying Catherine Wiens, a fellow teacher nearly twenty years younger than himself.[4] Although he is said to have been an effective teacher, his relations with parents and school boards were always contentious, and he moved frequently to different towns. His health was never stable, and he suffered with back trouble and deafness, as well as chronic nervous disorders. In spite of these difficulties he began publishing in the 1920s the books about life in the West for which he is still esteemed. His books did not sell well (royalties totaled $32.80 in 1930 and $0.10 in 1931), but he persisted in his efforts to establish himself as a writer. After the death of their only daughter in 1927, the Groves left Manitoba and moved to Ontario, where Grove unsuccessfully tried farming for a living. During the depression he found seasonal work in a canning factory while his wife continued to teach. In the 1940s he began to enjoy recognition for his work as a novelist, but in 1944 he suffered a paralytic stroke and died in 1948 after completing the autobiography. The latter, ironically, won a Governor General's Award for nonfiction.

The indifference and, sometimes, hostility that greeted Grove as a writer in Canada make it remarkable that he produced such a substantial body of work which, in addition to the twelve pub-

[3] See Douglas O. Spettigue, *FPG: The European Years* (Ottawa: Oberon Press, 1973). Desmond Pacey, Grove's official biographer, insisted on the veracity of Grove's story until the publication of Spettigue's book. This means there are inaccuracies and false assumptions in his writings about Grove, but his literary estimates of Grove's work, to be found in *Frederick Philip Grove* (Toronto: Ryerson Press, 1945, 1970), are sound.

[4] This period of Grove's life is carefully documented in the first three chapters of Margaret R. Stobie's *Frederick Philip Grove* (New York: Twayne, 1973).

lished volumes, includes numerous stories and novels in manuscript. But a clue to understanding Grove and the fictional characters he created lies in a conception of the artist as *isolato*, a man outside of society, so that the censure and neglect he encountered were possibly a form of inspiration to him. His best work can be found in his first published book, *Over Prairie Trails* (1922), a collection of sketches describing his experiences traveling alone through the Manitoba countryside. In 1917 Grove's wife took a teaching position in a location some thirty miles north of the town where Grove was principal of a high school. On weekends he visited his wife and baby daughter, making the journey through all kinds of weather by horse and buggy (by sleigh in winter). The book describes seven of those journeys, with detailed accounts given of the landscape and weather and the numerous natural hazards that Grove encountered on the way. What is most striking in *Over Prairie Trails* is the author's love of solitude and the powerful attraction he feels to the bleak, punitive aspects of the Manitoba landscape.

Grove's is a striking instance of the ascetic imagination which finds pleasure in what is humble and inconspicuous. He exults in "the silver grey, leathery foliage" which characterizes the northern woods, turning his back on the lush tropical lands that he claims he once visited.

The parrot that flashed through "nutmeg groves" did not hold out so much allurement as the simple grey-and-slaty junco. The things that are unobtrusive and differentiated by shadings only—grey in grey above all—like our northern woods, like our sparrows, our wolves—they held a more compelling attraction than orgies of colour and screams of sound. So I came home to the north.[5]

Like Thoreau, whom he admired, Grove observes and records the details of nature with an eye that compels in the reader a fresh seeing. His analyses of fog and snow and hoarfrost are like Thoreau's examination of the seaweed in *Cape Cod* or the phosphorescent wood in *The Maine Woods*.[6] He likes trees in winter, for they are stripped naked as truth, not without beauty:

[5] *Over Prairie Trails* (Toronto: McClelland and Stewart, 1957), p. 51. All references are to this text.

[6] Grove and Thoreau are linked as travel writers in Janet Giltrow's "Grove in Search of an Audience," *Canadian Literature* 90 (Autumn 1981): 92–107.

Winter reveals the bark and the "habit" of trees. All ornaments and un-essentials have been dropped. The naked skeletons show. I remember how I was more than ever struck by that dappled appearance of the bark of the balm: an olive-green, yellowish hue, ridged and spotted with the black of ancient, overgrown leaf-scars; there was actually something gay about it; these poplars are certainly beautiful winter trees. The aspens were different. Although their stems stood white on white in the snow, that greenish tinge in their white gave them a curious look. [pp. 72–73]

The book has moments of drama. On almost every ride the narrator must do battle with wind, rain, or snow to reach his destination. On one journey he is completely enclosed in fog and must trust the instincts of his horses to find the way; on another he must battle his way through huge snowdrifts that have completely obliterated his trail. Nature is temporarily the enemy, and the narrator must perform heroic feats to continue on his way. But Grove's sense of nature as the enemy is a playful one; in spite of the obstacles created by fog, wind, or snow, there is no full sense of danger. The real conflict lies just off the page—with society. In the preface Grove says, "I disliked the town, the town disliked me" (p. xiii). Again like Thoreau, the narrator of *Over Prairie Trails* finds nature a welcome escape from the difficult and unsatisfying transactions he has with his fellow man. On his solitary rides Grove is the only traveler abroad, and the desolate region he travels is virtually uninhabited. He finds an exquisite pleasure in being thus alone. During his drive through the fog he feels secure and comfortable in being isolated:

I was shut in, closed off from the world around. . . . It was like a very small room, this space of light—the buggy itself, in darkness, forming an alcove to it, in which my hand knew every well-appointed detail. Gradually, while I was warming up, a sense of infinite comfort came, and with it the enjoyment of the elvish aspect. [p. 32]

Similarly in the chapter "Snow" he writes: "None of the farms which I passed showed the slightest signs of life. I had wrapped up again and sat in comparative comfort and at ease, enjoying the clear sparkle and glitter of the snow" (p. 70). His weekend journeys, which take him away from the center of conflict, give him renewed strength. He writes: "Those drives took decades off my age, and in spite of incurable illness my few friends say that I look once more like a young man" (p. 45). The escape motif and the creation of an isolated shelter in the wilderness (what Grove called elsewhere a "domesticated island") are most fully dramatized in the image of the cottage and the young wife and child that await him at journey's end.

Although *Over Prairie Trails* belongs to a minor literary genre —the descriptive sketch—it is Grove's most successful book because of the writing. The author's affection for the humblest details observable in nature, his sense of the drama in nature, and his amused, ironic sense of his own relationship to the landscape are all communicated in a spare, supple prose that eschews the lyrical and sentimental. "Nature," he says, "with her utter lack of sentiment, is after all the only real soother of anguished nerves," and he communicates exactly that experience through an aesthetic of careful documentation.[7] When Grove went on to handle the larger elements of prose fiction—particularly scene and dialogue—he was considerably less successful and more uneven.

The first of Grove's novels to be published, *Settlers of the Marsh* (1925), is actually part of a trilogy that was to have been published under the title *Pioneers*. The first volume was a chronicle of the Big Marsh country recording the principal events in the pioneers' lives: house-building, well-digging, a marsh fire, a measles epidemic, births, deaths, new clearings, and so forth. The individual stories of the settlers were not so important as the story of the marsh itself. The second volume was a tragic novel about the inhabitants of the "White Range Line House," the most prosperous farm in the district. When he sent these two volumes in manuscript to McClelland and Stewart and to Macmillan, Grove was advised that "no book of the kind stood a chance in Canada." Ryerson Press eventually accepted a condensed, one-volume version of the work, which is published with ellipses that indicate material omitted from the original manuscripts. Grove dispiritedly referred to *Settlers of the Marsh*, when it appeared, as no more than a "garbled extract" from the original. Nonetheless, the book is often cited as Grove's finest achievement in fiction.

The merging of the two manuscripts produced a book with very marked inconsistencies. The chronicle about the Big Marsh

[7] There is an appreciation of the book as "nature-writing" in W. J. Keith's "Grove's *Over Prairie Trails*: A Re-examination," *Literary Half-Yearly* 13 (July 1972): 76–85.

had been written with literary assumptions very different from those of a tragic narrative. Writing about the evolution of a pioneer community in a bleak northern country, Grove was most interested in the effects of environment on his characters. He reveals, in the manner of the naturalists, how the harsh western environment erases from the European immigrants their pasts and their personalities. In the background of *Settlers of the Marsh* is a crowd of secondary characters—the Lunds, the Amundsens, Sigurdsen, Dunsmores, Dahlbecks, Hahns, and Kelms—who struggle against the elements to wrest a living from a stubborn land. There are few success stories: Mrs. Amundsen is destroyed by the hard farm labor and childbirth, and her husband is crushed to death by a chunk of ice in the creek; the old Icelander, Sigurdsen, overworks himself and dies grotesquely. The Lunds, a middle-aged European couple with some culture, are ill suited to pioneer life and disintegrate with the passing of time—he disappears from the district, and she abandons their claim. These people are defeated largely by their economic circumstances. Grove, the Naturalist, is concerned to show that their lives have become anonymous and without meaning, determined by forces that are blind to human purposes. When the Icelander dies, the hero of the novel reflects—"What was life anyway? A dumb shifting of forces"—and sees his dead friend as no more than inert matter: "Here lay a lump of flesh, being transformed in its agony from flesh in which dwelt thought, feeling, a soul, into flesh that would rot and feed worms till it became clay." [8]

When Grove merged his two manuscripts, the Naturalism of his Marsh story became muted and secondary to the tragic story of the Swedish immigrant, Niels Lindstedt. The focus rests on a man whose "nature was to be alone, even in a crowd" (p. 31). Niels is a young pioneer with the physical strength and the determination to create a prosperous farm. But his vision of the future, in opposition to his solitary nature, centers on a great house that he will build and a "wife that will go through it like an inspiration" (p. 39). His tragedy slowly takes shape as he tries to realize his dream in a flesh-and-blood woman.

[8] *Settlers of the Marsh* (Toronto: McClelland and Stewart, 1966), pp. 101–2. All references are to this text.

Niels is the type of man who views women as either virgins or whores exclusively, and in his search for a wife he becomes caught in the literal implications of this psychological trap.[9] The girl who answers his dream is a blond, hard-working Scandinavian, Ellen Amundsen, who has made a vow never to marry. She explains, in a passage which was considered obscene by the Canadian reading public in 1925, that her father had brutalized her mother, working her like a beast in the fields, forcing himself on her sexually even when she was sick, and making her miscarry unwanted babies. Ellen promised her mother that she would never let a man have power over her. When Niels is rejected by her, he turns to the flirtatious widow Clara Vogel, known to almost everyone in the community as a prostitute. Their marriage from the outset is a failure. Niels is instinctively repelled by his wife's sensuality—their life together "seemed to him almost an indecency" (p. 125). When he is aware that he has married the town whore who entertains men in their house, he kills her with a shotgun. The years in prison that follow are presented as a welcome release to Niels from his psychological torment.

When Niels is at a desperate pitch of anxiety and indecision, the author poses a fundamental question:

Are there in us unsounded depths of which we do not know ourselves? Can things outside of us sway us in such a way as to change our very nature? Are we we? Or are we mere products of circumstance? [p. 166]

The question is awkwardly phrased, but it illuminates a confusion at the center of the book's conception, a confusion which arises from the deterministic view of Naturalism being evoked alongside the concept of free will that is central to tragedy. Al-

---

[9] Grove's handling of women has been viewed in different ways. For example, Ronald Sutherland in *Frederick Philip Grove* (Toronto: McClelland and Stewart, 1969) sees Grove's characters shaped by the author's puritanism. Henry Makow, on the other hand, in "Grove's Treatment of Sex: Platonic Love in *The Yoke of Life*," *Dalhousie Review* 58 (Autumn 1979): 528–40, sees Grove's characters reflecting the dualism of Plato and the bondage of spirit to flesh. The higher spiritual existence, in this view, is symbolized by the "sexless" condition of the androgyne (represented by Ellen in *Settlers of the Marsh*), while man's fallen state is symbolized by division into male and female.

though in the following paragraph Grove describes Niels as a victim of circumstances outside his control ("He felt like a rider on horseback who tries to control his mount when it is under the influence of an uncontrollable panic"), the larger implications of the novel are that Niels's story is a tragedy. It is specifically a tragedy of innocence because Niels refuses to accept the implications of his sexuality and because he willfully flees the social bonds of a mature, adult life. The symptoms of his tragedy are evident in his attraction to Ellen. She is described as a strong, masculine woman, never in terms of feminine charm. When Niels pictures his future happiness with her, it is a wholly domestic scene without the complications of sex: "He saw himself and a woman in a cosy room, with the homely light of a lamp shed over their shoulders, while the winter winds stalked and howled outside and while from above the pitter-patter of children's feet sounded down" (p. 45). In contrast, Clara Vogel is described as a remarkably pretty woman, plump, smooth-skinned, with laughing eyes and a seductive voice, a woman who made all the other women in the room appear "neuter."

Niels feels a physical attraction to Mrs. Vogel, but he refuses to permit those feelings any place in his life. When he encounters her at a country wedding, he thinks "she looked very lovely . . . but she looked like sin" (p. 54). Niels is a puritan who interprets his natural desires as "low, disgraceful," and to ward off temptation he conjures up a vision of his mother, whom he idealized. When Clara makes her advances towards him, we are told "he longed to be with his mother, to feel her gnarled, calloused fingers rumpling his hair, and to hear her crooning voice droning some old tune" (pp. 55–56). When Ellen refuses his offer of marriage, his desire is to run away, be alone. He has a new dream, this time of leaving for the margin of civilization to clear a new farm and, when people settle in the area, to move again. That way, he reflects, his enormous strength would still have a meaning, but "woman would have no place in his life" (p. 119). Consequently Niels, whose choice is "to evade life's issues," is deceived by Clara Vogel and finds himself trapped in a marriage that is loathsome to him. Niels's self-repression is most effectively dramatized in his treatment of his horses, animals that traditionally symbolize sexual passion. As his revulsion for Clara and his marriage grows, he begins beating his Percheron team, Jock and Nellie; and when finally he kills Clara, he goes out to the stable and shoots Jock as well, an action symbolizing violence against his own sexuality.

Grove's attitude towards his hero is an ambiguous one. He sees very clearly the tragedy of Niel's puritanical nature, but one feels the author at the same time is extremely sympathetic to the lonely hero. He implies that Niels's crime is not so much the murder as the relationship which preceded it. In the solitude of the prison cell Niels enjoys a peace of mind he has not experienced before. When he is released, he goes back to find Ellen nearing middle age, flat-busted, wearing glasses, her hair streaked with grey. She will now marry Niels, with the desire to have children; she and Niels resume their old "brotherhood." Happiness for this couple is suggested at the novel's close, but in notes Grove made for a sequel their marriage is not a success, and Niels is dreaming again of living alone on the edge of the wilderness.

The novel is not without flaws (Grove's prose is often awkward and cacophonous, and there are long dramatic scenes which go beyond the realities of Canadian farm life); nonetheless, the dilemma of Grove's characters is authentic, and the circumstances in which they are trapped are fully documented. Grove's skill in describing nature adds considerably to the novel's artistry, most memorably perhaps in the storm scene which is a prelude to Ellen's refusal of Niels's marriage proposal. Grove describes the coming scourge, focusing on the clouds: "There are two, three waves of almost black; in front, a circling festoon of loose, white, flocculent manes, seething, whirling. . . . A winking of lights runs through the first wave of black" (p. 9). Another effective element is Grove's presentation, in brief vignettes, of the immigrant families struggling to make a new life in Canada. The Lunds are memorable for their genteel poverty, but also for their deadly contest with each other for mastery in marriage. When Niels comes upon this elderly couple struggling in a manure pile over a pitchfork, he is inwardly revolted and hurries away from the scene unnoticed. It reinforces in him the instinct to live by himself.

The pioneer's lonely struggle to prevail over a harsh, unyielding land is a central theme in all of Grove's western fiction. *Our Daily Bread* (1928) is another story of a man who has driven himself mercilessly in order to establish a prosperous farm. The tragedy for John Elliot is that his children do not want to inherit the family farm and maintain the homestead, but go off on their own. In the last part of the book, the abandoned patriarch, too old to keep up his farm, wanders aimlessly about the country visiting those of his children who will have him. He is never either welcome or happy and finally returns to his farm to die alone. The drama of the generations is also central to *The Yoke of Life* (1930). The hero, Len Sterner, is a sensitive youth raised in a northern area of subsistence farms; his intellect and imagination set him apart from the world of his dull, hard-working stepfather. Grove is anxious to reveal how an artistic temperament is thwarted by environment, but he is also at pains to tell once again the story of a lonely man who falls in love with an ideal. The woman Len loves, because of circumstances, becomes a prostitute, and his despair brings him to arrange their deaths.

Grove's classic novel of the soil, however, is *Fruits of the Earth* (1933). In this last of the prairie novels Grove brings together all of the major themes of his fiction—man's lonely struggle with the land, the difficult relationship between man and woman, the clash of the generations—and adds to these the dilemma of social change which alienates the pioneer from the community he has created. *Fruits of the Earth* is the story of Abe Spalding, who comes as a young man in 1900 to take up a claim in a sparsely settled region. Abe is described as an epic figure, like the hero of a saga, able to combat and control the opposing forces in nature and society. Grove said he once observed a man arrive from Ontario by train, file a claim, and that same day set to plow his land as the sun dropped below the horizon. Outlined against the sunset, the man looked like a giant, said Grove.[10] He gives Abe the same stature the first day he starts to work his unbroken stretch of prairie:

He was here to conquer. Conquer he would! Before long he had opened ten furrows; the sun was down; and still he went on. A slight mist formed

---

[10] *In Search of Myself* (Toronto: McClelland and Stewart, 1974), p. 259.

close to the ground, and he had the peculiar feeling as though he were ploughing over an appreciable fraction of the curvature of the globe; for whenever he turned at the north end of the furrow, he could no longer see his wagon, as though it were hidden behind the shoulder of the earth.[11]

The novel describes in detail the process by which he gradually masters the land and creates a prosperous farm, complete with brick buildings and modern agricultural equipment. He learns farming techniques to combat drought and flooding, and enjoys his greatest triumph in 1912 when he saves a bumper crop of wheat from rain by using the costly, old-fashioned practice of stacking his crop before threshing. His neighbors, who are amused by his caution, lose their harvests to an unexpected rain. The cash profit allows him to start building his magnificent home and barns. Abe's struggle with the land is presented in massive detail and is probably the definitive account of pioneering in western Canadian fiction.

But the single-mindedness and rigidity necessary to his being a successful pioneer impose tragic limitations on Abe in his relations with his family. *Fruits of the Earth* dramatizes the dilemma of a man and wife in a pioneer society. When Abe marries, he looks to his wife Ruth to serve as his helper and to bear and raise his children; there is little tender devotion or romantic feeling about sex in Abe. Ruth, who is "fitted for life in towns or cities," lives in isolation on the farm, becomes sullen and dispirited, and grows stout. She raises her four children to think of a better life away from the farm. Not until late middle age does she come to value her husband's courage and strength. But the principal tragedy for Abe is, not his wife's unhappiness, but the scattering of his children. While they are small, Abe is too preoccupied with his work to establish any kind of relationship with them. When they are older, it is too late for him to exert a significant influence over them. One son is killed accidentally on the farm, the other goes to town to become a mechanic; one daughter marries a lawyer, the other mixes with "bad company" and leaves the district pregnant and in disgrace. The patriarchal instinct in Abe is crushed.

[11] *Fruits of the Earth* (Toronto: McClelland and Stewart, 1965), p. 25. All references are to this text.

He says to his son, "I've built this house and these barns to keep my children on the farm. If you go, my work is for nothing." (p. 222).

Not only do his children leave, but the society that Abe has helped create rapidly changes. The district bears the Spalding name because Abe was the first man to clear the land and to build and establish a school. He was the natural leader, and everyone looked to Abe for counsel. But forces from outside the district begin to take power over the growing community, and Abe withdraws as leader, specifically over the issue of consolidating the schools. Grove was concerned to chronicle these rapid changes and focused particularly on the influence of the First World War:

The war had unsettled men's minds. There was a tremendous new urge towards immediacy of results; there was general dissatisfaction. Irrespective of their economic ability, people craved things which they had never craved before. Democracy was interpreted as the right of everybody to everything that the stimulated inventive power of mankind in the mass could furnish in the way of conveniences and luxuries. Amusements became a necessity of daily life. [p. 223]

Education takes Abe's older daughter away; the automobile takes his son. Most tragic for the hard-working puritan pioneer to watch is the restless quest after pleasure and adventure which leaves his younger daughter pregnant by a married man.

Earlier in the novel, when Abe installs electricity in his new buildings, he experiences the proudest moment of his life, not with his family or neighbors, but alone on the road, where we are told, "He raised an arm as though reaching for the stars" (p. 119). The gesture is symbolic of the pioneer's lonely dream and anticipates the older Abe who, isolated from his family and the community, becomes something of a tragic figure. Grove is at his most eloquent in conveying the isolation of the heroic individual set apart from his community and his defeat, not by society, but by time and change. The tragedy of the human condition as Grove conceives it—that of mutability—gives his old-fashioned novels a philosophical dimension that is universal and lasting. After his oldest son is killed, Abe begins to question the significance and permanence of his achievements. His great house is only five years old, but he notices that "already little sand grains embedded in the mortar were crumbling away; already the edges of the bricks were being rounded by a process of weathering." He thinks of what he has read about the ancient Babylonian cities and concludes: "The moment a work of man was finished, nature set to work to take it down again. . . . And so with everything, with his machines, his fields, his pool; they were all on the way of being levelled to the soil again" (p. 134). And when Abe visits the aged school teacher that once taught his children and finds him approaching senility, he is again deeply saddened:

The decay of the human faculties impressed him as part of the human tragedy inherent in the fundamental conditions of men's life on earth. . . . What as compared with this fact—that, having lived, we must die—did such inessentials matter as economic success or the fleeting happiness of the moment? [p. 199]

But Abe ultimately does not despair and retreat into bitter isolation. Grove has given the novel what might be considered a characteristically Canadian ending. Abe rejoins his society and commits himself to ridding the community of the immoral elements that have taken over during his absence. Abe would perhaps like to restore life as it was before the war, but he recognizes the inevitability of social as well as natural change, and his wisdom, we feel, will be a positive force in the community during his remaining years.

The American influence on western Canadian writers is strongly felt in Grove's work in both theme and structure. We know that although he looked upon contemporary North American writers as his inferiors, he read their works with considerable interest. In tone Grove's fiction is often reminiscent of Hamlin Garland's *Main-Travelled Roads* and *Rose of Dutcher's Coolly*; both writers present farm labor as back-breaking drudgery and view the prairie as a place of lonely exile. The exhilarating feature of the West was that it gave a man the opportunity to create his own world, and in his stories of men who carve large prosperous farms from the wilderness and try to escape their mortality, Grove gives voice to the oldest myth of the American frontier. His specific interest in *Settlers of the Marsh* in writing about immigrant settlement probably owes something to Willa Cather's fiction, to such pieces as "The Bohemian Girl" and especially to *O Pio-*

neers!, a novel which similarly combines two separately written stories—a history of pioneer immigrants and a tragic love story. Another American writer who may have influenced Grove was O. E. Rølvaag; we know that Grove likely read *Giants in the Earth* and *Peder Victorious* (he mentions them in letters), and one feels in Grove's work, especially in *Fruits of the Earth* and an Ontario-set novel, *Two Generations* (1939), the influence of Rølvaag's treatment of the generation conflict. One wonders also whether in his last novel, a satirical ant fable titled *Consider Her Ways* (1947), Grove does not owe something to Dreiser's ant story, "The Shining Slave-Makers," published in 1899.

Two other Grove books deserve brief mention. *A Search for America* (1927) is a picaresque story of a bewildered, sometimes pathetic young immigrant who wanders through the United States in search of the reality behind the American myth of utopia. *The Master of the Mill* (1944) is set in Ontario and is concerned with the effect of industrial automation on both individuals and society. Grove was the first Canadian writer to range over such a variety of subjects, employing so many modes and genres. He was also the first Canadian novelist to write on such universal themes as man's struggle with nature, the clash of the generations, and the advent of the machine age. His treatment of these themes is rooted concretely in the Canadian experience, but at the same time it is informed by a larger perspective on the human condition. Grove's lasting appeal as a novelist is undermined by the fact that he was a humorless and frequently awkward writer. But his somber vision of man alone, dramatized in the story of the pioneer, is authentic and compelling, and he remains a monumental figure in the history of Canadian letters.

Selected Writings

Over Prairie Trails. Toronto: McClelland and Stewart, 1922. Reprint, New Canadian Library, no. 1 (Toronto: McClelland and Stewart, 1957).

The Turn of the Year. Toronto: McClelland and Stewart, 1923.

Settlers of the Marsh. Toronto: Ryerson Press, 1925. Reprint, New Canadian Library, no. 50 (Toronto: McClelland and Stewart, 1966).

A Search for America. Ottawa: Graphic Press, 1927. Reprint, New Canadian Library, no. 76 (Toronto: McClelland and Stewart, 1971).

Our Daily Bread. Toronto: Macmillan, 1928. Reprint, New Canadian Library, no. 114 (Toronto: McClelland and Stewart, 1975).

It Needs to Be Said. Toronto: Macmillan, 1929.

The Yoke of Life. Toronto: Macmillan, 1930.

Fruits of the Earth. Toronto: Dent, 1933. Reprint, New Canadian Library, no. 49 (Toronto: McClelland and Stewart, 1965).

Two Generations. Toronto: Ryerson Press, 1939.

The Master of the Mill. Toronto: Macmillan, 1944. Reprint, New Canadian Library, no. 19 (Toronto: McClelland and Stewart, 1961).

In Search of Myself. Toronto: Macmillan, 1946. Reprint, New Canadian Library, no. 94 (Toronto: McClelland and Stewart, 1974).

Consider Her Ways. Toronto: Macmillian, 1947. Reprint, New Canadian Library, no. 132 (Toronto: McClelland and Stewart, 1977).

E. J. Pratt

Until the late 1920s Canadian poets were content to continue in the nineteenth-century Romantic tradition, writing landscape poetry and echoing the optimistic philosophies of the more sentimental Victorians. The work of the Confederation poets had become identified as the national literature, and younger poets were urged to emulate the standards set by Charles D. G. Roberts, Bliss Carman, and Archibald Lampman. But there emerged in Montreal in the twenties a group of young poets and critics, dominated by A. J. M. Smith and F. R. Scott, who challenged this concept of literary nationalism and argued for the values of cosmopolitanism and a contemporary sensibility. These poets were attracted to the modernist movement; they read the new poetry in the Imagist anthologies and in Harriet Monroe's *Poetry: A Magazine of Verse* and quickly mastered its techniques and idiom. They were particularly attracted to Imagism because its values of hardness, compression, and clarity seemed to them well suited to conveying the essence of the Canadian experience. At the same time, however, they could not share the literary cynicism of the postwar writers like Ezra Pound and T. S. Eliot. Canada was a new country, a lonely land but not a wasteland, and Canadian poets could not write about cultural decay when the country was at its beginning.[1] If anything, Canada had been exhilarated by the Great War, had come of age. These writers, then, turned away from Romanticism, not because they felt betrayed by its values, but because the new idiom allowed them to portray more directly and honestly the hard, rugged reality of the Canadian landscape. This new vision is set forth in Smith's "The Lonely Land," an

---

[1] The postwar cultural ethos is discussed in Sandra Djwa's "'A New Soil and a Sharp Sun': The Landscape of a Modern Canadian Poetry," *Modernist Studies* 2, no. 2, pp. 3–17.

Imagist poem similar to H. D.'s "Oread," and in a series of early poems by Scott, including "Devoir Molluscule," "Old Song," and "Laurentian Shield," which celebrate a stoical pleasure in confronting life's adversities and in hard-won truths.

Curiously, however, the writer most responsive to the northern vision of Canada was a poet who remained indifferent to the forces of modernism. E. J. Pratt is often considered Canada's most important poet, but because he is technically an old-fashioned writer, influenced by Browning and Tennyson rather than by his peers, he is virtually unknown outside the country. As one American critic observed in 1945 of Pratt's *Collected Poems*, he is "by our standards a hundred years out of date."[2] Another reason for Pratt's limited appeal is that he is an epic poet, treating specifically Canadian subjects such as the Jesuit missionaries of the seventeenth century, the building of the Canadian Pacific Railway, and the arduous existence of the Newfoundland fisherman. But perhaps the most parochial element in Pratt's work is the ethos it evokes of the academic poet, specifically that of the teacher from Victoria College, University of Toronto, where the austere bourgeois values of a small provincial city were mingled with Christian humanism and illumined by the wit and erudition of a classical tradition of learning. Yet for the very reasons that he has gained so little attention outside the country, Pratt stands as a figure of unique significance in Canadian letters.

Edwin John Pratt was born in Western Bay, Newfoundland, in 1882 and was educated at Saint John's Methodist College. Like his father before him, Pratt worked as both a minister and a teacher on the island, living in the small fishing communities where life changed little from generation to generation. In 1907 he left the island and enrolled at Victoria College, Toronto, graduating with a Bachelor of Arts in 1911, a Bachelor of Divinity in 1913, and a Doctor of Philosophy degree in theology in 1917. Although he was ordained, Pratt did not take up the ministry, probably because of a crisis in his religious beliefs. Instead, he joined the Department of English at Victoria College, where he was a much loved teacher, poet, and raconteur until his re-

---

[2] Winfield Townley Scott, "Poetry and Event," *Poetry: A Magazine of Verse* (Chicago) 66, pp. 329–34; rpt. in *E. J. Pratt*, ed. David G. Pitt (Toronto: Ryerson Press, 1969), pp. 50–53.

tirement as professor emeritus in 1953. During his lifetime he published some eighteen collections of poems, many of which quickly found their way into anthologies of verse used in Canadian schools. When he died in 1964, Pratt was mourned as a national figure whose work was emblematic of the country's literary culture.

Although E. J. Pratt is best known for his long narrative poems on epic subjects, his first published book, *Newfoundland Verse* (1923), is a collection of lyrics. In this book, however, many of the themes and assumptions of the major poems are given their first significant expression. Here Pratt establishes himself as a poet whose vision takes root in the hard realities of life in a bleak northern land, where men and women wage an endless struggle to make a living from the sea. Loss of life on the water is the occasion around which several poems take shape. In "The Toll of the Bells" the community mourns the fishermen whose frozen bodies are recovered and brought to shore. In "On the Shore" a woman keeps vigil over the waters, but her loved one, we are told, will never return. In "The Ice-Floes" men on a seal hunt are separated from their ship and drift south to certain death on the ice. The brutal harshness of this life and its effect on the people are captured most concisely in a brief lyric poem titled "Erosion," where we are told that it took the sea a thousand years to carve the features of the cliff, but only an hour of storm (in which presumably a husband or son is lost) to sculpt granite seams upon a woman's face. As well as the human tragedy, the image conveys the unity of humankind with the natural environment. In the poem "Newfoundland" Pratt writes that the tides ebb and flow "within the sluices of men's hearts," that the winds "breathe with the lungs of men."[3] But at the same time, purposeful men and women are separate from the world of tide, wind, and rocks, and we have projected one of the central conflicts in Pratt's verse—humanity's origin and kinship with nature, but its potential for a larger life through intelligence and spirit.

Central to Pratt's imagination is his fascination with all forms of strength and power. Such an interest is announced by the sub-

[3] All quotations are from Pratt's *Collected Poems*, 2d ed., ed. with an introd. by Northrop Frye (Toronto: Macmillan, 1958).

jects of his major poems: dinosaurs, whales, the luxury liner *Titantic*, a transcontinental railroad. As critics have often suggested, that fascination is articulated in Pratt's poetry in a central metaphor of evolution, wherein human intelligence gradually replaces brute nature as the most powerful force in the world and where a moral order is projected to supplant a natural one.

Pratt views the bedrock of existence to be in the natural forces of wind, water, and rock. There water nurtures life, but must also kill in order to feed "the primal hungers of a reef." The poet is spellbound by primordial forms of life, by nature "red in tooth and claw," which from a human vantage point appears wantonly cruel and destructive. In the early poem "The Shark," Pratt creates a symbol of something terrifying and malignant in nature, a creature "tubular, tapered, smoke-blue," more frightening than a vulture or wolf because its blood is cold. Pratt repeatedly makes the reader shudder as he or she is forced to consider the origin of life in elements and forces remote from human intelligence and emotion. But at the same time, the poet marvels at the evolutionary process that produced human beings with their capacity for wonder, joy, and compassion.

The evolutionary theme comes strongly to the fore in Pratt's second collection of lyric poems titled *Many Moods* (1932). "From Stone to Steel" defines succinctly Pratt's view of humanity and the nature of civilization. The poem begins:

> From stone to bronze, from bronze to steel
> Along the road-dust of the sun,
> Two revolutions of the wheel
> From Java to Geneva run.

Humanity's evolutionary progress is charted in terms of technology and government—a movement from the stone implements and tribal warfare of prehistory to the manufacturing of steel and the fashioning of a League of Nations in the twentieth century. But according to Pratt humanity has not entirely shed the brutal phases of prehistory, and he warns that "the snarl Neanderthal is worn / Close to the smiling Aryan lips." Human beings are both flesh and spirit, are poised, says Pratt, between the cave and the temple, which is to say that they are torn between the primitive instincts to kill and the ideal of compassion and self-sacrifice:

> Between the temple and the cave
> The boundary lies tissue-thin;
> The yearling still the altars crave
> As satisfaction for a sin.

The proximity of contrary instincts in human beings is reflected in the rituals of religion, where a killing, a sacrifice, is part of the act of worship. In the final stanza Pratt observes that Christianity too is based on a sacrificial death, for "whether to the cross or crown / The path lies through Gethsemane."

Christ, however, is for Pratt the highest point that humanity has thus far attained in the process of evolution. In "The Highway," Pratt asks whether humanity has perhaps missed the whole point of history and the evolutionary process. The poem begins in the time when the planets are put in orbit and the creation of the brightest star is announced; the second stanza shifts to geological time when the appearance of vegetation on earth culminates in the emergence of the rose; then, in the third stanza, the human species appears "late in the simian-human day," and the creation of a human being as perfect in turn as the star and the rose takes place in the appearance of Christ. The final stanza, however, implies that the purpose of evolution has been missed, that humanity, putting Christ to death and ignoring his message, is lost.

> But what made *our* feet miss the road that brought
> The world to such a golden trove,
> In our so brief a span?
> How may we grasp again the hand that wrought
> Such light, such fragrance, and such love,
> O star! O rose! O Son of Man?

The image of humanity traveling on a long road towards a better life is examined in the light of Christian faith in an earlier poem titled "The Iron Door (An Ode)" published in 1927. The poem was occasioned by Pratt's grief at his mother's death and enquires into the possibility of an afterlife. Pratt had written his doctoral dissertation on Pauline eschatology, so the Christian arguments for life after death were an intimate part of his thinking. But the poem, cast as a dream vision with the quality of a scene from Dante's *Purgatorio*, is an ambiguous testament of faith at best. In the dream a company of mortals, supposedly the souls of the dead, come to a high cliff by the sea where stands an iron door in the shape of a cross, but with a death's crest carved on its lintel. The petitioners seek to pass through the door, to know whether there is a greater life beyond. They come from various walks of life: a child is there searching for his "father," an aged master mariner asks for directions for "the unknown ocean" ahead, and there is the poet's mother who proceeds with calm, unshaken faith. Another woman, who seems to represent humanity at large, asks why, after the price paid by a woman's travail and love, evil should still be brought into the world:

> Why all the purchase of her pain
> And all her love could not atone
> For that incalculable stain:
> Why from that tortuous stream, —
> Flesh of her flesh, bone of her bone, —
> Should issue forth a Cain.

As the petitioners sink into despair contemplating evil and universal death, the door swings slowly open. The narrator watches the crowd pass through, although he himself sees nothing beyond the door. However, he catches a sense of light and life beyond:

> And while it was not given me to know
> Whither their journey led, I had caught the sense
> Of life with high auroras and the flow
> Of wide majestic spaces;
> Of light abundant; and of keen impassioned faces,
> Transfigured underneath its vivid glow.

The poet is left with a positive feeling, although as he awakes and daylight returns, he is blinded again to the next world. The poem gives a visionary or imaginative sanction to Christian faith, but does not insist on its reality. Pratt's position on Christianity remains personal and ambiguous, but it does assert without reservation the importance of faith in a moral order and of Christian ethics as a counterforce to the existence of evil in human affairs.

Pratt views nature as part of the cosmic process, which is amoral and without intelligence. Humankind has evolved out of nature but does not conform to its laws, for it has intelligence and will and a capacity to choose the way to live. Pratt's most rousing affirmation of humanity in the face of an amoral, mechanistic cosmos is found in "The Truant," a long poem published in his last collection of lyrics, *Still Life and Other Verse* (1943). In this poem the god of the universe is called the great Panjandrum (a pretender to power), and his world is the mechanical order of the cosmos. Man, the truant, is brought protesting to the throne of the Almighty by the Master of the Revels and made to give an account of himself and his irregular ways. The Master of the Revels assures the Panjandrum that tests have been done and that man consists of the fundamentals, "calcium, carbon, phosphorous, vapour." However, man has a will and concepts "not amenable to fire" and will not obey the laws of the cosmic dance. There is no conflict for Pratt in describing a mechanistic universe in terms of dance, because he saw the machine as a metaphor for all forms of energy and rhythm, from physics and physiology to politics and the arts.[4]

The point of the poem is that human beings are more than a function of chemicals; they have a capacity for pain and joy and love and rebel against all mechanical and formal systems. The Panjandrum threatens man with physical deterioration ("I shall make deaf the ear, and dim the eye / Put palsy in your touch . . . shoot / Arthritic needles through your cartilage") which is in fact a literal account of what happens to mortal beings. But man, who through history has suffered untold agony in wars, still refuses to conform to the Panjandrum's laws, and in a noble speech of defiance he asserts the moral law of human love and brotherhood (Pratt's response to Darwin and Huxley):

> We who have met
> With stubborn calm the dawn's hot fusillades;
> Who have seen the forehead sweat
> Under the tug of pulleys on the joints,
> Under the liquidating tally
> Of the cat-and-truncheon bastinades;
> Who have taught our souls to rally
> To mountain horns and the sea's rockets
> When the needle ran demented through the points;
> We who have learned to clench

---

[4] See Louis Dudek, "Poet of the Machine," *Tamarack Review* 6 (Winter 1958): 74–80; rpt. in *E. J. Pratt*, ed. David G. Pitt, pp. 88–94.

> Our fists and raise our lightless sockets
> To morning skies after the midnight raids,
> Yet cocked our ears to bugles on the barricades,
> And in cathedral rubble found a way to quench
> A dying thirst within a Galilean valley—
> No! by the Rood, we will not join your ballet.

Although the human species has evolved out of nature, evolution has created in men and women an ethical impulse that raises the species above its primitive, savage origins.

In "Come Away, Death," critically regarded as Pratt's finest lyric, the poet describes the possibility of humanity being thrown back to a state of savagery through its own self-destructive impulses. The poem is a reflection on death in response to the bombing of Britain during World War II. The cataclysmic horror of technological death is contrasted with its ritualization in earlier periods of history. In the first stanza the poet reminds us that all living things must die:

> However blow the winds over the pollen,
> Whatever the course of the garden variables,
> He [Death] remains the constant
> Ever flowering from the poppy seeds.

In the second stanza the medieval dance of death is evoked to convey death's constancy and unpredictability, but the idea of death is softened by chivalric personification ("He offered sacramental wine" and "led the way to his cool longitudes / In the dignity of the candles"), just as it is romanticized in the allusion to the Clown's song (*Twelfth Night* 2.4) in the poem's title.

The third stanza, however, asserts that chivalric death is no longer possible. In the twentieth century it takes the form of tanks used in the First and Second World Wars:

> The *paternosters* of his priests,
> Committing clay to clay,
> Have rattled in their throats
> Under the gride of his traction tread.

The fourth stanza describes the bombing of an English village by the sea, focusing on the terrifying moment of silence before the bomb explodes:

As the winds stopped to listen
To the sound of a motor drone—
And then the drone was still.
We heard the tick-tock on the shelf,
And the leak of valves in our hearts.
As calm condensed and lidded
As at the core of a cyclone ended breathing.

In the final stanza the bomb is described as "a bolt / Outside the range and target of the thunder" which makes human emotions return to savage modes of terror. The bomb also has the power to obliterate civilization, to return humankind to the primitive condition of the Java caves. Death in the twentieth century is an apocalypse that returns humanity to its origins in savagery. The poem, rich in literary and cultural allusions, is probably most memorable for the intensity of those phrases in which the impact of physical fear is recorded.

Most of the important ideas that inform Pratt's poetry are set forth in the lyrics, but his reputation as a major poet rests with the long epic narratives. Altogether Pratt wrote ten long poems which deal with different phases of the evolutionary process—in *Titans* with the evolution of superior forms of animal life, in *Brébeuf and His Brethren* with civilization, in *The Titantic* with human technology, and in *Towards the Last Spike* with the development of Canada as a nation. The conflict in these poems is man versus nature, or, perhaps more precisely, the conflict between highly evolved, sophisticated forms of life and primitive, less-developed forms. Pratt grew up beside the North Atlantic, and the struggle with a harsh environment blind to human purposes was printed indelibly on his spirit. Accordingly, his imagination is most fully engaged when he is writing about those stark, primordial forms of nature which threaten to destroy civilization—the shark, the iceberg, the pitiless savages of the forest, the granite cliffs of a rocky coastline on which human beings continue to endure. As Northrop Frye has observed, there is a kind of innocence to the epic conflicts that Pratt describes because there is enmity without hatred. The enemy is outside the human community; the conflict is part of the evolutionary process.[5]

[5] Frye, introduction to the *Collected Poems*, p. xvii.

In 1926 Pratt published a pair of long narrative poems in a book he called *Titans*. The first poem, "The Cachelot," is the story of a gigantic sperm whale who fights and triumphs over his primitive foe, the giant squid, but who is in turn destroyed by a higher form on the evolutionary scale—humankind. E. K. Brown contends that Pratt had not read *Moby Dick* when he wrote the poem, but the description of the whale as well as the action of the poem suggest that he likely had.[6] Pratt gives an exuberant account of the whale's magnificence, outside and in:

> His iron ribs and spinal joists
> Enclosed the sepulchre of a maw.
> The bellows of his lungs might sail
> A herring skiff—such was the gale
> Along the wind-pipe. . . .
>
> . . . .
>
> And there were reservoirs of oil
> And spermaceti; and renal juices
> that poured in torrents without cease
> Throughout his grand canals and sluices.

In the final struggle between man and the whale, between two different stages of the evolutionary scale, the poet curiously exhibits some sympathy for the lower order. We experience not only the whale's death agonies but his conscious humiliation in being brought down by a thing called a second mate. But men also suffer in this conflict: the poem ends, like Melville's novel, with the whale dragging down the ship and crew:

> Then, like a royal retinue,
> The slow processional of crew,
> Of inundated hull, of mast,
> Halliard and shroud and trestle-cheek,
> Of yard and topsail to the last
> Dank flutter of the ensign as a wave
> Closed in upon the skysail peak,
> Followed the Monarch to his grave.

[6] E. K. Brown, *On Canadian Poetry* (Toronto: Ryerson Press, 1944), p. 149. See also Sandra Djwa's valuable study, *E. J. Pratt: The Evolutionary Vision* (Montreal: McGill-Queens University Press, 1974), p. 71, and the introduction, p. 147 n. 3.

The other poem in *Titans*, "The Great Feud," is subtitled "A Dream of a Pleiocene Armageddon" and takes place in Indonesia at a time of evolutionary crisis, just before the Ice Age and the emergence of the human species. The action of the poem is a great battle between the creatures of the land and those of the sea—the dispute is over territorial rights to the shoreline. The central character is a female ape who precipitates the battle in the name of a righteous cause: she wants revenge on the cold-blooded sea creatures because an alligator has eaten one of her young. What is significant is that her aggressive purpose comes as she exercises a rudimentary form of reason, which results in the moral law of an eye for an eye, a tooth for a tooth. The other chief character is a dinosaur, *Tyrannosauros rex*, whose race is extinct but who is hatched from an egg preserved in pitch and mothered by an ostrich. He joins the battle, which is directed by the female ape and which is described with all the classical conventions of military epic. But the dinosaur becomes confused and attacks land creatures, who in turn start tearing him apart and each other as well. The dinosaur seems to recognize that he is an anachronism and throws himself off a cliff into the ocean. The battle is brought to a swift conclusion by the eruption of a nearby volcano. Only the ape, with her combined instinct and intelligence, realizes what is going to happen and travels inland before lava covers the Indonesian coast.

"The Great Feud" is a comic poem with a regular octosyllabic meter and a rhyme scheme that underscore the farcical element throughout. Much of the humor resides in the great gusto with which Pratt applies his love and knowledge of Latin words to his prehistoric subject. But as in most animal fables, the purpose of the poem is deadly serious. The question asked is whether evolution brings a new moral order. "The Great Feud" is an allegory about war and the perversion of reason, a theme that can be found in other twentieth-century writings, such as the poems of Robinson Jeffers and William Golding's *The Inheritors*. Pratt, who had reflected deeply on World War I, asks whether there is progress in evolution when reason serves the purposes of aggression.

In *The Titanic* (1935) humanity has evolved to a point where it has almost complete technical mastery over the environment.

The central irony throughout the poem is that humanity assumes it is absolutely safe on this splendid ship, when in fact the ship will sink in a few hours and many lives will be lost. Pratt leans heavily on the irony of the ship's proclaimed seaworthiness:

> An ocean life boat in herself—so ran
> The architectural comment on her plan.
> The wave could sweep those upper decks—unthinkable!
> No storm could hurt that hull—the papers said so.
> The perfect ship at last—the first unsinkable,
> Proved in advance—had not the folders read so?

This continues in the description of the luxuries on board ship during the voyage, the gourmet dinners served in the first-class dining room, and especially in the description of a poker game. The gambling motif underscores in the poem the idea of chance, that the people are not in complete control of their fate.

The antagonist in the poem is the iceberg with "a palaeolithic outline of a face" and "a sloping spur that tapered to a claw." The iceberg is also described with religious imagery, "facade and columns with their hint / Of inward altars and steepled bells." Nevertheless, the iceberg in its beauty represents the brute power of nature that humanity has attempted to master through technology. Humanity is still vulnerable, betrayed not only by its mechanical inventions but by pride as well. Self-confident, the ship proceeds at full speed through the dangerous ice floes and, colliding with the iceberg, sinks before another ship can effect a rescue.

Humanity endangered, however, displays nobility. The real significance of being human emerges at this point in the poem, as men and women perform courageous deeds to save others, show restraint and self-sacrifice. Pratt touches only briefly on ignoble behavior; the incident of the stoker who almost murdered the wireless operator for his life jacket illustrates the primal instinct for self-preservation. He focuses instead on those who make a positive moral choice to save others—the young men who give up their places in the lifeboat to the women from the steerage, Mrs. Strauss's decision to stay on the sinking ship with her husband.

The poem ends with a powerful description of the iceberg "still the master of the longitudes." But humanity has triumphed in the beleaguered community at sea. The moral choice has prevailed, and men and women have proven themselves capable of courage, restraint, and self-sacrifice. What is especially important is that they achieve heroism, not through individual acts, but as members of a group. The high value placed on community in Canadian life is nowhere better illustrated than in Pratt's epic narratives. As poet and critic Frank Davey has put it, "The story of the Titanic is . . . a story of the necessity of social responsibility, of group action and group heroism, of men uniting in a common cause and gaining strength and inspiration from their own communality."[7]

These same values are central to Pratt's masterpiece, *Brébeuf and His Brethren* (1940). *The Titanic* is a highly polished poem, structurally sound and written in vigorous iambic pentameter, but Pratt plays so heavily on the central irony of the ship's history that the poem almost loses credibility. This is not true of *Brébeuf*, where conflict with savagery is not simply an occasion for self-sacrifice but is a matter of historical destiny. Technically, one of the great advantages in the poem is Pratt's use of blank verse which moves away from the comic and academic overtones of his earlier writing. In this poem Pratt brings his themes of evolution and the noble endurance of "corporate man" to a genuinely epic level.

Brébeuf and His Brethren is set in the period of the seventeenth-century Counter-Reformation and tells of the Jesuit mission to the Indians in New France. It is the story specifically of a martyrdom—a saint's legend cast in heroic form—which moves relentlessly forward to the inevitable destruction of the mission at Huronia and the torture and deaths of Brébeuf and Lalemant. The epic scope of the poem is established in the panoramic opening sequences which describe the rekindling of the old faith throughout France and the call of the missionaries to the frontier of the Canadian wilderness. The zeal and devotion of the missionaries in their attempt to convert and civilize the Indians is developed in twelve separate sections (following the conventional epic design) and concludes, not with the destruction of the mis-

[7] Frank Davey, "E. J. Pratt, Apostle of Corporate Man," *Canadian Literature* 43 (Winter 1970): 64.

sion in 1649, but with an awakening to the values of belief and
self-sacrifice in the twentieth century. Because the story of the
Huron mission is a familiar one (the poem's sources were the
Jesuit *Relations* and Francis Parkman's *The Jesuits in North America*), Pratt was free to develop the narrative in a leisurely fashion
using a mosaic of vignettes, dramatic dialogues, letters, and related documents which extend and enrich the religious design of
the story.

Pratt's desire to write about an epic hero (somewhat frustrated
by the democratic character of the twentieth century) is here fulfilled in the figure of Father Brébeuf, an aristocratic descendant
of the crusaders, a man of heroic physical stature and exemplary
spiritual courage. Brébeuf is larger than life, both during his mission (the Indians call him *Echon*, "he who pulls the heaviest
load") and during his twelve-hour torture when he answers his
tormentors "roar for roar." Some critics have felt that Brébeuf is
presented ironically as a victim of hubris, that Pratt shared Parkman's view of the Jesuit mission as heroic folly;[8] but Pratt has too
much admiration for Brébeuf, is too much in awe of his strength
and courage to view him as less than a great hero. His heroism,
however, is not that of a defiant individual, but represents the
bravery of the Jesuit community, and the glory Brébeuf achieves is
for his faith, not for himself.

The heroic religious sonority of the poem culminates in those
passionate, rhetorical lines where the father's final torture and
death are described:

> Where was the source
> Of his strength, the home of his courage that topped the best
> Of their braves and even out-fabled the lore of their legends?
> In the bunch of his shoulders which often had carried a load
> Extorting the envy of guides at an Ottawa portage?
> The heat of the hatchets was finding a path to that source.
> In the thews of his thighs which had mastered the trails of the
>   Neutrals?
> They would gash and beribbon those muscles. Was it the
>   blood?

---

[8] See Vincent Sharman's "Illusion and an Atonement: E. J. Pratt and Christianity," *Canadian Literature* 19 (Winter 1964): 21–23.

> They would draw it fresh from its fountain. Was it the heart?
> They dug for it, fought for the scraps in the way of the
>   wolves.

The answer to the question posed, of course, is faith. Pratt writes that Brébeuf's strength was not in love of country or in love of religious doctrine,

> But in the sound of invisible trumpets blowing
> Around two slabs of board, right-angled, hammered
> By Roman nails and hung on a Jewish cross.

These lines do not necessarily assert Pratt's own belief in the literal truth of Christianity, but as one critic has observed, they do show "that belief itself is a reality that can transform life and give even the sceptical earth-bound mind a vision of beauty and meaning."[9] In terms of Pratt's evolutionary vision, Brébeuf's story represents the conflict between civilized man and savagery, a conflict which again testifies to humanity's potential for great acts of courage and compassion.

The last of Pratt's long narratives is about the building in Canada of the first transcontinental railroad and is titled *Towards the Last Spike* (1952). On one level the conflict in the poem is between the country's first prime minister, Sir John A. Macdonald, who envisions the unification of the country, and his political opponent, Edward Blake, who says: "A Road over that sea of mountains. . . . It can't be done." But the heart of the poem is Pratt's old theme of humankind united against nature, here in the form of the geographical obstacles that lie in the path of the railroad's construction. The most memorable passage in the poem is Pratt's description of the Laurentian Shield as a sleeping reptile, a dragon to be vanquished in order to run the railroad over its back. Pratt's perennial fascination with power assumes a comic form in the poem, where he gives an elaborate account of how oatmeal is digested by Scots laborers and becomes the energy needed to attack the shield's great bulk. *Towards the Last Spike* bristles with conceits and witty abstractions; it is the most academic of Pratt's long poems and the least successful.

Pratt is a quintessentially Canadian poet, for he had a northern

[9] Peter Buitenhuis, preface to *Selected Poems of E. J. Pratt* (Toronto: Macmillan, 1968), p. xv.

vision of life's intractable hardness and responded to the immensity and bleakness of the Canadian landscape by writing on subjects of commensurate proportion and austerity. The documentary precision in the presentation of his subjects, whether modes of torture in New France or the workings of a modern transatlantic liner, gives his poems their characteristic Canadian feeling of reality. And his emphasis on group action rather than individuality marks him from most American writers. Pratt was a highly original poet; he worked outside the mainstream of modernism and with a fine disregard for literary fashions, fulfilling his own needs for imaginative expression. Accordingly, Pratt wrote with direct simplicity about some of the heroic phases of Canadian history and became one of the country's significant myth-makers.

Selected Writings

Newfoundland Verse. Toronto: Ryerson, 1923.

The Witches' Brew. London: Selwyn and Blount, 1925.

Titans. London: Macmillan, 1926.

The Iron Door: An Ode. Toronto: Macmillan, 1927.

The Roosevelt and the Antinoe. New York: Macmillan, 1930.

Many Moods. Toronto: Macmillan, 1932.

The Titanic. Toronto: Macmillan, 1935.

The Fable of the Goats and Other Poems. Toronto: Macmillan, 1937.

Brébeuf and His Brethren. Toronto: Macmillan, 1940.

Dunkirk. Toronto: Macmillan, 1941.

Still Life and Other Verse. Toronto: Macmillan, 1943.

Collected Poems. Toronto: Macmillan, 1944.

Behind the Log. Toronto: Macmillan, 1947.

Towards the Last Spike. Toronto: Macmillan, 1952.

The Collected Poems of E. J. Pratt. 2d ed. With introduction by Northrop Frye. Toronto: Macmillan, 1958.

Ethel Wilson

Ethel Wilson, the author of six novels and several short stories, holds an anomalous place in the history of Canadian literature. Because she lived in the West and because she did not publish until late in life, she was not part of the literary community of her generation. Her ties, if any, were with British writers. Ethel Wilson was born in 1888 in South Africa, where her father was a Methodist missionary. Orphaned at an early age, she was raised in British Columbia by relatives who were among Vancouver's founding families. She was educated in England as well as Vancouver, and between 1907 and 1920 she taught in Vancouver's public schools. In 1921 she married Dr. Wallace Wilson, a distinguished physician who was for a time head of the Canadian Medical Association. Mrs. Wilson began writing stories in the 1930s, but it wasn't until 1947, when she was nearly sixty years old, that she published her first novel.[1] Most of her fiction is set in British Columbia and beautifully captures the atmosphere of place, but her writing is never simply regional: it takes up human problems of universal import. Its originality was still being discovered at the time of her death in 1980.

The characteristic concerns of Ethel Wilson's imagination are revealed by her style. In a letter to Desmond Pacey she says that what she likes best is "the English sentence, clear, unlush, and unloaded . . . the formal and simple sentence."[2] Yet while the simple style forms the matrix of her prose, her writing is at the same time full of stylistic quirks—curious repetitions, illogical

[1] Her papers, however, in the Special Collections division of the University of British Columbia library reveal that she was seriously trying to write a novel as early as 1930 and that the image she cultivated of a socially prominent doctor's wife with an amusing hobby was not wholly accurate.

[2] See Desmond Pacey, *Ethel Wilson* (New York: Twayne, 1967), p. 179. The letter is dated 12 July 1953.

statements, ellipses, lacunae—which arrest our attention, direct us to something unspoken, covert. The failure to communicate is a thematic corollary to such a style, the gaps in the writing constituting palpable forms of arrest and discontinuity in the flow of human relationships. Indeed, Mrs. Wilson gauges in her fiction the many ways by which human contact is broken—through guilt, shyness, fear, jealousy, hate. The recurrent story in her work is that of a woman who withdraws from familiar surroundings and sets out on a lonely quest of self-discovery. This woman usually has no mother and, deprived of this intimate bond of family, must establish on her own a link with the larger human community. The pattern is mythic and familiar, but what involves and disturbs the reader of Ethel Wilson's fiction is a certain *froideur* in the narrative voice, an implied emotional preference for retreat, evasion, and distance, which is always in tension with the author's vision of unity and her theme of human responsibility.[3]

In Ethel Wilson's first novel, *Hetty Dorval* (1947), the theme of human community is struck at once in the epigraph from Donne, the familiar "No man is an Iland, intire of it selfe."[4] The heroine of the title is a spoiled, attractive woman whose life illustrates the very reverse of Donne's counsel: Hetty Dorval islands herself in a world of selfish comforts and amusements and leaves behind her a long string of broken attachments. Her story is narrated by Frankie Burnaby, a young school girl who is initially infatuated with Hetty, but who eventually comes to see her without romantic illusions. At the outset of this pastoral novel Frankie is going to school in Lytton, a pioneer ranching community in British Columbia, when the mysterious Hetty Dorval takes a bungalow near the town. In a few brief scenes the author defines the relationship of the young girl and the older woman. In the eyes of young Frankie the various images of Hetty (on horseback, watching a flight of wild geese, in the cottage surrounded by her elegant furnishings and library of yellow books) all fall together to create a

[3] In his book *Ethel Wilson*, Desmond Pacey has made a study of the large themes in Mrs. Wilson's fiction, focusing particularly on her humanist's concern for love and friendship in a universe that frequently reveals itself to be destructive and without purpose.

[4] *Hetty Dorval* (Toronto: Macmillan, 1947). All references are to this edition.

forbidden, romantic picture of sophistication and freedom. This is enhanced by Hetty's unwillingness to become involved in the mundane affairs of the small town.

But Hetty's romantic image eventually tarnishes. After a period of school in Vancouver, Frankie goes to live in England, and on the ship crossing the Atlantic she and her mother encounter Hetty deep in intrigue to marry a wealthy old gentleman. Previously Mrs. Burnaby had confided to her daughter that an ugly story had followed Hetty from Shanghai to Vancouver. Frankie thinks of Hetty's refusal in Lytton to become involved in the community, and at the same time she thinks about Donne's admonition. What was once for Frankie a romantic manifesto—"I will *not* have my life complicated"—now becomes a complex problem for the girl: "'No man is an Iland, intire of it selfe;' said Mother's poet three hundred years ago, and Hetty could not island herself, because we impinge on each other, we touch, we glance, we press, we touch again, we cannot escape" (p. 72). Hetty appears again in Frankie's life, this time smashing up the friendships Frankie has made for herself in England. Frankie grows to hate Hetty, and when the latter leaves for the continent and another marraige, Frankie finds that she cannot bear to have her life complicated either.

The human community theme dominates the book, but one feels there is a further emotional drama that is not fully revealed. The simple style of *Hetty Dorval* in fact conceals much of the experience that is at the heart of the novel. In the following excerpt from the novel's first paragraph, notice the number of words and phrases repeated:

Mr. Miles, the station agent, was in his shirt-sleeves; the station dog lay and panted, got up, moved away, lay down and panted again; and the usual Indians stood leaning against the corners of the wooden station (we called it "the deepo") in their usual curious incurious fashion, not looking as though they felt the heat or anything else. The Indians always looked as though they had nothing to do, and perhaps they had nothing to do. Ernestine and I had nothing much to do, but school was out and supper wasn't ready and so we had drifted over to the station. [p. 1]

The repetition of course crystallizes the feeling of monotony in a small town on a hot summer afternoon, but it also creates an opaque surface here and elsewhere in the narrative which directs the reader away from the portentousness of the events being described. On closer scrutiny *Hetty Dorval* is a complex emotional drama of initiation involving the relationship of mothers and daughters, older women and young girls.

Hetty initiates Frankie into life's disillusionments (a process symbolized by the Fraser River that muddies the Thompson), but why, we ask, does Frankie come to dislike Hetty so intensely? Possibly it is because her relationship with Hetty is the first in a series of guilty involvements. Frankie's early affection for Hetty is guilty because it is secretive (Frankie is forbidden by her parents to keep company with Hetty) but also because it encroaches on the young girl's love for her own mother. The climactic scene of the novel turns on a guilty mother-daughter relationship when Hetty discovers that her chaperon, whom she has always treated with impatience, is in fact her mother. Frankie for a time abandons her mother's love, and so the guilty revelation implicates her as well.

But there is a further reason for Frankie's bitterness—Hetty becomes her rival for a young girl's affection. In England Frankie looks forward some day to marrying a young man named Richard Tretheway, although in the meantime it is the innocent and gentle charms of his sister Molly that she enjoys most. Hetty establishes the same relationship with the Tretheways and threatens to steal their love away from Frankie.

Hetty Dorval can be described as a pastoral of experience— one of those stories of a remote rural childhood which focuses ultimately on a disturbing memory of growing up, leaving home, and finding a place in the larger world. Hetty is the catalyst that brings change in Frankie's life and leaves her ill prepared to meet adulthood. Near the end of the novel Hetty comes to share Frankie's bed for a night, but Frankie is so filled with jealousy and guilt that she gives Hetty a hard smack on her "round silken bottom" and renounces the life of desires and involvements altogether. The negative implications of Frankie's actions are made clear in a final sequence where we are told that Hetty has gone to live in Vienna, but around that city in 1914 there has grown up a wall of silence—the negation of human community and involvements writ large.

Ethel Wilson's second novel, *The Innocent Traveller* (1949), is very different from *Hetty Dorval*; it celebrates in loving fashion the life of a woman who lives to be one hundred years old, but who learns less about living in that time than does Frances Burnaby in one night with Hetty Dorval. The subject of this major novel is the author's family history. The character of Topaz Edgeworth, effervescent, irrepressible, superficial, is one of the most delightful creations in Canadian literature. The book is a pastoral of innocence celebrating the domestic joys of family and old age rather than youth and erotic love. There are unforgettable comic episodes such as great-grandfather Edgeworth's courting at the age of ninety, and later Topaz, also in her nineties, thinking that she has suffered a stroke when her bloomers drop around her ankles on the street. The whole world, as seen through the eyes of Topaz and the older members of the family, is providentially ordered and secure. Great-grandfather Edgeworth, drowsing in the sunshine of his garden, is content because "his world was a good world. His Queen was a good Queen. His country was a good country. . . . His family was a good family and God was good." [5] For Topaz's saintly sister, Annie Hastings, the world is a reflection of the divine order of the next world, while for Topaz herself it is completely defined by the existence of her father, Queen Victoria, and Mr. Gladstone. Even the Canadian wilderness in this book has the childish and animate aspect of a pastoral landscape—with mountains that "skip like rams" and "the innumerable laughter" of the sea. But above all it is the sense of family which gives the world its unity.

The escapist pleasures of celebrating an innocent and uncomplicated past, however, are undercut by the narrator's preoccupation with time and meaning. We are told, in a particularly effective metaphor, that gradually the members of the family "slipped one by one with acceptance or amazement through the strangely moving curtain of Time into another place" (p. 16). Death is softened through the various strategies of pastoral style (the death of Topaz's mother is a comic ritual of dress and decorum, Topaz's

---

[5] *The Innocent Traveller* (Toronto: Macmillan, 1949), p. 73. All references are to this edition.

father and sister die of "ripe old age"), but its inexorable presence is an important part of the family history. More difficult, however, is the question of life's meaning. The author describes bubbly Topaz with such evident pleasure, but there is always the nagging problem of the significance of her life—of what "use" was she? Mrs. Wilson writes: "Aunty's long life . . . inscribes no significant design. Just small bright dots of colour, sparkling dots of life" (p. 243). In the course of the narrative she is described as a "warbling unimportant bird," a creature as ephemeral as "the dimpling of the water caused by the wind," and, most memorably, as a water glider who skims along the surface of life "unaware of the dreadful deeps below." When she has died, she is but a "memory, a gossamer." Seen from something like a cosmic eye, Topaz looks foolish and pathetic in all her commotion of living.

As an innocent, Topaz has within the reference of her family a kind of comic sanctity. But outside that framework she is a creature of little worth—without resources, without imagination or character. In a finely crafted chapter, "The Innumerable Laughter," often anthologized, the author exposes that innocence by taking Topaz (one of Mrs. Wilson's motherless orphans) on a brief journey into isolation. The chapter opens with a comic sequence: Topaz, who is on holiday with the family at their summer cottage, discovers nine young men swimming naked in the ocean. She dashes off to tell her niece Rachel and says she wishes she could identify them: "If they would only turn right side up I might be able to see." (Mrs. Wilson is capable of delightful bawdy humor; when Topaz's father decides to remarry, we are told in a series of double entendres that there is "Something Up," that he is going to Switzerland, which on the map is "pink," and that he is going to bring back a "piece" [pp. 13–14].) Topaz's experience at the beach is followed by the threat of Yow, the devilish Chinese cook, to put a snake in the supper stew. That night Topaz decides to sleep outside on the porch alone. She takes all the accoutrements of her civilization with her—shawl, walking stick, umbrellas, biscuits—but gradually the sounds of the night begin to frighten her. She thinks of the bearded decorum of her Victorian father and relations and then of the nude men swimming. She imagines she hears a flute and she "panics"; as the etymology of that word implies, she fears a revelation that will turn her mad. One can hardly miss the sexual implications. The day's experiences (the nude men bathing, the invincible Yow with the snake) culminate in sexual terror: "Inside the white satin body of Topaz . . . there opened a dark unknown flower of fear. . . . Her whole body dissolved listening into fear which flowed into the terrible enclosing night" (p. 193). She rushes inside the cabin, and Rachel, to quiet and comfort her, gently massages her body, restoring her to the protected world of the family. In this chapter we see that Topaz's innocence is pathetically dependent on a social order which is evasive and artificial. Topaz is not exposed in this manner again; she remains a water glider who never probes beneath the surface of appearances. But her innocence has been discredited, and in the images of Topaz being absorbed at death like a drop of water in an endless cycle or like one of the gulls going out to sea, there is something just a little sad, for we are made aware not only of her insignificance but that as a human being she never lived fully or with a purpose.

The breadth of Ethel Wilson's imagination is reflected in her ability to write in different literary modes. From writing pastoral and family chronicle, she turned in her third book to composing two works in the satirical, or critical, mode. *The Equations of Love* (1952) opens fittingly with the image of a golden dawn yielding to "mere flat day." The book comprises two novellas and as epigraph takes a question from Dickens's *Bleak House*—"What is the common sort of Terewth?" The answer in the first story, "Tuesday and Wednesday," is that man is vain, sentimental, and pretentious, and only his egocentricity, ironically, saves him from recognizing the meaningless, destructive void in which he lives. The story describes two days in the lives of several lower-class characters living in Vancouver, characters whose minimal humanity and purpose are beautifully reflected in flat, throwaway statements like "Because he had to get up some time or other, he got up."[6] The lives of Myrt and Mort Johnson and their acquaintances are without pattern and purpose, and yet to emphasize this

---

[6] *The Equations of Love* (Toronto: Macmillan, 1952), p. 3. All references are to this edition.

by contrast Ethel Wilson creates an intricate literary design around their activities, especially Mort's death.[7]

Two of the characters hold a special place in Ethel Wilson's fiction. Vicky Tritt, a neurotically withdrawn spinster, is representative of countless lonely individuals whose lives are depicted or suggested in the course of Wilson's writing. Vicky lives alone in a boardinghouse; her room is lit by one bare bulb hanging from the ceiling. She has work in a notions shop, but except for church services and an occasional visit with her cousin, Myrt Johnson, she has no other human contacts. Her one pleasure in life, carefully meted out, is to read a movie magazine each week. The shyness and pathetic anonymity of this girl/woman are contrasted sharply with the "golden effulgence" of Mrs. Emblem, a woman whose geniality and human success emphasize to Vicky Tritt her lack of "the golden possession—popularity." This grotesquely maternal woman is another figure which appears frequently in Ethel Wilson's fiction. Yet even for Mrs. Emblem the best part of the day is when she is alone, tucked up in bed, reading "the Personal Column" of the newspaper. Ethel Wilson, like American novelist Edith Wharton, is fascinated with people whose lives are completely anonymous and depersonalized, people who live in lonely retreats with only the barest essentials of existence. In Ethel Wilson's short stories probably the most memorable figure of this type is Mrs. Bylow, the old woman in "Fog" whose monotonous, empty life is relieved by reading the ads in the newspaper and by chatting briefly each day with two women who hurry past her little house on their way to work.

The central figure in the other novella, "Lilly's Story," can be grouped with the above; her life too is minimal in terms of human relationships. Lilly is another of Mrs. Wilson's orphans— her mother abandons her when she is still a girl—and her life is a lonely journey. The emotion which prevents her from establishing lasting relationships with others is fear, an animal instinct which keeps her "on the run" all her life. The different phases of her life are marked by experiences of terror. When she is a child

[7] Beverley Mitchell's "Ulysses in Vancouver: A Critical Approach to Ethel Wilson's "Tuesday and Wednesday," *Atlantis* 4 (1978): 111–22, argues that the novella is a literary parody in the manner of Joyce's *Ulysses*.

living with her mother in a wretched cabin in Vancouver, she is questioned by the police about her part in delivering stolen goods and afterwards has nightmares and whimpers "the police, the police" in her sleep. Her first lover brings her stolen gifts, which starts her running in earnest from the police. On Vancouver Island Lilly takes shelter temporarily with a Welsh miner who fathers her child. When her daughter Eleanor is born, Lilly resolves to bring up the child respectably and moves to another part of the island where she will not be known. She fabricates a story about her past and her husband's death, but fear that she will be recognized and exposed keeps her on the move. Throughout the story she is described as a frightened animal seeking a secure hiding place in which to raise her child.

Fear estranges Lilly from other people, but for another group of women social relations are anxiety-ridden because of shyness and lack of self-confidence. Ethel Wilson has never written an artist's story, but one glimpses something like a self-portrait in the heroine of the short story "Mrs. Golightly and the First Convention." It is written in a transparently simple, almost confessional style: "Mrs. Golightly was a shy woman. She lived in Vancouver. Her husband, Tommy Golightly, was not shy. He was personable and easy to like." The story describes the plight of a Canadian woman attending a convention with her husband in California. Her husband, who has the "gorgeous possession" of social ease, leaves his wife to get on as best as she can with the other wives. In spite of her desperate desire to conform and please, situations become awkward for Mrs. Golightly, her speech faltering. At one point during a car ride arranged for the wives, she escapes her situation temporarily by glorying in the sportive freedom of the seals in the ocean. (Animals are frequently an index to intense emotional experiences in Ethel Wilson's fiction.) The story comes to a climax when, to her horror, Mrs. Golightly insults a woman, only to discover later that the woman is not aware she has been injured. The supposed victim says to the apologetic and fumbling Mrs. Golightly, "You are too earnest, my child." Mrs. Golightly then recognizes the necessary superficiality of society and its operations, which gives her confidence but which, ironically, disappoints her just a little as well.

In *Swamp Angel* (1954), a quest romance usually regarded as her masterwork, Ethel Wilson develops the theme of running from human responsibility into a complex and subtle piece of symbolic fiction. Here to catch the ebb and flow of experience, to create surface texture in the prose that will mirror Mrs. Wilson's vision of a formless, chaotic world, the style is strikingly elliptical and fragmented. Chapters do not always appear to follow one from another; scenes are juxtaposed beside each other without linear connectives in the narrative. The failure of human beings to connect with each other is reflected in tiresome monologues, in speeches tortured with slang, and in chapters which consist of only one clipped statement or an advertisement from the newspaper. But beneath this jarring, rough-textured surface there is a pattern of interconnected symbolic incidents which, carefully considered, have much to say about human relations, especially the dilemma of modern woman.

The plot itself reveals little. A woman named Maggie Vardoe, living in Vancouver, leaves her husband and starts life over as a cook at a fishing lodge in the interior of British Columbia. Her success and satisfaction with her new life are marred by the jealousy of the lodge owner's wife. In the meantime Maggie's husband is rejected by a series of women, and her friends, the Severances, continue their lives in the city—Hilda Severance marries, and her mother Nell, after a little accident, dies. A more rewarding approach to the novel is through its title, which is also the book's central symbol. As Pacey has pointed out, the two images yoked together suggest the range of human experience—from the primal and inchoate emerges the human form divine.[8] Even more suggestive is the title's historical origin explained in the novel's epigraph: "Swamp Angel. An 8-inch, 200 pound . . . gun, mounted in a swamp by the Federals, at the siege (1863) of Charleston, S.C." The gun had its origin in a battle fought to decide the issue of slavery. The Swamp Angel is an image of power; its possession

---

[8] Pacey, introduction to the New Canadian Library edition of *Swamp Angel* (Toronto: McClelland and Stewart, 1962). All references from the novel are to this edition. For a study of the journey into isolation in *Swamp Angel*, see John Moss, *Patterns of Isolation* (Toronto: McClelland and Stewart, 1974), pp. 129–49.

and relinquishment symbolically describe a drama of will and power in the novel.

The Swamp Angel of Nell Severance, "a powerful and wilful old woman," is a family pistol. Nell was once a brilliant circus performer. The gun, which she used to juggle, symbolizes her past triumphs, but it is still a potent weapon in the present, for it represents her power over her daughter Hilda. For Hilda, the gun is an emblem of her unhappy childhood, a childhood filled with shame at the fact that her mother was a vagabond with the circus. In the elliptical, non sequitur style of the novel the reader is given a glimpse of Hilda's confused relationship with her mother: "She loved her mother dearly and hated her a little. People should not be so powerful. People should not always succeed, and so she made tea" (p. 49). The gun also carries the phallic association of male authority. In her interviews with the rejected Eddie Vardoe, Nell twirls the gun menacingly, and in bed she keeps it pressed against her thigh. The gun enters directly into the symbolic action of the novel when Mrs. Severance, grown very heavy over the years, falls on the street and sprains her ankle. The gun tumbles out of the old woman's grasp, and a small scandal ensues involving the police. Mrs. Severance feels she is no longer strong enough to control its destiny, and so she sends the Swamp Angel to Maggie for safekeeping.

The transfer of the gun opens up the significance of Maggie's story. Maggie is Nell's spiritual heir, for, like Nell, she is a strong woman who wants to be free and to have control over her own life. Maggie is also one of the author's motherless women who, the reader is told, was "brought up from childhood by a man, with men" and "had never learned the peculiarly but not wholly feminine joys of communication, the deshabille of conversation." (p. 32). Our first impressions of Maggie are wholly positive. She is calm, intelligent, resourceful; and when we meet her husband Vardoe, a truly unsavory individual, we admire her courage in breaking away. Her strong, creative instincts are such that she can build up the fishing resort in one season, forget her tragic past in New Brunswick (her first husband, child, and father have all died), and, before the first season is over at Three Loon Lake, save from death a wealthy businessman, Mr. Cunningham, who offers her a position in the East as a reward. But we must ask whether Maggie's actions are entirely admirable; remembering that Mrs. Wilson is fascinated with the meshing of contraries, one can expect a negative side to the heroine's character as well. Why, we should ask, does Maggie break her marriage vows and leave Vardoe? Certainly he is an unpleasant man, and the two- and three-sentence chapters about his life after Maggie leaves (chapters 28–35, 37–38) encapsule brilliantly the emptiness of his character. But from Maggie's point of view the one reason given and dwelled on is the "nightly humiliation" she endured while she lived with Vardoe. She thinks of her marriage as a period of "slavery." When she is preparing to leave Vardoe, she thinks only of freeing herself from the outrage of "the night's hateful assaults." But if Maggie does not enjoy the marriage bed, why did she marry Vardoe in the first place? The implied answer is that she was attracted to his weakness. Vardoe, the poor boy with "spaniel eyes" working in her father's store, physically unfit for the army, seems to have attracted Maggie by those very qualities which elicited pity in others. Perhaps Maggie subconsciously felt she could dominate this man and that marriage would not mean any loss to her freedom. We are told nothing about Maggie's first marriage to Tom Lloyd, but the one time she thinks of him, her thought is cold and almost comic in its impersonal, stylized nature: "Dear Tom, casting perhaps, with a crystal fly for a quick jade fish in some sweet stream of heaven" (p. 54). Vardoe, however, turned out to have very conventional ideas about marriage (male supremacy, female subjugation), so Maggie leaves him.

Swamp Angel is peopled largely by strong, forceful women and weak men. In the world Maggie creates for herself at Three Loon Lake, her contact, Henry Corder, is old, the proprietor, Haldar Gunnarson, is crippled, and Alan Gunnarson is still a boy; in her service are the biddable Chinese brothers, Angus and Joey Quong. Only the jealousy of Gunnarson's wife spoils Maggie's haven, for it curbs her freedom (she must constantly watch herself so that Vera's suspicions are not aroused). The irony is that Maggie does not want Vera's husband or son; she prefers no social obligations or responsibilities. Yet Vera's jealousy creates them. "Human relations . . . how they defeat us," thinks Maggie (p. 142).

Mr. Cunningham's offer of a position in the East is the turning point in the novel. Will Maggie "run away" again from a difficult situation (she has run from New Brunswick and from Vancouver), or will she stay with the Gunnarsons and try to make their relationship work? Mrs. Severance's visit with Maggie is decisive. The old woman accuses Maggie of escaping to the woods from the reality of human relationships: "Everything of any importance happens indoors," she insists (p. 149). Then she urges Maggie to recognize that all things are interconnected in "the everlasting web" of creation, and the Donne theme "No man is an Iland" is sounded again in Ethel Wilson's fiction. Earlier in the novel Maggie had an intimation of this herself, first when she considered the harmony of the Chinese family in Chinatown, and later when she thought about how many people were involved in designing and creating the English crockery Mr. Cunningham had sent her as a gift. In this conversation Mrs. Severance admits that, preoccupied with her juggling and her mate Philip, she had lived on an island herself and had made Hilda suffer—binding her to any unhappy childhood and a search for maternal love. Only after the old woman has given up the gun (symbol of selfhood and power) does Hilda begin to live a "normal" life. The latter marries Albert Cousins, another of the novel's gentle, unaggressive men, and though Mrs. Severance describes Albert as a "lamb," she also tells Maggie that "he rules [Hilda] with a rod of silk" (p. 127)—perhaps Ethel Wilson's ideal vision of the marriage relationship.

The final scene in the novel shows Maggie, after Nell's death, throwing the Swamp Angel into the lake; the act is coincident with her decision to stay at the lodge and strive for a workable relationship with the Gunnarsons. The reminder of Excalibur in this gesture and the grail in Maggie's yellow Chinese bowl (her "household god") suggest a specifically Christian dimension to Maggie's quest, as does her instinctive act of compassion in kneeling and rubbing the feet of both Mr. Cunningham and Vera Gunnarson when they come out of the cold water of the lake. This is further enforced by the symbolism of the geography: Maggie's journey into the wilderness, through the town of Hope, past three crosses planted on a hillside to the waters of a remote lake, suggests the stages in a pilgrimage toward self-discovery and Christian humility.[9] But the larger significance of Maggie's throwing away the gun is her relinquishment of power and freedom in order to become part of the web of creation, part of the human community. As the gun settles to the bottom, we are told in a repetition of phrases that knits things together that "the fish, who had fled, returned, flickering, weaving curiously over the Swamp Angel. Then flickering, weaving, they resumed their way" (p. 157).

Death is the agent of separation and loneliness in Ethel Wilson's last published novel, *Love and Salt Water* (1956). This novel is a romance in the sense of Shakespeare's last plays, where characters are tested through a series of misfortunes and misunderstandings before being fully integrated into society. As in every one of Mrs. Wilson's major pieces of fiction, the journey motif is the central element of structure. Here it is coupled with a symmetrical narrative design that takes the heroine from the unity of a happy family life to almost total isolation, then back again into the larger fabric of the human community. *Love and Salt Water* is the least successful of Mrs. Wilson's novels, but it dramatizes more powerfully than any of the other books the author's conviction that chaos lurks beneath the smooth surface of events, that humankind lives "on a brink."[10] The action of the novel is studded with gruesome accidents, maimings, and sudden deaths.

As epigraph to *Mrs. Golightly and Other Stories*, Ethel Wilson quotes from Edwin Muir: "Life '. . . is a difficult country, and our home.'" The line reflects the creative tension in Mrs. Wilson's art: feelings of estrangement circumscribed by reasonable and philosophical acceptance. Human relations, their complexity, and their fragility, is Ethel Wilson's intimate theme, and an oblique, elliptical style is the special signature of her prose. But to say this does not invalidate or detract from the philosophical vision of her novels. Rather, Ethel Wilson's sense of the universe as

[9] See Paul Comeau's "Ethel Wilson's Characters," *Studies in Canadian Literature* 6 (Summer 1981): 32.

[10] See Frank Birbalsingh's "Ethel Wilson, Innocent Traveller," *Canadian Literature* 49 (Summer 1971): 35–46; and Blanche Gelfant's "The Hidden Mines in Ethel Wilson's Landscape (or an American Cat among Canadian Falcons)," in *The Ethel Wilson Symposium*, ed. Lorraine McMullen (Ottawa: University of Ottawa Press, 1982), pp. 119–39.

an ungoverned void (an existential, twentieth-century version of the Canadian wilderness motif) carries conviction because it is approached by characters who, for complex reasons, have lived for a time in isolation and without motive. Similarly, her insistence on the humanistic values of love and faith and her almost mystical preoccupation with unity, "the everlasting web," assert as antidote the powerful, and historically Canadian, need of community.

Selected Writings

Hetty Dorval. Toronto: Macmillan, 1947. Reprint, Laurentian Library, no. 6 (Toronto: Macmillan, 1967).

The Innocent Traveller. Toronto: Macmillan, 1949. Reprint, New Canadian Library, no. 170 (Toronto: McClelland and Stewart, 1982).

The Equations of Love. Toronto: Macmillan, 1952. Reprint, Laurentian Library, no. 19 (Toronto: Macmillan, 1974).

Swamp Angel. Toronto: Macmillan, 1954. Reprint, New Canadian Library, no. 29 (Toronto: McClelland and Stewart, 1962).

Love and Salt Water. Toronto: Macmillan, 1956.

Mrs. Golightly and Other Stories. Toronto: Macmillan, 1961.

Earle Birney

Earle Birney is the first major poet to come from western Canada. He was born in Calgary, Alberta, in 1904 and brought up in the mountain country of Banff and Creston, British Columbia, where he did farm labor and worked as an axman on survey crews to earn money to attend the University of British Columbia. After graduating in 1926, he spent ten years at various schools working toward a doctorate in English literature. His studies were interrupted by financial difficulties, which resulted in his teaching for a time in Utah, and by political commitment to Trotskyism, which took him to London to work for the British Independent Labour Party. He finally completed a doctoral dissertation on Chaucer at the University of Toronto and taught there from 1936 until 1942, when he joined the army, serving overseas as a personnel selection officer. It was during World War II that Birney began to write poetry; although he started relatively late, the high quality of his work was quickly recognized, and he won Governor General's Awards for his first two books of verse. In 1946 he became a professor of English at the University of British Columbia, where he eventually established the Department of Creative Writing. On leaving the University of British Columbia in 1966, he became writer-in-residence at several Canadian universities, making his home in Toronto, traveling widely, and continuing to write and give readings and lectures.

Perhaps it was inevitable that a poet born in a rough, thinly settled part of the country still known as the Northwest Territories would begin with one of the oldest themes of Canadian literature—man's relationship to the wilderness. What characterizes Birney's treatment of nature and, by extension, informs his world view as a poet is a set of attitudes peculiar to the mountain man, that most western form of the North American frontiersman. The mountain man (explorer, trapper, fighter, guide) views the wilderness as a place of freedom and adventure, but recognizes at the same time its brutal indifference, sometimes its active hostility, to his presence. The wilderness is always a place of testing. There is in the mountain man a characteristic feeling for violence as the measure of reality and an exaggerated preoccupation with masculinity. But what is particularly relevant to the poet is that the mountain man, alone in a world with geological rather than human features, develops a cosmic vision of life's cycles and measures time in millenia. The mountain man takes a long perspective on human activities, recognizes man's cosmic insignificance. The experience and vision of the mountain man constitutes a relatively small portion of Canadian literature, but in Howard O'Hagan's *Tay John*, a mythic tale of a half-breed Indian, and in the poetry of Earle Birney and Patrick Lane it has found particularly eloquent expression.

Birney's most famous poem, "David," published in *David and Other Poems* (1942), issues directly from Birney's experiences as a boy growing up in rugged mountain terrain and from a view of nature as both idyllic and monstrous. "David" is a narrative about two youths who are working for a summer on a survey crew and who, on weekends, go mountain climbing to escape the crowded camp and to test their young muscles. Much of the poem describes the physical exuberance they experience in climbing the mountains and the pleasure they enjoy in their friendship with each other. Youth with its sense of unlimited power gives a heightened, Olympian scale to their adventures: "Mountains for David were made to see over, / Stairs from the valleys and steps to the sun's retreats."[1] But in each section of the poem there are foreshadowings of danger—a goat's skeleton, a broken-winged robin, ice-covered rock, the tracks of a grizzly—which are reminders of nature's cruelty and indifference to individual lives. Then David, helping the narrator get his footing, falls from the top of the mountain to a ledge fifty feet below. The narrator finds him there still alive, but his back is broken and his legs "splayed beneath

[1] All quotations, except as noted, are from Earle Birney's *Selected Poems*, 1940–1966 (Toronto: McClelland and Stewart, 1966).

him." David pleads to be spared a life in a wheelchair, and the narrator pushes him over the edge. We are told that only "the sun and incurious clouds" mark the place where David died.

As critics have noted, the setting is the most vividly realized dimension of the poem.[2] It conveys the narrator's changing perception of the world. In the early part of the poem when the two companions are reveling in their sport, the mountain landscape seems like a living thing, full of energy and purpose. The diction used to describe the landscape, words like "flashing," "floating," "sprawling," "sunalive," endow it with a vitality commensurate with the spirit and hardihood of the young men. Moreover, the five-stress lines with their irregular number of unstressed syllables, a measure suggested by Archibald MacLeish's *Conquistador*, and the assonant rhymes which fall short of being full rhymes give, as Desmond Pacey has noted, the effect of climbing, of stress and movement.[3] After the accident the diction radically changes; motion words to describe nature are replaced by static adjectives such as "fanged," "spectral," "wrinkled," "grave-cold." The physical energy of the lines is broken by dashes that force a pause. The idea implicit in the poem's nature imagery is that the narrator attributes to the landscape whatever joy or cruelty he perceives there, that nature is in fact "incurious" about human affairs. Significantly, as the narrator descends the mountain, he no longer sees a swamp "that quivered with frog-song," but a bog rank with purple toadstools.

"David" is an elegy on the theme of male friendship. It strikes more deeply than the conventional pastoral elegy because the narrator conceives a guilty involvement in the death of his friend. He failed to test his footing on the Finger, and his friend slipped helping him to regain his place. The narrator's horror and revulsion at what has happened are dramatized in his nightmarish descent from the mountain with its "running and falling" and "pounding fear." The landscape is "fanged" and "blinding," obscene with phallic shapes—toadstools and slugs—and with the

[2] Frank Davey, *Earle Birney* (Toronto: Copp Clark, 1970), p. 93.
[3] Ibid., p. 91; Desmond Pacey, *Ten Canadian Poets* (Toronto: Ryerson, 1958), p. 306.

pain of some animal that yelps in the dark. The depth of the narrator's guilt suggests that he had an unconscious desire to end the idyllic friendship with David, that his friend's death was psychologically necessary before he could join the camp and become part of society. Birney makes his initiation theme explicit in the last line, where the narrator recalls that day on the Finger as "the last of my youth."

The dark side of mountain life (the harshness of winter, madness, death) is also dramatized in "Bushed," where a man living alone in the woods loses his sanity, convinced that the wilderness has intelligently chosen to destroy him. His dream of a pioneer life takes concrete form in a cabin beside a mountain lake, where he rises at dawn, learns to cook porcupine meat, and dresses himself with animal skins. But in this isolation he begins to perceive nature as animate and willful, preparing for hostilities against him:

> He found the mountain was clearly alive
> sent messages whizzing down every hot morning
> boomed proclamations at noon and spread out
> a white guard of goat
> before falling asleep on its feet at sundown

He sees the ospreys as valkyries "choosing the cut throat," imagines the woods full of moose and bears circling him. He takes refuge in his cabin, refusing to go outside, convinced that the mountain peak is poised like an arrowhead at his heart. Although Birney makes clear that nature's malevolence exists primarily in the mind of the human observer, nature's force is nonetheless powerfully felt in the poem.

In "Vancouver Lights" Birney begins to take the long, cosmic perspective and extends his double vision of nature to include humankind; in a dark universe, humanity with its intelligence is both the source of light and its extinguisher. This frequently anthologized piece is written in one of Birney's favorite forms, the descriptive-reflective poem. The scene which triggers the poet's thoughts consists simply of the twinkling lights of the city as seen from the side of the mountain. Nature is beautiful but frightening—the poet observes the "mountain's brutish forehead" and feels "the terror of space." Night embodies all the emptiness the poet feels surrounding him in the universe, while the city lights signal humankind's attempt to create an intelligent order in the darkness. The fragility of the human species is emphasized: "We are a spark beleaguered / by darkness." Humankind's capacity to create light, however, is always threatened by a primal instinct for violence and destruction. The poem, written during the uncertain days of World War II, ends with a powerful statement on the irony of humanity's ambiguous powers:

> These rays were ours
> we made and unmade them   Not the shudder of
>   continents
> doused us   the moon's passion   nor crash of comets
> In the fathomless heat of our dwarfdom   our dream's
>   combustion
> we contrived the power   the blast that snuffed us
> No one bound Prometheus   Himself he chained
> and consumed his own bright liver   O stranger
> Plutonian   descendant   or beast in the stretching
>   night—
> there was light

If the light fails, it is not because nature destroyed it, but because human beings destroyed it. There is in all of Birney's poetry a strong and persistent conviction that humanity has the power to create its own destiny. He delineates the choice succinctly in the final stanza of the epigrammatic "Time Bomb," with its characteristic mountain image of primal violence:

> Within the politician's ribs,
>   within my own   the time-bombs tick
> O men be swift to be mankind
>   or let the grizzly take

In the face of nature's brute indifference on the one hand and humanity's capacity for self-destruction on the other, Birney asserts the importance of love and fidelity. These values in his poetry carry the conviction of one who has brooded in solitude on the human condition and has been numbed by the realization that the species' existence is without consequence to the workings of the universe. "The Road to Nijmegen," inspired by Birney's war experiences, might be taken as a personal philosophical statement. The theme is set forth in the first two lines:

> December my dear on the road to Nijmegen
> between the stones and the bitter sky was your face

As has been suggested, the stones here symbolize the ruins of war, hence war itself, while the bitter sky symbolizes the harshness of nature. The face between is a symbol of human love.[4] The poem proceeds through a series of images which picture the ravages of war ("graves with frosted billy-tins for hats / bones of tanks beside the stoven bridges"), but the remembered face gives the soldier-narrator hope and a reason to march on. At the center of the poem is an affirmative creed based on faith in human kindness: "Only the living of others assures us / the gentle and true we remember."

Birney's humanism is also expressed in his perennial concern for social justice. At times he assumes the mask of the satirist, nowhere perhaps more effectively than in "Anglosaxon Street," a portrait of contemporary urban society written in Anglo-Saxon verse form. Here Birney reveals both the scholar's and the poet's fascination with language, describing a modern city in richly alliterative lines with strong caesural pauses and compound words. His frontier imagination, however, is never wholly absent from his poetry; in his use of Anglo-Saxon versification he creates an ironic contrast between a primitive, heroic civilization (appealing to a mountain man) and its diminished present day counterpart. Birney's vision of the modern city is not that of a wasteland, but of a smug, conformity-ridden society sustained by prejudice rather than imagination.

In his verse play, "Damnation of Vancouver," first published in *Trial of a City* (1952), Birney approaches the question fundamental to his humanism: can the human species create for itself a meaningful future, or will it ultimately destroy itself through its instincts for cruelty and greed? The play takes the form of a public hearing on the future of Vancouver—whether the city should be destroyed or not. Witnesses for the prosecution include the explorer Captain Vancouver, who says that on the whole he pre-

[4] Pacey, *Ten Canadian Poets*, p. 312.

ferred "the sweep of fir and cedar," a chief of the Salish Indians who eulogizes the simplicity and abundance of native life, and Gassy Jack Deighton, a pioneer saloonkeeper, who believes that only the roisterers and pretty girls, those who really enjoy life, are worth saving. Birney's socialism and his medieval interests inspire the inclusion of Long Will of Langland, who sums up the case for the prosecution by describing the harried, browbeaten working people and the frenzied scramble of the middle class for money, the worship of Lady Meed:

> Beyond the tamed shores that no tide cleansed
> Rose the raped mountains, scarred with fires and finance,
> And raddled with the lonely roofs of the rich,
> Of barristers and bookies, and brokers aplenty
> Of agents for septic tanks, for aspirin, or souls.

The counsel for the defense is P. S. Legion, a slick entrepreneur who speaks in the language of the Chamber of Commerce admen. His defense defines the city as a commercial enterprise, a "fast-buck" center:

> Well all I need to say is, we've got faith in B.C.
> Our motto's "We Prosper by Land and By Sea."
> There's billions still to be made from our greenery
> And the mountains will always be there for scenery.
> We're the hub of Tomorrow, the Future's baby,
> We're here to stay, and I don't mean maybe.

But Legion is a false witness, a greedy capitalist living off the common folk by pretending to serve them. Late in the play he is replaced by a housewife, Mrs. Anyone, whose defense of the city is based solely on the simple joys of living: her pleasure in the mountains and ocean, concern for the birds and flowers in her garden, her love for her husband:

> I woke today with my husband,
> To the bronze clashing of peaks,
> To the long shout of the ocean,
> And the blood alive in my cheeks.

She believes that the human instinct to live and enjoy the things of this earth will always prevail over greed and the urge to despoil the earth. The play ends with her defense, asserting Birney's belief in the importance of the common man participating in the destiny of the community.

The high value Birney places on the common man is given succinct expression in "El Greco: *Espolio*" with its mordant religious ironies. Birney is close to E. J. Pratt in his fascination with nature's strength and with his concern for man's moral progress, but he does not view the life of Christ as the pattern for man's highest achievement.[5] In "El Greco: *Espolio*" (inspired by the great painting) it is the carpenter who made the cross who is celebrated; his skill with the awl is seen as more valuable than the activities of that other "carpenter's son who got notions of preaching." Birney places emphasis on the physical reality of the carpenter's work: the hardness of the wood, the exact pressure needed to get the holes straight and deep enough to hold the spikes. The carpenter's craft, building "temples or tables, mangers or crosses," carries forward the slow progress of human culture, while the preaching of the "convict" (Christ) results only in gambling, punishment, and death. The carpenter at work is wholly oblivious to the hands of Christ held out over his head; ironically, this oblivion is his salvation and his guarantee of peace on earth.

Some of Birney's most popular poems derive from his mid-century travels to countries far from Canada. These poems contain the reflections of a sophisticated scholar-poet, an urbane twentieth-century man; yet the mountain man is present in these pieces as well. His habit of far-seeing is stimulated by his travels, where the strangeness of a situation suddenly brings into relief the larger, universal dimensions to experience. In "The Bear on the Delhi Road" the poet is startled to find an animal so familiar to his mountain home in such a strange context. He watches two Kashmir men trying to train a bear to dance so they can exhibit it for money. Through the western poet's eyes the crowded order of an old civilization is evoked, but the poem transcends this regional interest: when the narrator observes that "It is not easy to free / myth from reality," he suggests a parallel between the work

[5] Peter Aichinger in his book *Earle Birney* (Boston: Twayne, 1979) stresses the point that Birney does not believe in God. See, for example, pp. 86–87.

of the bear trainers and his own activities as a poet. By making it dance instead of amble in the berries, the men of Kashmir are trying to impose a human form on the bear; they are trying, like the poet, to give an artistic shape to crude reality.

In another travel poem, "A Walk in Kyoto," the tall man from the mountains is for a time unable to get his bearings in a culture so subtle and discreet as Japan's. Birney has described the poem as "a record of a day's half-conscious hunting for a bridge of identity between my raw Canadian self and the complexities of Japan's ancient capital, Kyoto."[6] The narrator finds himself, like Gulliver in Lilliput, unable to relate to the people. He is told by the maid at the inn that it is Boy's Day, also Man's Day, in Japan, but maleness in the Western sense of size and aggression he finds missing in this country. Everything is small, discrete, and delicate as a watercolor. Clearly there is sexual vigor in these islands teeming with life, yet it remains hidden from the speaker with his "phallic western eye," as confusing as *kabuki*, theater where the roles of both sexes are played by men. He concludes that just as the military power of the shogun's palace is reduced to a tourist site, so the overt sexuality of the people has been erased by the "hermaphrodite Word" of Buddhism wherein all earthly differences are ultimately transcended. But having come to this unsatisfactory conclusion, which he considers a defeat, he is given a revelation: the maid at the inn smiles at him, like a lotus opening, and points over his shoulder at a fish-shaped kite rising in the air, being flown as part of the Boy's Day festival. The narrator's perception has finally adjusted to this alien culture, and he is able to decipher the hieroglyphics of its sexuality in the female lotus, the phallic fish. Only when the speaker ceases to impose his own ideas on the foreign landscape can he begin to perceive its reality.

In "Cartagena de Indias" the poet is visiting the South American seaport, Cartagena, once known, according to the epigraph by José-Maria de Heredia, as the queen of the ocean. In contrast to the poet's virgin frontier home, Cartagena is a city of decay, a place of obscene poverty and disease where "old crones of thirty"

---

[6] Earle Birney, *The Cow Jumped over the Moon: The Writing and Reading of Poetry* (Canada: Holt, Rinehart & Winston, 1972), p. 96.

beg in the streets and "poxed, slit-eyed savages" offer their women as prostitutes. Again the lonely poet feels disoriented and alone, this time oppressed by the fact that to these people he is not only "tall as a demon" but he is one of the world's privileged, a tourist "from outer space . . . plainly able to buy." He searches for a "bridge" other than commerce or charity by which to reach these people. He finds it in a pair of concrete shoes, a curious monument erected to the memory of Colombian poet Luis Lopez. A taxi driver explains to the bewildered tourist that Lopez, who had castigated the people of his native city for their laziness and backwardness, had at the end of his life conceded a love for Cartagenians, "that love a man has / for his old shoes." Hence the monument. The narrator no longer feels repelled by Cartagena, but is filled with love for a city which honors even its most critical poet. The speaker reflects bitterly that in his vigorous new land his poetry is seldom read by his townsmen, whereas here in decayed Cartagena even the taxi driver knows Lopez's work and its critical reputation. He concludes the poem, not with a final reflection on Cartagena's "rancid disarray," but with a statement of love for the city which taught him the true bonds of human brotherhood and, by implication, the insufficiency of his own prosperous, material culture:

> Descendants of pirates   grandees
> galleyslaves and cannibals
> I love the whole starved cheating
> poetry-reading lot of you   most of all
> for throwing me the shoes of deadman Luis
> to walk me back into your brotherhood

One of Birney's best known pieces is "November Walk near False Creek Mouth," a long meditative poem on the human condition. In Birney's canon this is a summary poem bringing together his perennial preoccupation with nature's indifference to humanity, the instinct in people for violence, and the inadequacy of human cultures structured solely on material gain. Here he also gives expression to his cosmic vision of life's cycles and man's inconsequence in terms of geological time. The poem, set in Vancouver, is written in the descriptive-reflective form that Birney favors and relies heavily on the melancholy mood of late autumn for its emotional impact and its thematic significance. Intermittent stanzas in italics carry a persistent reminder that time and nature's process slowly but irreversibly erode:

> *The beat is the small   slap   slapping*
> *of the tide sloping   slipping*
> *its long soft fingers into the tense*
> *joints of the trapped seawall*

The dense homophony, stylistic trademark of Birney's writing, is here used to great advantage to convey the physical process of nature's never-ceasing motion. Beyond this world with its rhythm of change and decay there are only "the desert planets," then the "unreached unreachable nothing."

This sober reflection on humanity's cosmic insignificance and an ultimate void is made darker by the poet's premonition that the human species is approaching the end of its history. As critics have pointed out, the poem is haunted by a vision of humankind's self-destruction by atomic weapons, hence the opening lines: *"The time is the last of warmth / and the fading of brightness / before the final flash and the night."* As the narrator of the poem walks along the beach in the November sunset, he views his fellow citizens engaged in "the separate wait / for the mass dying," people soon to be obliterated by "the unimaginable brightness":

> At this edge of the blast
> a young girl sits on a granite bench
> so still as if already only
> silhouette burned in the stone

The poet on the beach is poised between the disregard of nature, with its eroding waves, and the chaos of humankind's violent world: "between the lost salt home / and the asphalt ledge where carhorns call." Like Matthew Arnold in "Dover Beach," Birney also sees himself on the remotest edge of civilization from which the sea of faith and belief has retreated. As Birney himself has pointed out,[7] there is a trail of mythic references in "Novem-

[7] "Epilogue," in *Earle Birney*, ed. Bruce Nesbitt (Toronto: McGraw-Hill Ryerson, 1974), p. 211.

ber Walk" (Greek, Hebrew, Buddhist, Christian, Norse, Indian) which point to the absence of faith in this prosperous western city where antennae on aseptic penthouses rise "above the crosses" and "pylons march over the peaks / of mountains without Olympus." Like Arnold, the poet is left at the end of the poem "*on the sliding edge of the beating sea*" waiting for the dark and imminent conflict. "November Walk" with its powerful seasonal mood appropriated to a "twilight of the gods" theme is a moving reflection on humankind's transient destiny. The poem's scope and achievement are perhaps best summarized by A. J. M. Smith, who sees the poem as crystallizing a man's efforts to come to terms with nature, society, and the macrocosm in his brief moment of allotted time.[8]

Earle Birney is an eclectic poet who employs a variety of forms—the narrative poem, the nature lyric, the meditation, satire, and ode. In his later years he experimented broadly with form, particularly typography and spelling, and followed younger poets on the road to concrete verse. He believes firmly that poetry, like everything else, must change in order to stay alive; and consistent with this view, he is a frequent reviser of his work, refusing to issue a final version of collected works. But throughout his career what is consistent and most characteristic is his love of language and all its resources of sound, pattern, and meaning, a love that is present in his early intoxication with Anglo-Saxon alliteration through to his late sound poems.

Birney also published two fictions that are worthy of brief mention. *Turvey* (1949), designated by the author as a "military picaresque," is a comic novel about the misadventures of a Canadian private during World War II. The hero, Thomas Leadbeater (Tops) Turvey, is a stock character of war comedy, the foolish private who always outwits his clever superior officers. The plot follows Turvey's military career from enlistment through numerous Canadian and European barracks, train trips, and hospitals, to his eventual discharge in Toronto. The best parts of the book are in-

[8] A. J. M. Smith, "A Unified Personality: Birney's Poems," in *Early Birney*, ed. Bruce Nesbitt, p. 148. There is a good reading of this poem in Les McLeod's "Irony and Affirmation in the Poetry of Earle Birney," *Essays on Canadian Writing* 21 (Spring 1981): 130–57.

dividual scenes where, in order to break the boredom of barracks life, Turvey goes drinking, gambling, or whoring and in the tradition of Chaucer's fabliaux gets into some highly comic situations. *Turvey* has been compared to Jaroslav Hasek's *Good Soldier Schweik* because the hero repeatedly suffers for the incompetence of his superior officers. But Birney's book is concerned as much with the purely comic possibilities of character and events as with the ironies of war and army life.

By contrast, *Down the Long Table* (1955), a less successful book, is a wholly serious fiction. It tells the story of Gordon Saunders, an academic who during the thirties was involved with Trotskyist politics. The framework of the story is a United States congressional committee hearing into the political background of influential academics. Saunders is called before the committee, and as he looks down the table, he recalls his activities and the confusion he experienced as a young man, particularly in relationship to a married woman, a group of Toronto Trotskyites, and a close friend, Professor Channing. Saunders participates in the significant events of that decade, crossing the country by riding the rods, standing in the bread lines, raiding a relief office, and milling about with thousands of others in Vancouver's Victory Square. Birney captures the spirit and feel of the period by using headlines and news stories from the papers in the manner of Dos Passos. His evocation of the social unrest of the thirties is the book's strongest achievement and in Canadian literature is matched by only one other novel, Irene Baird's *Waste Heritage* (1939). The book is of greater value as a social documentary than as a psychological study of a young idealist and will continue to be read largely for its social history.

Earle Birney's career is characteristic of the creative writer who has had a life as a gifted academic as well. During what might have been his most productive years, collections of poems appeared infrequently, and the productivity of the novelist was similarly limited. Birney speaks often of the frustration of the creative writer whose inspiration is drained away by his duties as a teacher. Nonetheless, with poems like "David," "Bushed," and "November Walk near False Creek Mouth," Birney created some important landmarks in Canadian poetry. Specifically, these are the works of the poet as mountain man, and they bring their unique voice and vision to the national literature.

Selected Writings

David and Other Poems. Toronto: Ryerson, 1942.

Now Is the Time. Toronto: Ryerson, 1945.

The Strait of Anian. Toronto: Ryerson, 1948.

Turvey. Toronto: McClelland and Stewart, 1949.

Trial of a City and Other Verse. Toronto: Ryerson, 1952.

Down the Long Table. Toronto: McClelland and Stewart, 1955.

Ice Cod Bell or Stone. Toronto: McClelland and Stewart, 1962.

Near False Creek Mouth. Toronto: McClelland and Stewart, 1964.

Selected Poems, 1940–1966. Toronto: McClelland and Stewart, 1966.

Rag and Bone Shop. Toronto: McClelland and Stewart, 1971.

What's So Big about Green? Toronto: McClelland and Stewart, 1973.

The Collected Poems of Earle Birney. Toronto: McClelland and Stewart, 1975.

Fall by Fury. Toronto: McClelland and Stewart, 1978.

Sinclair Ross

Sinclair Ross ranks as a major Canadian author on the strength of
As for Me and My House, a novel about the drought and depression of the 1930s that stands in a class with the fiction of John
Steinbeck and Nathanael West from the same period. When it
was published in 1941, *As for Me and My House* received a scattering of favorable notices and then dropped from sight. However, the book had made a lasting impression on some of its early
readers; and in 1957, when McClelland and Stewart initiated the
New Canadian Library, a paperback series, *As for Me and My
House* was one of the first novels to be reissued. Since that time
the book has grown steadily in readership and critical reputation
and is now one of the few critically acknowledged classics of Canadian literature.

James Sinclair Ross was born in 1908 on a homestead near
Prince Albert, Saskatchewan. The birthplace is significant because the harshness of the northern prairie and the struggle of the
farmers to wrest a living from their bleak environment always
form an important backdrop to Ross's best writing. Ross's parents,
of Scottish ancestry, separated while he was still a boy, and when
Ross was sixteen, he left school in order to support his mother,
with whom he made his home. His first position was with the
Royal Bank of Canada, and he lived in a series of small prairie
towns, like the Horizon of *As for Me and My House*, until he was
transferred to more permanent posts, first in Winnipeg, then in
Montreal. Except for three years of service during the Second
World War with the Royal Canadian Ordnance Corps, he worked
for the same firm until his retirement.

In the 1930s Ross began writing and publishing a series of
short stories which are among his finest achievements. His first
piece, "No Other Way," won third prize in a competition judged

by Somerset Maugham and Rebecca West and was published in 1934 in *Nash's Magazine* in England. Most of the others appeared in the Canadian academic journal *Queen's Quarterly*, from which a selection was compiled and published as *The Lamp at Noon and Other Stories* in the New Canadian Library series (1968). In all of these stories written during the 1930s and 1940s, Ross describes the heroic efforts of prairie farmers pitted against a hostile environment, and in the taut, spare style of Ross's writing there is a precise articulation of humanity's tenacious struggle to endure. Humankind is shown as determined by environment, by the power of the land, and by the savage assaults of the weather. In "The Lamp at Noon" a dust storm takes away a woman's sanity and the life of her baby; in "A Field of Wheat" a family's hopes for the future are destroyed by a sudden hailstorm, which flattens a promising harvest; and in "Not by Rain Alone" a woman freezes to death when a winter blizzard penetrates the house while she is giving birth to a child. Yet in the face of these tragedies the characters exhibit amazing strength and courage to continue.

The lives of Ross's characters are also determined by a rigid pattern of relationships. The stories focus on three main figures —the farmer, his wife, and their son. The farmers are physically strong men who bear up under the terrible strain of repeated crop failures and the necessity of providing for their families. Their struggle with the unyielding seasons is heroic, but these men are inarticulate: they repress their anger and frustrations and remain grimly silent and aloof from their families. Only rarely does Ross show these stoic figures crumble. In "A Field of Wheat," after the devastating hailstorm, the farmer breaks down and sobs against the mane of a horse in what he believes to be the privacy of the barn. The wife and mother figure longs for a closer relationship with her husband and for the society of others; typically she is alone in the farm house, cut off from neighbors by dust storms or by miles of frozen prairie. She dreams of the family's moving away from the lonely farm and sometimes resorts to desperate acts, like the woman in "The Lamp at Noon" who runs out into a dust storm and smothers her child.

The tension between the men and the women in these stories has a profound effect on the lives of their children. The single motive which keeps both the men and women struggling on is the hope that their children will some day be able to enjoy a better way of life, but their visions of a better life are so disparate that the child is unable to fulfill their expectations. In "Cornet at Night" this conflict is dramatized when the boy must choose which parent to obey: the wheat is ripe and the father needs his son's help with the harvest, but the mother argues that the Sabbath must not be broken and that the boy must attend school if he is ever to have a better life than his parents. The pattern in Ross's stories is for the boy to escape his dilemma by entering into an imaginative world of his own making, suggested by a fragment of music in "Cornet at Night," or made real by the spirit and freedom of a horse in "The Outlaw." The imaginative boy in Ross's fiction temporarily eludes the dilemma of his parents' lives, but the fragile nature of his escape suggests that he too will eventually be trapped by his environment.

"The Lamp at Noon," "Cornet at Night," and "One's a Heifer" are among the best short stories to be written in Canada in the 1930s, yet Ross's masterpiece is *As for Me and My House*, the story of a preacher and his wife living in a small prairie town during the depression. The story is told in the form of a diary kept by the wife, Mrs. Bentley, who craves for intimacy with her silent, aloof husband and who plots their escape from the town. From the first pages we are aware of the cheerless, frustrated existence this couple leads; in twelve years of marriage neither Philip Bentley nor his wife has found any lasting source of happiness. Philip is miserable in his vocation as a preacher; he had wanted to paint, to be an artist, but he could not afford an education. Furthermore, he knows himself to be a hypocrite not believing what he preaches. Mrs. Bentley, who has not been able to bear children, lives only to make her husband happy, but her attentions are always met with indifference. She writes in her diary: "To have him notice me, speak to me as if I really mattered in his life, after twelve years with him that's all I want or need." The novel has little plot; Mrs. Bentley's scheme to save enough money so that Philip can leave the ministry and open a secondhand book store in the city is a unifying thread. Otherwise the novel records life's smaller passages: planting a garden, caring for an orphan boy, a summer holiday, a concert, friendships, and above all the weather—the seemingly endless winter, the hot, dry summer, and the wind that never stops blowing.

The surface monotony of the book may have alienated a 1941 readership weary of depression, dust storms, and religious hypocrisy. The book, moreover, offered neither socialist insight nor escapist entertainment, but gave back a picture of one of the bleakest periods in modern history. Public attention by then was focusing on the Second World War, and novels with war themes were beginning to appear. In 1941, when the world was moving rapidly into another age, *As for Me and My House* seemed curiously dated. But critics and discerning readers since then have come to appreciate the universal and timeless character of the story as well as its historical authenticity. The imaginative complexity of the book is reflected in the widely different interpretations that have been offered: Warren Tallman sees the novel as exemplifying the life-strangling forces of puritanism, while in the opposite vein Sandra Djwa finds an affirmative pattern of spiritual crisis and rebirth subtly manifested in the novel's biblical allusions. Roy Daniells sees the narrator, Mrs. Bentley, as a candid, heroic figure, while W. Cude argues that Ross's purposes go beyond Mrs. Bentley and questions her honesty and reliability as narrator.[1]

In a 1974 interview Ross said that as a young man he attended church regularly, sometimes playing the organ for Sunday services, and that he was once asked whether he would not consider being a minister. The idea did not interest him, yet at the same time he tried to imagine what such a life would be like, and gradually the novel took shape in his mind. The conflict in Philip Bentley between artist and preacher likely went back to the novel's earliest conception. Similarly drawn from Ross's immediate experience are the small-town setting, the drought, and the depression.

[1] See Warren Tallman, "Wolf in the Snow," *Canadian Literature* 5 (Summer 1960): 7–20, and 6 (Autumn 1960): 41–48; Sandra Djwa, "No Other Way: Sinclair Ross's Stories and Novels," *Canadian Literature* 47 (Winter 1971): 49–66; Roy Daniells, introduction to *As for Me and My House* (Toronto: McClelland and Stewart, 1957); and W. Cude, "Beyond Mrs. Bentley: A Study of *As for Me and My House*," *Journal of Canadian Studies* 8 (Winter 1973): 3–18.

When asked about literary influences on his writing, Ross has been less specific. Certainly Ross's knowledge of the Bible informs the novel throughout. Sometimes biblical references—such as the book's title from Josh. 24:15 ("As for me and my house we will serve the Lord")—function ironically as a measure of spiritual failure. In other places the biblical character of such motifs as wind, dust, plagues, and harvest gives the novel an epic coloring. Ross has said that among novelists he especially likes Hardy, and in his picture of the wind-ravaged prairie that Mrs. Bentley describes as a "quivering backdrop, before which was about to be enacted some grim, primeval tragedy," there is the same connection as in Hardy's writing between landscape and man's fate. Ross does not mention a particular interest in Hawthorne, but his book reminds one of that classic American study of Puritanism, *The Scarlet Letter*, which also features a hypocritical minister guilty of secret sin. A different kind of inspiration for Ross, the young writer, might have been the publication in 1925 of Martha Ostenso's *Wild Geese*, which won a Dodd, Mead prize of $13,500—an award which drew a great deal of attention to the book and its author. Ostenso's novel was one of the first to use the Canadian prairie realistically as a fictional setting. Farm life and the western landscape are intimately tied to the smoldering drama of the characters' lives. An aspiring Canadian writer in the West would hardly fail to note the critical and financial success of *Wild Geese*. There may have been a more specific literary influence on Ross in a trilogy of western novels, *The Prairie Wife* (1915), *The Prairie Mother* (1920), and *The Prairie Child* (1922) by the popular professional writer Arthur Stringer. Canadian-born, Stringer worked and found his largest audience in the United States, where he made his home for many years, although much of his fiction is set in various parts of Canada. His prairie trilogy concerns the struggles of a young couple to homestead on the Canadian prairie, raise a family, and secure for themselves a measure of comfort and happiness. Stringer's characters are not westerners, but sophisticates from the eastern states, and the tone of the books throughout is witty and self-consciously smart in the fashion of the late 1910s and early 1920s. But the three novels, which did enjoy some popular success, are narrated through the medium of the wife's letters and diary, and the strongest impression they leave is of an intelligent, courageous woman betrayed by her humorless husband.

The diary form in both Stringer's books and Ross's *As for Me and My House* emerges directly out of the western experience. The journal, or diary, assumed a special importance for pioneer women, who frequently had no close female company with whom to confide their intimate feelings. Many women who were taken west felt alienated from their men, and writing things down in a diary was a way of keeping their sanity and securing a few moments of privacy. The West of Ross's novel is barely a generation removed from the time of the pioneers, and Mrs. Bentley, like the early homesteaders, is moved from place to place with her silent husband as her only companion. Often overwhelmed by loneliness and frustration, she uses her diary to get a grip on her emotions and to wrestle with the tormenting knowledge that she is not loved. Like the diaries of pioneer women, Mrs. Bentley's daybook is grounded in concrete, everyday details—the weather, what is to be cooked for supper, the purchase of a new hat. And as in most private writings, there is little or no reference to public life; the conditions of the 1930s define the book's setting, but there is no reference to the depression, no mention of country or politics. As a form of writing indigenous to the story's setting, the diary is the basis of the realism in *As for Me and My House*—we feel that a complete world has been created. At the same time, the diary allows the author a high degree of artistic selection, for we do not expect detailed comprehensiveness in a private journal. Most important, the secretive, repetitious nature of the entries gives precise voice to the puritan experiences of repression and self-examination out of which the novel is made.

The diary form also accounts for another of the novel's remarkable features—Ross's great success in creating a woman narrator. Mrs. Bentley is wholly credible, and whether we view her as heroic or see her as self-deceiving and manipulating, she commands our attention and sympathy. The type of individual forever rejected in love, in her most unguarded moments she gives us a glimpse of her desperate loneliness: "I must still keep on reaching out, trying to possess him, trying to make myself matter. I must, for I've left myself nothing else . . . I've whittled myself hollow that I might enclose and hold him, and when he shakes me off I'm just a shell."[2] She is also capable of acute insight into the nature of human relationships, particularly in matters of love: "It's the reason perhaps I still care so much, the way he's never let me possess him, always held himself withdrawn. For love, they say, won't survive possession. After a year or two it changes, cools, emerges from its blindness, at best becomes affection and regard. And mine hasn't" (p. 65).

But Ross wanted to tell more than Mrs. Bentley's story; he wanted us to know as well about the life of the frustrated artist.[3] On a first reading Philip is likely to remain a shadowy background figure enclosed in his study, such is the immediacy and authentic voice of the narrator. But in fact the novel's deepest pattern is rooted in the psychology of Philip. Mrs. Bentley tells us that he was born a bastard, that he nursed a deep aversion for his waitress mother, and that he romantically idealized his dead father, a student preacher whose ambition was to paint. Whether Mrs. Bentley realizes it or not, she and her husband are cast in similar roles, and Philip's desire to duplicate his father's life binds them together in a negative relationship. Mrs. Bentley, a mother figure without a first name, has a maternal desire to possess and comfort her husband. But his aversion for his real mother extends to all women and explains the hopelessness of the narrator's situation. The more affection Mrs. Bentley shows her husband, the more he "winces" and withdraws from her. But the perverse logic of emotions is such that the more Philip exhibits a hurt attitude, "as if he were a boy in trouble," the more Mrs. Bentley yearns for him and is determined to possess him. In lieu of sensuous womanhood, Philip calls forth in his wife a sacrificial and protective compassion, which is at once the dignity and deception of her appeal as a fictional character. At the same time, Philip's desire to be like his father leads him to be a preacher and a painter and to reenact his father's primal sin, thus producing another bastard and unwittingly providing Mrs. Bentley with the son she so des-

[2] *As for Me and My House* (Toronto: McClelland and Stewart, 1957), p. 75. Also available as a Bison Book (Lincoln: University of Nebraska Press, 1978). References are to those editions.
[3] See Tallman, "Wolf in the Snow."

perately desires. This does not mean, however, that the outcome
of the story is a happy one, for Judith's child is being introduced
into the same world as its father, and so the progress from one
generation to the next is hopelessly repetitive and circular. The
wind and the dust, metaphors for the suffocating sterility of the
characters' lives, reappear at the end of the novel, and Mrs.
Bentley, perhaps more prophetically than she intends, reflects on
how their lives in the past year have run a "wide wheel."

Reading the novel in the light of Philip's psychology not only
reveals the inevitable shape of the plot but enables us to appreciate more intelligently the nature and limitations of the narrator.
We recognize that Mrs. Bentley's dowdiness and sense of failure
are the projection of Philip's response to women. Mrs. Bentley
tells us that he "recoiled" from his mother "with a sense of griev-
ance and contempt," and Mrs. Bentley elicits the same response
from her husband. Accordingly, her love for Philip is never returned, and she sits alone by her lamp at night, consumed by a
passion that draws her on, as the moths are drawn to their death
at her lamp. Further, Mrs. Bentley's reliability as narrator assumes more complex dimensions, for her words must always be
measured against her desire to possess Philip and be a mother.
The integrity of her motives appears to be unquestionable: when
she confesses that her sole ambition for twelve years has been
to possess Philip and that she has caused him to fail, her self-
knowledge would seem complete. Yet her actions belie her words.
She arrives at motherhood, not through sexual love, but through
a series of petty deceptions: pretending not to notice the attraction
between Philip and Judith, pretending to be asleep when they are
making love, and pretending for a long time not to know the
identity of Judith's lover so that neither shame nor pride will stand
in the way of her acquiring Philip's child. Though she recognizes
that she has smothered Philip, her resolve to change carries little
conviction. Towards the end of the novel her power to deny Philip manhood is still there when she says over the assembling of
the stove for winter, "Why can't you do things like other men?"
Though she takes great pains to remove the family from Horizon,
only the setting will change; her possession of "Philip" is just
beginning.

As for Me and My House is on the surface a vivid exposé of

puritanism and small-town life, but their rejections are deeply rooted in Philip's psychology, most powerfully stated when Mrs. Bentley tells us that Horizon is "a world of matrons and respectability." We see none of the men in the town except Paul, who is an outsider; it is women that make daily existence in Horizon the petty and stifling round that it is. The novel is colored for us by Philip's distaste for matronly women. Attention is drawn to female physical ugliness: town women like Mrs. Finley and Mrs. Bird are described as portly and aggressive, while the country women at Partridge Hill are described collectively as "wind-burned, with red chapped necks and sagging bodies." Repression is the sanctioned modus vivendi of the small town, and its debilitating effect is powerfully evoked in such details as Philip's fear of being caught smoking and Mrs. Bentley's use of the soft pedal when she plays the piano.

But the propriety and repressive decorum of the town are only a surface reflection of the grim tension between husband and wife. Images of repression delineate the inescapable reality of their lives and make up one of the most powerful elements in the novel's artistry. Mrs. Bentley refers to the "silence and repression and restraint" in the house that are "screwed down tight upon [them] like a vise" and to "brittle meals through whose tight-stretched silences you can fairly see the dart of nerves." Philip's withdrawal from his wife into his study is one of the central gestures in the novel, a part of that *noli me tangere* revulsion to women which in bed renders his shoulder "a lump of stone" or "a wall" when his wife reaches out for him. When Mrs. Bentley feels her every movement "furtive and strained" and the silence in the house hardening over her "like glass," her fear is, not public censure, but dread lest she irritate and further alienate Philip. Images of immobilization by repressed emotions reach a climax in Mrs. Bentley's description of herself at the door of the lean-to shed where Judith and Philip are making love: "I just stood there listening a minute, a queer, doomed ache inside me, like a live fly struggling in a block of ice, and then crept back to bed" (p. 123).

Just as Mrs. Bentley's failure to win her husband's love can be traced back to his maternally inspired contempt for women, so

Philip's actions are determined by his desire to be like his dead father, the student preacher who wanted to paint. Identification with his father locks Philip's life into a similar mold of failure in which art provides the only escape from the drab reality of the waitress mother's world. Art is the only part of his life that is real, but at the same time it is a reminder to him of failure, for he is a preacher instead of a painter. His paintings and sketches of the prairie and the towns have become increasingly bleak and hopeless, casting back a reflection of "thin, cold, bitter life." But Philip's quest to be like his father also becomes a quest for a son. Mrs. Bentley tells us at the beginning that Philip likes boys and wants one "in his own image." Steve, the boy they try to raise, at first promises to fill that need; like Philip he is of doubtful birth and an outcast in the town. Philip isolates Steve from other boys and encourages him to draw and make fun of Mrs. Bentley's world—Steve does a sketch of Mrs. Bentley emerging from the outhouse. But despite Philip's efforts to mold the boy in his own likeness, Steve turns out to be "just an ordinary boy" and repays Philip's attentions with insolence and condescension. Only when Steve is taken away from the Bentleys does he become the boy Philip desired, "an idol tarnish-proof." That image of Steve as artifact circles back to the one of Philip as a boy looking at his father's photograph and Mrs. Bentley's observation: "Let a man look long and devotedly enough at a statue and in time he will resemble it."

Throughout the novel there are elaborate patterns of mirror imagery and parallelisms which underscore Philip's imaginative quest to discover his true features as a man. Steve, as the town reprobate, provides Philip with a replica of his own youth. The farmer, Joe Lawson, resembles Philip physically (long and lean, he has "the same turn and gestures, the same slow strength"), and he loses a twelve-year-old son who has been crippled by a runaway horse. The loss of a son parallels not only the removal of Steve from Horizon but also the Bentleys' stillborn child that would have been twelve years old if it had lived. The parallelisms and repetition of detail give the novel a highly stylized quality. Like Philip, who is invariably described as "white-lipped" and "wincing," Judith is remarkable for "that queer white face of hers," and Mrs. Bentley notes that "her smile comes so sharp and vivid that it almost seems there's a wince with it." Through his compulsion to imitate his father's sin and through his self-love, Philip is inevitably drawn to Judith, who resembles him. Resemblances to Philip even extend to the dog, El Greco, who like Philip is restless and constrained in the town. Mrs. Bentley observes "the two of them so long and gaunt and hungry-looking, both so desperately in need of being consoled."

The descriptions of Philip's sketches and drawings provide another approach to understanding the novel. When Philip, Paul, and Mrs. Bentley go out to Partridge Hill schoolhouse for their first service, Philip sketches the likenesses of all three on the blackboard. While he gives Paul's face a slightly screwed-up expression, he renders his own face "expressionless and handsome like an advertisement for underwear or shaving cream." The image suggests not only Philip's narcissism but also his detachment and impersonal manner. His actions bear out this self-image: when Mrs. Bentley has a cold, he gets her tissue from the store not for humanitarian, but aesthetic reasons. But there is another side to Philip, for sometimes in his sketches he renders his Main Streets and their cowed inhabitants with pity and insight when, according to his wife, they should be laughed at. The conflict between an aesthetic and a humanitarian response is at the core not only of Philip's creativity but of Ross's as well. The creation of Mrs. Bentley as a sympathetic and admirable character is tautly balanced by the ironic view of her as manipulator and petty deceiver. At one point Mrs. Bentley describes three of the subjects of Philip's art: a man plowing a field, a handsome youth, and a woman "staring across a wheat field like a sybil." The relationship of these three figures (father, mother, son) in effect represents the emotional "tangle" out of which Ross's fiction is made. But to counter the personal and emotional aspects of art, Philip argues that the literal associations do not count for anything, only form matters, and the real test of a picture's value is to turn it upside down: "That knocks all the sentiment out of it, leaves you with just the design and form" (p. 154).

This is what Ross himself does in the middle sequence of the novel when the Bentleys, Paul, and Steve holiday on a ranch further west. Here the whole pattern of the novel is reversed: they are in the hills instead of on the prairie, in the country instead of the town, and the nearest town is new and booming rather than set-tled and economically depressed. The prevailing mood is one of freedom rather than inhibition, and the characters are able to ex-press themselves. Mrs. Bentley finds an interest in other people at the ranch, and Philip feels a renewed desire to paint and to suc-ceed. In contrast to the endless hours spent alone in his study fur-tively sketching, Philip paints Laura's stallion with a genuine de-sire for appreciation. But although the setting and the mood have changed, the imaginative design of the novel remains the same. In town on Saturday night Mrs. Bentley dances with a young cowboy who gives her considerable attention, but she is filled with regret that the man courting her is not Philip. The experi-ence only sharpens her desire for him. At the same time Philip's aversion for women is accentuated in his confrontation with Laura, who has open contempt for weak men. At one point when he is painting he shouts at her to leave him alone and throws away the hat she brings him to wear against the sun. Temporarily released from routine, the characters are also able to see more clearly the nature and design of their lives in Horizon: "Without knowing it we relaxed a little out there, looked back and saw our-selves. Maybe Laura helped us. We didn't like it when she sneered, but she was right . . . she saw us pretty well for what we are" (p. 107).

The success of As for Me and My House rests in a design, the daybook, which gives powerful expression to the repression and the soul-searching of the characters. In succinct fashion the title, As for Me and My House, embodies the confessional dimension of the book and the characters' self-absorption. And what is in-structive is the way the real meaning, the confession, lies veiled beneath a false front, a religious slogan. Remarkable in the novel's form is Ross's use of a narrative voice which is external to the psy-chology from which the novel has been created. Mrs. Bentley's viewpoint is a sympathetic one, but at the same time its limita-tions preserve the mystery that surrounds creative genius; for though Philip is a failure, he is still an artist. Finally, if we view the artist's story as a paradigm of the imaginative life, then Ross's As for Me and My House is a novel of universal consideration.

When As for Me and My House failed commercially, Ross

seems to have given up writing—just three short stories appeared in the next sixteen years. It was only after interest in *As for Me and My House* was kindled by its reissue in paperback that he began writing again. Two subsequent novels were unsuccessful; in neither did he find the right form to give economical and compelling shape to his material. *The Well* (1958) tells the story of a young fugitive from the law who finds work on a prairie farm and becomes entangled in the disastrous marriage of the elderly farmer and his young wife. *Whir of Gold* (1970) is the story of another young man forced to choose whether to live in a man's or a woman's world. Ross's theme in these two novels is the nature of crime, and both in part use Montreal backgrounds. Although both novels contain some good individual scenes, they are conventionally plotted, and Ross's usually taut Naturalistic style is somehow slack, unstrung.

In 1968 Ross retired from the bank and moved to the Mediterranean, first Greece, then Spain, and although he was living at a great distance from the Saskatchewan prairie that inspired his best work, he managed to use that setting to considerable effect in his fourth novel, *Sawbones Memorial* (1974). Again he found a unique narrative form to give point and precision to every word in the book.[4] The form approaches drama and obeys the classical unities of time and place. The townspeople of Upward, Saskatchewan, are gathered together at a party to say farewell to Doc Hunter, who is retiring after forty-five years of practice in the area, and to mark the opening of the new district hospital. The book consists of conversation amongst the townspeople during the evening, interspersed with memories in stream-of-consciousness form as various characters reflect alone for a moment on the past and their relationship to the doctor. There is no narration as such, no "He said" or "She said." The narrative structure is the party itself as it moves naturally to the point in the evening where refreshments are served, speeches made, and the doctor is presented with a watch in honor of his long service to the community. The form is organic and fragmented, yet dramatic tension is created as memories and viewpoints fall together to create a mosaic of the community and its past. The form is economical; through jux-

[4] See Lorraine McMullen, *Sinclair Ross* (Boston: Twayne, 1980), pp. 119–21.

taposition of fragments it suggests the whole without being at pains to describe it. Indeed, one of the central characters in the book is Nick, the new doctor and former town outcast, but he is not even present for the party. Because of its form the novel is best read in no more than a couple of sittings—to sustain its dramatic tightness.

Like *As for Me and My House*, much of *Sawbones Memorial* is concerned with exposing the special prejudices and hypocrisies of a small prairie town. This function of the novel adheres in the nature of the central character, Doc Hunter; at seventy-five, he reminds one of a crusty Mark Twain with few illusions about human nature. His "Thank you" speech near the end of the book becomes a bitter reflection on the way man's innate goodness, visible during crisis, dissipates into everyday spite, gossip, and jealousy.

The success of *Sawbones Memorial*, written when Ross was in his sixties, discounts the easy notion that he had only one novel to write and heightens in turn the sense of loss surrounding this author whose work was long ignored and who missed the chance of making his living as a writer. *Sawbones Memorial* does not quite rank with *As for Me and My House*; it does not have the historical importance of the dust-bowl experience and the depression setting. But it significantly extends the range of Ross's treatment of the prairie experience: where the short stories, filled with deaths and madness, are frequently written in a tragic mode and *As for Me and My House* is a satire on the hypocrisies of a small town, *Sawbones Memorial* is essentially a comedy that affirms man's goodness and his instinct to labor for a better life. Ross's contribution to Canadian literature is quantitatively small, but it is a vitally important one; certainly *As for Me and My House* is one of those books, like *Huckleberry Finn* or *The Great Gatsby*, by which a country measures its imaginative life.

Selected Writings

As for Me and My House. New York: Reynal and Hitchcock, 1941. Reprint, New Canadian Library, no. 4 (Toronto: McClelland and Stewart, 1957), and Bison Book (Lincoln: University of Nebraska Press, 1978).

The Well. Toronto: Macmillan, 1958.

The Lamp at Noon and Other Stories. New Canadian Library, no. 62 (Toronto: McClelland and Stewart, 1968).

Whir of Gold. Toronto: McClelland and Stewart, 1970.

Sawbones Memorial. Toronto: McClelland and Stewart. Reprint, New Canadian Library, no. 145 (Toronto: McClelland and Stewart, 1978).

The Race and Other Stories. Ottawa: University of Ottawa Press, 1982.

Ernest Buckler

The reputation of Ernest Buckler rests, like that of Sinclair Ross, on one novel. Buckler, born in 1908 and raised in the Annapolis Valley of Nova Scotia, lived there as a farmer most of his life. As a young man he went to university in Halifax and did a graduate degree in philosophy at the University of Toronto, but after working for a Toronto actuarial firm for five years, he decided to return home and take up farming in Bridgetown, Nova Scotia. He published his first story in *Esquire* in 1940, but his first book, *The Mountain and the Valley*, did not appear until 1952. As with Ross there was a decline in Buckler's work after the publication of a first novel. Again we have an instance in Canada of a major writer who had great difficulty in establishing himself and who was never able to live solely from his writing, but whose small body of work includes one of the country's finest pieces of fiction.

One can trace a progression in Buckler's writing. The early stories that he published in such magazines as *Esquire, Saturday Night*, and *Maclean's* were sketches of family life that would eventually form part of *The Mountain and the Valley*, his masterpiece. Most of the stories are tentative and incomplete. Eventually published as *The Rebellion of Young David and Other Stories*, they are of interest largely as early drafts of the novel.

The Mountain and the Valley tells the story of an artist growing up in the Annapolis Valley and also chronicles three generations in the life of a Nova Scotia farm family. It was first published in the United States, where Buckler was widely acclaimed as an accomplished writer of fiction, and his talent was likened by several reviewers to that of Thomas Wolfe. Like Wolfe, he writes in a reminiscent mood and in an intensely lyrical style. But in the four books published since his classic *Bildungsroman*, Buckler moved steadily away from fictional narrative. His second book,

The Cruelest Month (1963), has been described as an anatomy or symposium; six characters spend a vacation together in a Nova Scotia farmhouse where they analyze each other's personalities and problems.[1] Narrative in terms of plot or action is minimal. Buckler's third book, *Ox Bells and Fireflies* (1968), which he described as a memoir, is a collection of lyrical sketches evoking the physical and emotional landscape of his childhood. The movement toward nonfiction implicit in *Ox Bells* is almost wholly realized in Buckler's last two books. *Nova Scotia: Window on the Sea* (1973) consists of photographs of Buckler's native province and a complementary text which might be described as a lyrical documentary, while *Whirligig* (1977) is a collection of humorous anecdotes, jokes, and limericks.

Critics have been disappointed that Buckler did not write more novels in the vein of *The Mountain and the Valley*. But Buckler's movement towards semifictional and documentary forms of writing follows thematically from that novel, where the artist hero, David Canaan, dies before he can write a novel. The death of the artist, poised on the threshold of his career, is a significant departure from the classic pattern of the *Künstlerroman* and makes a negative statement about both art and the future. Some critics have felt that David Canaan's death on top of the mountain is a gratuitous device for ending the novel on a high dramatic note. But I suspect for Buckler it was the inevitable ending and that among other things David's death questions the value and efficacy of novel writing.

There is a tragic theme in *The Mountain and the Valley* which lies in David Canaan's vision of what his novel will accomplish. *The Mountain and the Valley* is the familiar account of the spiritual growth of a sensitive young man, but it is also a study of human relationships within the family context where deep personal differences are in conflict with kindred love and loyalty. In his struggle to emerge a free and inviolate spirit, David Canaan is the cause of many ruptures in the family life; his sense of remorse makes him peculiarly sensitive to all the pain and disappointment suffered within the family group. When he resolves to write a

[1] Gregory Cook, Introduction to *Ernest Buckler* (Toronto: McGraw-Hill Ryerson, 1972), p. 3.

novel, David becomes delirious with joy to think that for his family he will be able to give "an absolving voice to all the hurts they gave themselves or each other—hurts that were caused only by the misreading of what they couldn't express."[2] In other words he believes his novel will set right all the wrongs that the members of his family did to each other. Moreover, David believes he will free himself from his own guilty sense of the past: "They will see that anyone who must have loved them so well, to have known them so thoroughly, could never have denied them once, as sometimes they might have thought I did." But then abruptly he dies, as if it were best to have had that vision and then see no more. In fact David's final vision is an illusion. His mother and father are dead, his brother and sister have moved far away; any restitution David might try to offer in the words of his novel will come too late. For while art can bring its creator to a point of understanding and acceptance, it cannot restore or change the past. David dies a pathetic rather than a tragic figure, for he is victim of this fervently willed illusion. But there is a tragic dimension in Buckler's view of the impotence of art which perhaps explains the direction his subsequent writings have taken. As a classic fiction *The Mountain and the Valley* deserves close scrutiny for its own structure and themes and for its status as a Canadian novel.

Like Wolfe's *Look Homeward, Angel, The Mountain and the Valley* is a pastoral novel wherein the imagination seeks to recover a time when all life existed in simple harmony and when the individual was not conscious of being separate from the rest of the world. Buckler realizes the pastoral dream by recreating the world of childhood with an enclosed rural setting, a tightly knit family, and shared community life.[3] But pastoral art turns on the paradox that the vision of unity it celebrates is only a memory; people live instead in a complex world of social ills and physical mutability. This paradox emerges in a tension between the novel's content and its form. As David Canaan's story is told, the narrator

[2] *The Mountain and the Valley* (Toronto: McClelland and Stewart, 1961), p. 300. All references are to the New Canadian Library edition.

[3] See Alan R. Young, "The Pastoral Vision of Ernest Buckler in *The Mountain and the Valley*," *Dalhousie Review* 53 (Summer 1973): 219–26.

presents scenes of childhood filled with ecstatic wonder and wholeness for the boy. But the novel's form, its chronology in six parts, invalidates the underlying emotional quest for unity, because the passing of time continuously moves David away from the point of childhood and brings the sober recognition that the past can never be repeated. Thus scenes of happiness and momentary fulfillment in the novel give way to disorder, despair, and isolation.

On another level *The Mountain and the Valley* is the story of a potential artist and his special defeat by the demands he places on his craft.[4] David Canaan believes that by writing a novel about his family and community he will be able to reorder the past so that it will become the perfect world of his earliest memories. But the undoing of David's dream rests in words. From the beginning David's acute imaginative response to life finds expression through words. At the same time, his ability to use words intelligently separates him from the members of his family whose thoughts are not "word-shaped" and forces him to recognize that he is different and essentially alone. Words for David have the power to recreate and unify experience, but the synthesis always remains visionary, private. The novel is structured around moments of unity which quickly fade but which, more significantly, elude the potential artist's attempt to give them permanence in language.

The prologue, which takes place on the afternoon of David's death, contains one of the novel's central images—the rug David's grandmother is hooking out of old pieces of family clothing. With its circular pattern the rug is a symbol of unity and wholeness, and with its fabric of family memories it is a counterpart to the novel that David some day hopes to write. But the image of unity suggested by the rug is undercut by a number of sobering, realistic details: the winter landscape, the senile grandmother, and the village recluse, Herb Hennessey. These images focus the tension between memories of past happiness and the experience of loss and estrangement for David, who is now a man in his thirties.

[4]D. J. Dooley, "Style and Communication in *The Mountain and the Valley*," *Dalhousie Review* 57 (Winter 1977–78): 671–83, relates Buckler's novel to Joyce's *Portrait of the Artist as a Young Man* (rpt. in Dooley's *Moral Vision in the Canadian Novel* [Toronto: Clarke, Irwin, 1979], pp. 49–59).

Each of the novel's six parts is similarly developed around images or scenes in which unity and perfect happiness are suggested, but ultimately elude the young hero.

The two events central to part 1, "The Mountain," are the trip up the log road and the Christmas play. To climb to the top of the mountain with his father, Joseph, and his brother, Chris, is for young David something like an initiation rite into manhood; it bespeaks a camaraderie he has never experienced with men before, a shared experience that will transcend words. But the trip is cut short when the Canaans are met by the loggers returning to town with the bodies of two neighbor men who have drowned. In retrospect the abortive venture up the mountain becomes an early instance of David's failure to realize a cherished ambition and to move forward to maturity. Until the day of his death many years later, the mountain looms as an obstacle which he has conquered neither physically nor imaginatively. On Christmas Eve when all the members of the family join together in a ritual which is both domestic and sacred, David approaches one of the most intense experiences of unity in the novel. The moment of transfiguration occurs when Joseph brings the tree into the house: "No one spoke as he stood it in the space in the corner. It just came to the ceiling. It was perfect. Suddenly the room was whole. Its heart began to beat" (p. 64). The magic of Christmas, however, is broken at the school concert, where David behaves foolishly on stage. For a few moments David feels that his acting is truly inspired, that he is creating for the people of his village a synthesis of the actual and the imaginary, but his illusion is shattered when he kisses the girl in the play, toppling the crown she is wearing, and someone from the audience laughs at the silly spectacle. Then David is bitterly angry at himself for being duped by his emotions and at the villagers for openly ridiculing him. The Christmas holiday is in ruins for David, and he rejects the comfort of his family. Years later he regrets his hurtful attitude to those who tried to comfort him and as a potential artist seeks to make amends to his family by giving voice to words of reconciliation in his art.[5]

[5] In "David Canaan: The Failing Heart," *Studies in Canadian Literature* 1 (Winter 1976): 64–75, Douglas Barbour argues that David's projects fail because he is self-centered and therefore unable to communicate with others.

The two principal scenes in part 2, "The Letter," describe the family ritual of tending the graveyard and David's first lovemaking with Effie. The tension in pastoral art between passing time and the desire to remain in the protected world of childhood is expressed in the opening paragraph of part 2: "David was thirteen now; yet the day they went to fix the graves in the old cemetery had still its shut-in magic for him." The little graveyard under the pine trees, with the lake gently lapping on one side, is physically a pastoral retreat; its "magic" for David lies in the oneness of the family working together, for the day they tended the graves "the family was indivisible." The scene in the cemetery has the formal elements of Renaissance pastoral art: a picnic holiday in a green setting, with the graves a reminder of mutability—*Et in Arcadia ego*. For a time David's feeling of unity with his family and the generations gone before is so complete that even the granite gravestones feel "warm as flesh to the touch." But that unity is broken by the presence of an outsider, Charlotte Gorman, and when she and Chris slip away from the group to make love, time is set in motion again.

David feels challenged by his brother to prove that he too is becoming a man, but his seduction of Effie the following summer becomes one of those guilty experiences for which David the adult novelist would do penance through his writing. This sequence of the book also begins with a vision, with a description of life like an eternal summer. But the boys' idyll at the local swimming hole is disturbed by their growing awareness of their bodies, and when David is teased about sex, he pridefully insists that he has had experience with a girl. To substantiate his boast he takes Effie, his trusting and innocent friend, into the woods and quickly and mechanically makes love to her. He uses Effie to prove himself to the other boys; it is a betrayal of her trust in him, and the guilt he feels is reflected in the pathetic details surrounding the girl—the tear in her skirt, the scratch on her leg, and her lost berry kettle. The wholeness of summer disintegrates further in the remaining incidents of part 2. There is a letter from the penpal, Toby, which speaks of a world larger than David's village; David's brother feels the first edge of dissatisfaction with Charlotte, his parents have a silent quarrel over another woman, his grandmother's mind begins to wander out of control for the first time.

Part 3, "The Valley," opens with a seasonal headpiece, but instead of the conventional celebration of spring or summer, it evokes the haunting loveliness and sadness of autumn. The description of the farm in October, with special attention to light and color ("the thin October light of after-ripeness . . . the albino light") gives the whole sequence the quality of a painting—a Constable or a Turner. The scene concludes with an image of David's parents, Martha and Joseph, on their knees gathering potatoes, and from a distance they look as if "in the dusty steeping light" they are praying, the pastoral scene assuming the qualities of a biblical *tableau vivant*. The harmony of this scene, however, is broken (according to the persistent pattern of the novel) when Joseph goes to the barn for more potato bags and stops to talk to the doctor passing along the road. When he comes back to the field, a break in the unity of the family has taken place, for it has been decided that David's sister, Anna, will go to school in town and live with the doctor and his wife.

David's ardent longing to feel true kinship with another person is temporarily fulfilled when his pen-pal Toby comes for a visit. But friendship with a sophisticated boy from the city makes David feel ashamed of his family's simple country manners and the crudity of his friends at the swimming hole. He tries to impress on Toby the idea that he is superior to his country origins, and to show off in front of his friend he takes Effie into the meadow for a quick lovemaking while Toby waits on the road. David's betrayal of his people turns back upon him in a flood of guilt and remorse. The vulnerability of his family and friends is focused in the pathetic figure of Effie, who dies a few days after David takes her into the damp meadow. He does not know that she has died of leukemia; rather, he is consumed with guilt thinking that he has caused her death. In the novel's imagery the valley has become the "valley of the shadow of death," the place of guilt and sorrow, while the mountain is the locus of vision, achievement, and, above all, absolution. Significantly, it is at this point that David conceives the idea of building a camp at the top of the mountain and writing a book. Buckler at the same time subtly discredits art by revealing that its motive derives from a pathetic feeling of guilt and a failure to meet fully life's exigencies.

If the novel has a turning point, it comes at the beginning of part 4, "The Rock," when David is suddenly faced with the choice of running away to the city or staying at home on the farm. Part 4 opens with a eulogistic account of farm labors in the manner of Virgil's *Eclogues*. Fullness of life for David's parents finds its expression in tasks well done, the house lovingly cared for, the fields tilled by the same family from generation to generation. But for the first time in the novel David has become impatient with the routine and cyclical patterns of village life; he yearns to get away to the city and to college. The tension accumulating in David spills over to the work he is doing with his father. Angry words are spoken, Joseph strikes his son, and David decides to leave the farm at once. As so often in the novel, the break between David and one of his family focuses on the articulation of feelings. Joseph feels wounded "not by David's anger, but by the words he'd used." Speech is David's weapon to assert his superiority over a man whose slow thoughts cannot find words. But when, shortly after, David is driving away with a city couple, he is overwhelmed with shame at his actions and with love for his family, and he turns back. The incident is crucial, because David never leaves home again, though he is never really part of the village thereafter either. Buckler writes: "He began to sob. He sobbed because he could neither leave nor stay. He sobbed because he was neither one thing nor the other" (p. 171).

The latter half of part 4 follows the familiar pattern of a unified moment which gradually disintegrates. The members of the family, in a high holiday mood, decide to take a picnic up to the top of the mountain where Joseph is planning to cut a large tree for a ship's keel. Anna and Toby join them, which makes the adventure more complete; but they travel in Toby's new car, which mires in a soft spot on the road, and they are forced to turn back. The misadventure is not of great consequence to the others, but for David it is another promise of happiness symbolized by the mountain top, which fails to be realized.

In part 5, "The Scar," David is cast as a sacrificial figure. The identification is never explicit, but accrues from the mood and suggestive details of the scene where the pig is butchered and David falls from the beam of the barn roof. The butchering, by nature of its timeless economic necessity, has the cast of a primitive, seasonal rite, like the dismemberment of a god to ensure continued fertility and harvest. The scene focuses on the ritual-like assemblage of butchering tools, the killing of the pig, the bleeding, trussing, and dissecting of the animal for winter storage, all of which are accompanied by a series of familiar and repeated sexual jokes, including a mock castration. David senses that the men do not really need his help at the butchering, and in a mood of self-pity and defiance he alternately identifies with the doomed animal and takes the lead in its slaughter. The agony for David is in waiting for the animal to be killed. His brother whispers to the others that "Dave don't like to see anything killed," suggesting that he is different from other men. Then, as if bent on self-crucifixion, David rips the back of his hand on a nail, strikes his palm sharply with a gam stick, and defiantly mounts the scaffold to the big beam in order to loose the rope for hanging the carcass. David is on his cross, with the men below like a mob of indifferent strangers. When he falls, his romantic self-dramatization is complete, and thereafter, like the biblical Adam and like Christ, he is painfully conscious of his flesh, a man of sorrows. The details of this sequence are not shaped in an allegorical pattern (Buckler may not have consciously intended to evoke the Christ story), but they gather associations which hover over the scene and connect with other details in the narrative, like the biblical names of the characters, to give a mythic dimension to David's plight. The fact that he dies on a mountain when he is in his early thirties is another of those suggestive details.

The events in the remainder of part 5 focus on ruptures in the family which can never be mended, but which David hopes his novel will somehow heal. When he is lying in bed after his fall, Chris comes to be forgiven, but David will not speak to his brother. There follows another tragic rupture—a quarrel between Martha and Joseph, and the subsequent death of Joseph when he is cutting down the great tree on the top of the mountain. Both Martha and Joseph wanted to be reconciled, but their inarticulateness in the wake of hurt pride prevents their ever being united again. This scene looks forward directly to David's resolve at the end of the novel to speak for his family—"to give an absolving voice to all the hurts they gave themselves or each other."

In part 6, "The Train," David and his grandmother are the only ones left living on the farm. A man different from the others in the valley, David is identified with the recluse Herb Hennessey. But his loneliness is perhaps the essential factor in his potential as an artist, for it sustains in him "a condition for universality." He has no one place where he fits in, but, rather, "he could be old with the old, or young with the young." David's lack of identity is brought into relief during Toby's and Anna's visit to the farm. When David tries on Toby's sailor hat, Anna exclaims how much David looks like Toby. That night David stands alone in front of the mirror wearing the hat, assuming Toby's easy smile and thinking they could be the same person. Earlier in the novel the grandmother had thought to herself that David "seemed to have no face of his own." David enjoys Toby's friendship, but they are very different, for Toby lives for the present moment, has no plans or regrets. The great difference between the two friends is illuminated by the scene at the end of part 6 when Toby leaves on the train to go back to war. David stands in the fields, watching the train, ready to wave at his friend, but Toby is already talking and joking with another sailor and never looks back to the farm. David then recognizes with a final crushing intensity that he will "always be a stranger to everybody." The passing train symbolizes life moving forward without David and when his grandmother reappears, she fittingly calls David "child."

The epilogue, "The Mountain," returns to the beginning of the novel where David's grandmother is hooking a rug and he is about to feed the chickens. When he first steps outside, the frozen winter landscape mirrors back his state of spiritual dryness. But as he begins to ascend the mountain road, the world comes alive again ("The face came back to everything") and he achieves at last a transcendental vision of life unified: "Everything seemed to be an aspect of something else. There seemed to be a thread of similarity running through the whole world. A shape could be like a sound: a feeling like a shape; a smell the shadow of a touch" (p. 287). Correspondingly, time is no longer linear movement, but flat "like space," so that memory is not a returning to the past, but is being there again for the first time: "No one has been away, nothing has changed."[6] Art is to be David's means of sustaining his vision of unity, and soon the faces and voices of all his memories begin to swarm upon him and demand expression. For a moment he experiences a kind of madness at the prospect of life's chaotic multiplicity and the impossibility of writing down in words all that has been and all that might have been. But then he realizes that the artist must select from his experiences and "find their single core of meaning." Most important, David feels that art will be a compensation for life's failures and a form of penance and forgiveness. Filled with "the warm crying of acquittal" and a vision of life replenished by art, David dies on top of the mountain in the snow. His grandmother is left calling for her "child," while his spirit metamorphosed into a bird slips over to the valley on the other side of the mountain.

The complexity of thought, the passionate integrity, and the evocative prose in the *The Mountain and the Valley* make it a novel of universal worth. But it also bears the marks of its Canadian origins. The hero's reluctance to leave the valley, his failure to get over the mountain, are aspects of what Northrop Frye describes as Canada's "garrison mentality." His death in the snow is an instance of the pattern that Margaret Atwood describes as pervasive in a literature about losers.[7] His death, moreover, means that his ambition to be an artist is never realized, so that David Canaan is another one of those figures like Ross's preacher, Philip Bentley, whose creative ambitions are frustrated and ultimately doomed. But Buckler's novel also emphasizes the importance of the community in the hero's life, even though he sees himself as a man set apart. David Canaan may be reluctant to leave his village, but his reason is as much love for his people as it is fear of the larger world. The values of the community are not challenged as in American literature, but reaffirmed.[8] In this respect

[6] In "The Past Recaptured," *Canadian Literature* 65 (Summer 1975): 74–85, J. M. Kertzer posits two modes of time as the source of tension in David's life: "valley time," which is chronological, and "mountain time," which is timeless transcendence.

[7] See Margaret Atwood, *Survival* (Toronto: Anansi Press, 1972).

[8] There is a brief but interesting rebuttal to the negative implications of Atwood's thesis in David Savage's "Not Survival but Responsibility," *Dalhousie Review* 55 (Summer 1975): 272–79.

The Mountain and the Valley is not so much like Thomas Wolfe's novels as like James Agee's *A Death in the Family*, a favorite novel about family life of Buckler's. David Canaan is frustrated by the confines and mediocrity of his world in the valley, but he also loves the world and its people with a passionate intensity.[9] Like *As for Me and My House*, *The Mountain and the Valley* records one of the essential phases of Canada's imaginative life.

In the books that followed *The Mountain and the Valley*, Buckler moved, like so many Canadian writers, to more documentary, less dramatic forms of writing. The importance of the artist figure in these books is steadily diminished as well. In *The Cruelest Month* Buckler tries unsuccessfully to build a novel around the conversations of six people vacationing in a Nova Scotia farmhouse. The resulting fiction is contrived and sustains little interest. Two of the characters might be described as artist figures, but the one, Morse Halliday, a brutally cynical novelist from the States, has given up writing by the time he comes to Nova Scotia, while the other, Paul Creed, a shy farmer who owns the farmhouse, has filled several notebooks with ideas but has never written a book.

Ox Bells and Fireflies, a much more successful book, returns the reader to the pastoral world of *The Mountain and the Valley*, but it is a world significantly altered. In this memoir Buckler achieves a vision of innocence and unity by excluding plot and narrative altogether. Many of the scenes from the novel are recreated (Christmas, the boys at the swimming hole, gathering potatoes in October), and the death of a neighbor is again the opening sequence of the book. But the dramatic import of these scenes has been removed. Mary (the name changed from Martha) and Joseph gathering potatoes in the fall is not the prelude to a quarrel or a separation in the family, but remains a harmonious memory. Similarly, Christmas in this book is not spoiled by the school concert, but is preserved as a wholly ecstatic and joyous time. This is possible because the setting in the book is Norstead, or "no

---

[9] David's dual vision and his failure to develop a separate identity are seen in M. Doerksen's *"The Mountain and the Valley*: An Evaluation," *World Literature Written in English* 19, no. 2 (Spring 1980): 45–56, as "paradoxically both a defeat and a triumph."

place," and the time is the timeless one of childhood. Unity is achieved in the style by the conjunction *and*, which joins together different kinds of perceptions and experiences—thus chapter titles like "Chords and Acres," "Wicks and Cups," and "Soft Soap and Drawknives," and the title of the book itself, *Ox Bells and Fireflies*. Only by writing a series of sketches rather than a novel is Buckler able to knit together the happy world of his childhood memories and dreams. The artist figure as such disappears from the book, although there is a vestige of him in the sketch entitled "Another Man," which describes Syd Wright, a village recluse like Herb Hennessey. In the line from David Canaan (and Herb Hennessey) through Paul Creed to Syd Wright, the artist becomes increasingly ineffectual, more shadowy and anonymous.

In *Nova Scotia: Window on the Sea* the artist figure has disappeared altogether. In contrast to David Canaan, the artist in *Window on the Sea* has merged himself totally with the people and the landscape of the book. The author's abiding quest for unity is realized here in a people inseparable from their geography. In an extended metaphor, Nova Scotia is likened to a living body (in the manner of William Carlos Williams's *Paterson*), and human beings and the land share a "common bloodstream." The text of the book is a prose poem that celebrates human physical identity with the landscape. In the photographs we are again reminded of scenes from *The Mountain and the Valley*; there is an old grandmother hooking a rug from pieces of family clothing, a son associated in the imagery of the accompanying text with the crucifix. But these characters and vignettes are not personal; rather, they are part of a vision of universals to be found in the daily life of Nova Scotia farmers and fishermen. However, in the concluding section of *Window on the Sea* Buckler sees the organic relationship of men and women to landscape disappearing: "The land is beginning to smother beneath all the crockery of man that is being heaped on it . . . Shopping Centres . . . spring up where once were orchards. Television aerials comb the night for dross or screams where once the night kissed righteous muscles with the balm of rest." Again the vision is not just personal; it implicates us all.

But the elegiac note sounded at the end of *Window on the Sea* is still the special signature of Buckler's prose. In whatever form his writing takes, whether novel, memoir, anatomy, or documentary, his work is always predicated on a tragic recognition of the limitations of art. The novel cannot rewrite family history, the anatomy cannot change personality or the direction of one's life, nor can a memoir or a documentary that celebrates a vanishing way of life restore that order again. The haunting, lyrical power of Buckler's prose is steeped in the knowledge that art can bring awareness and understanding, but can never replenish life.

Selected Writings

The Mountain and the Valley. New York: Henry Holt, 1952. Reprint, Signet Book (New York: New American Library, 1954), and New Canadian Library, no. 23, 1961.

The Cruelest Month. Toronto: McClelland and Stewart, 1963. Reprint, New Canadian Library, no. 139 (Toronto: McClelland and Stewart, 1977).

Ox Bells and Fireflies. Toronto: McClelland and Stewart, 1968. Reprint, New Canadian Library, no. 99 (Toronto: McClelland and Stewart, 1974).

Nova Scotia: Window on the Sea. With photographs by Hans Weber. Toronto: McClelland and Stewart, 1973.

The Rebellion of Young David and Other Stories. Selected and arranged by Robert D. Chambers. Toronto: McClelland and Stewart, 1975.

Whirligig. Toronto: McClelland and Stewart, 1977.

Gabrielle Roy

The history of French-Canadian literature and its relation to the writings of English Canada finds a significant focus in the work of Gabrielle Roy. Until the Second World War most of Quebec literature belonged to the rural school, which celebrated traditional values, principally love of the land, adherence to the church, and preservation of French language and customs. This school had its apotheosis in Louis Hémon's novel *Maria Chapdelaine* (1917) where the heroine, who is offered marriage and the advantages of life in an American city, ultimately chooses to stay on a backwoods farm and affirms the myth that in Quebec nothing will ever change. But in fact the static world of the French-Canadian *habitant* was coming to an end, and it was Gabrielle Roy's 1945 novel *Bonheur d'occasion (The Tin Flute)*, set in a working-class slum of Montreal, which first documented that profound change in French-Canadian life and brought Quebec literature into the mainstream of English-Canadian and international writing.[1]

The circumstances of her life determined, perhaps, that Gabrielle Roy would be a voice for the whole of Canada. She was born in 1909, not in Quebec, but in Saint Boniface, Manitoba, where her grandparents had pioneered and where her father worked for the government's Department of Colonization. She obtained a teaching diploma from the Normal School in Winnipeg and for nine years taught in rural areas of the province, gathering experiences which later inspired some of her best fiction. In 1937 she left Canada to study drama in Europe (first Paris, then London), returning to settle in Montreal, where she worked as a writer for newspapers and magazines. Her experi-

---

[1] For a concise history of French-Canadian literature in English, see Jeannette Urbas's *From Thirty Acres to Modern Times: The Story of French-Canadian Literature* (Toronto: McGraw-Hill Ryerson, 1976).

ences in Montreal provided her with the material for her first book, *The Tin Flute*, which won her the prestigious Prix Femina in France, a singular honor, since she was the first writer from Canada to win the award. In 1947 she married Dr. Marcel Carbotte, also from western Canada, and subsequently made her home in Quebec City.

Gabrielle Roy has published ten works of imaginative prose which cover an exceptional range of characters and themes. At one extreme she has written novels of powerful social criticism, at the other pastoral idylls of great charm and delicate lyricism. In setting, moreover, her work encompasses almost the whole of the country, the Northwest Territories, the prairies, urban and rural Quebec, the Ungava, and the Eskimo regions of Labrador. Although she writes in French, her novels have quickly been translated into English and have become central to the traditions of Canadian literature in both languages.

Artistically the least finished of Gabrielle Roy's books, *The Tin Flute* remains the novel for which she is best known. Set in Montreal during the depression and the early years of World War II, it tells the story of a working-class family of fourteen where the father is unemployed. Written in a Naturalistic, quasi-documentary style, the book has as its chief purpose the exposure of the far-reaching effects of poverty and chronic employment on the members of a French-Canadian family who are powerless to alter their situation. The setting, or perhaps more specifically the environment, determines all the other aspects of the novel.[2] The characters are presented as extensions of that environment; the plot, or story line, consists of their individual attempts to escape its crushing confines.

The novel opens with a portrait of young Florentine Lacasse, the family's oldest daughter and principal wage earner, who works in a five-and-ten store. Like the place where she works, Florentine is common, pretty in a cheap, superficial way, but without significant intelligence. She is a natural part of the noise and the tinsel glare that fill the store. As a character, however, she is re-

[2] For a discussion of Roy's city novels in a social, political and economic framework, see Ben-Zion Shek's *Social Realism in the French-Canadian Novel* (Montreal: Harvest House, 1977), pp. 65–111, 173–203.

deemed by her loyalty to her family and by her will to survive. A central strand in the plot of the novel is Florentine's love affair with Jean Levesque, a cynical young opportunist who is attracted by Florentine's charm and her innocence, but repelled by the air of poverty that clings to her. He takes advantage of her physically, but deserts her when she becomes pregnant.

The other main strand in the plot is the family's search for a new place in which to live. Each spring as the family's resources dwindle further, the mother, Rose-Anna, takes to the streets to find cheaper lodgings. The constant moving, the smaller, more crowded rooms, the birth of yet another child are all conditions which eventually cause the family to fall apart. Each member of the family tries in his or her own way to escape the wretched limitations of everyday life. For Florentine, it is through a dream of romantic love with Jean Levesque, while for a younger girl, Yvonne, it is through religion and the dream of someday becoming a nun. Rose-Anna's means of temporarily escaping from her pressing responsibilities and from the sordid reality of the slum district is to think about her childhood in the country and to dream of visiting, perhaps someday living, there again. One of the small boys, Daniel, is consumptive, and when he goes to hospital, he escapes reality through a little toy flute his mother brings him and through the kindly attentions of a nurse. His final escape, which gives the English title of the novel such poignancy, is through death.

Although they do not realize it, death is the escape that the men in the family choose when they decide to go to war. The father, Azarius, once a skilled carpenter, has been demoralized by years of unemployment during the depression. When the war breaks out, his romantic nature finds a meaningful purpose in the idea of saving "La France." The oldest boy, Eugene, in despair of finding work and needing money, has been drifting towards petty crime, but the war promises an escape from this hopeless existence. Here lies Gabrielle Roy's indictment of her society. The terrible irony is that for the inhabitants of the Saint-Henri slum the war will be their salvation, for it will bring jobs in the munitions factories and a steady income to those who enlist in the army. Rose-Anna will at last be able to afford a better home.

There is in *The Tin Flute* the same kind of epic purpose as in

Steinbeck's *Grapes of Wrath*, which is to show the plight of a whole people. The Lacasses are representative of thousands of families suffering the effects of social and economic injustice. As we watch Florentine working in the store, we are told that she is just one of many such girls, and as Rose-Anna walks the streets in search of another house, she is joined by countless others in the same predicament, "a universal migration every spring." In this epic vein the book ends with a picture of the troops leaving from Saint-Henri on the train.

Although *The Tin Flute* is a powerful portrait of the ills of urban life, of the squalor of existence in overcrowded rooms and streets filled with the cacophony of railroad crossings and factory whistles, Gabrielle Roy does not propose a solution to the economic dilemma of modern man. In interviews after the novel's publication, the author said she hoped that by exposing conditions as they were she would help bring about a change for the better.[3] But Gabrielle Roy's imagination is not principally concerned with social injustice. Her deep and abiding theme, one which gives great power to *The Tin Flute*, is the power of human love and compassion, especially as it is focused in the relationship of mothers and children. The special creation in *The Tin Flute* is, not the vain little heroine, Florentine, but Rose-Anna, the strong mother who struggles to keep her family together. In all her gestures she assumes a larger-than-life dimension: on the road every spring looking for a new house, working tirelessly day after day at her spinning wheel which "turned as the earth turned," and towards the end of the novel giving birth to another child with "not one moan." But at the same time she is, as Hugo McPherson has phrased it, a *mater dolorosa* who can never give enough in either love or material things to prepare her children for a world that is full of poverty and suffering.[4]

The limits of a mother's love are viewed in the relationship between three generations. In the country Rose-Anna rediscovers

---

[3] "Réponse de Gabrielle Roy," in *Société Royale du Canada*, no. 5 (1947–48), pp. 35–48.

[4] Hugo McPherson, introduction to *The Tin Flute*, trans. Hannah Josephson (Toronto: McClelland and Stewart, 1958). All references are to the New Canadian Library text.

her mother, Madame Laplante, as a dour old woman who has never believed in happiness. She sits in her rocking chair dispensing "pious old bromides" and talking of the family's troubles. She has raised fifteen children, providing for their every need, but she has never, Rose-Anna reflects, given them love. Ironically, this is how Rose-Anna in turn appears to her children. When she stops at the five-and-ten, Florentine notes sadly that her mother speaks immediately of family difficulties. The need for love is brought into focus most poignantly when little Daniel finds such happiness with the nurse at the hospital. Rose-Anna, like her mother, offers only material things, pathetic substitutes for love like the toy flute. Her reaction to Florentine's eventual appeal for help is, not sympathy, but horror. And again after Florentine has married Emmanuel Letourneau, a compassionate and idealistic young man, she too expresses her love for her unborn child by calculating how much she can afford to buy for her family. These women all give things instead of love; it is the true measure of their poverty.

Gabrielle Roy's characteristic portrayal of women in terms of the mother imago assumes a completely different aspect in her second novel, *La petite poule d'eau* (1951), translated as *Where Nests the Water Hen*. In this story of a French-Canadian family living in a remote and sparsely populated region of northern Manitoba, the mother, Luzina Tousignant, is a wholly positive figure, a seemingly boundless source of inspiration and love for her husband and large family of children. She is a woman who, although she lives "so far from the world," finds life truly wonderful and, through her inquiring eyes and eager interest, makes others aware that they have reasons for being happy too. In the first section, "Luzina Takes a Holiday," she concludes from her travels that "human nature everywhere is excellent." Her joyful, maternal nature assumes almost a mythic dimension when we learn that her holidays, usually in the early spring, are taken to bring a new baby into the world. This information withheld until the end of the trip gives emphasis to the idea of maternity as life's greatest and most wonderful mystery.

In the second section, "The School on the Little Water Hen," Luzina is concerned, despite their remoteness, to provide her children with education. Her husband builds a little schoolhouse on the island where they live, and she arranges with the government for a teacher to spend the summer months with them. In successive summers three teachers come to the Water Hen district with very different ideas about education. The first summer it is the young and very charming Mademoiselle Côté, who endears herself to the family and inspires in the children both a love for learning and a desire to see the world. She imparts to them a heroic vision of Canada as explored and settled by courteous and adventurous Frenchmen. The second year, in sharp contrast, they are taught by an embittered and pathetic old maid from Ontario, a Miss O'Rorke, whose vision of the world is tied to the order emanating from the king of England. Miss O'Rorke is followed by a philosophical young man, Armand Dubreuil, who proves to be much more interested in hunting than in teaching and whose pedagogical ideals are nature and freedom. When he is supposed to be in the schoolhouse, the children find him asleep in his boat among the reeds, worn out from shooting ducks.

Where Nests the Water Hen, with its sheep-covered island and its cottage full of happy children, is an idyll celebrating the joys of family life in a remote region of the earth. It is informed by the pastoral dream of a simplified, harmonious existence from which the complexities of society and natural process (age, disease, and death) are eliminated. But the condition of human existence is temporal (time is the element in which all things have their being), and even to the static life of the Water Hen there come changes. In the latter half of part 2 the children grow up and leave the island in order to seek education and make their living in the larger world. Armand Dubreuil, who had given the children the strongest taste for it, had been the most skeptical about learning:

What would be the outcome of all this? A great deal of sorrow, perhaps, for Mama Tousignant. What, indeed, would come of it? Discontent first of all, which lies at the root of all progress? And afterward?[5]

[5] *Where Nests the Water Hen*, trans. Harry L. Binsse (Toronto: McClelland and Stewart, 1961), p. 75. All references are to this edition.

Dubreuil's stories for the children were not about elegant French heroes or English kings, but unhappy exiles wandering the face of the earth.

Josephine, the oldest girl, wants to be a teacher like Mademoiselle Côté, and when she leaves the island, the family see her off as if they were going to a funeral. Although it fulfills Luzina's dream of progress for her children, it is also for her an event of sadness:

Now she remained behind, and it was the children who were leaving. After a fashion, Luzina was seeing life. And she could not believe what her stout heart told her: already life, to which she had given so abundantly, little by little was leaving her behind. [p. 87]

By the end of part 2 almost all her children have gone, and the little schoolhouse, fallen into decay, has become a storage house for grain and lumber during the long winters. To the grown-up children in the city receiving letters from home, the Water Hen is no longer the center of the world, but a tiny dot on the map, remote in place and time, just a memory.

What distinguishes *Where Nests the Water Hen* from other pastoral novels is the third part, "The Capuchin from Toutes Aides," which fulfills the dream of all pastoral art and returns the reader wonderfully to the Water Hen and to that first summer when Mademoiselle Côté came to teach the children. The perspective, however, has shifted from the Tousignant family to that of Father Joseph-Marie, the aging priest who comes to the Water Hen country every year to hear confessions and preach a sermon. His is the larger perspective of the outside world; for this polyglot priest born in Latvia of Belgian and Russian parentage the Water Hen is not home, but a faraway country in a melancholy region of lakes and wild water fowl. He loves this country peopled with wandering exiles like himself, feels closer to God the further north he travels, but he has also greatly loved the cultured cities of old Europe and the art and music of its great civilizations.[6]

---

[6] In "Gabrielle Roy; ou, L'être partagé," *Études françaises* 1, no. 2 (June 1965): 39–65, Albert Le Grand sees opposing values as central to Roy's fiction—security and liberty, primitive and civilized, and so forth. These opposing attitudes and feelings, writes Le Grand, are necessary for growth and self-discovery in Roy's characters.

In returning to her story from the vantage point of the priest, Gabrielle Roy seems to be asking whether there is a meaning to life larger than the temporal and natural one of the Tousignants. The nostalgia we feel at the end of part 2 for a time and place that are gone is replaced in part 3 by a view of life that transcends a specific time or place. The priest's immediate experience of time habitually dissolves into memories of other times, and he is reminded of other places by the many different languages being spoken around him. Father Joseph-Marie is not unlike Luzina, for he loves to travel, and, like Luzina, he feels a surge of love for humankind and for God when he takes to the road. He sees his whole life as a trip and thinks: "Oh, yes! The world was a pleasant place of sojourn! and to think that it would be better yet in Heaven!" (p. 102). The priest's vision is a truly ecumenical one in which men and women from different regions and races are brought together by divine love. The human capacity for love and compassion is the larger vision that Gabrielle Roy brings to her novel. We have seen it in Luzina with her children. But what are its larger bounds, what its limits?

When the priest hears a dozen or more languages being spoken in the little village of Rorketon, he reflects, "On the whole, was it not in a small crowd of well-mixed races, such as he saw before him, that stood revealed, in its most simple, natural fulfilment, the precept 'Love one another!'" (p. 107). He feels he draws singularly close to God "in this so fraternal a confusion of languages and faces." The priest's vision is not an abstraction, but is compounded from his experiences in his parish. He recalls how he furnished his little chapel with gifts and talents of people from many different religions: the harmonium, for example a gift from a Methodist lady, played on Sundays by a Presbyterian; or the gift of money from the Jewish animal trader for his statue of Saint Joseph. The little chapel stands in a field of wild mustard, and we are reminded of the parable of the mustard seed and connect it with the novel's theme of love that extends itself to encompass the whole world.

Father Joseph-Marie finds, however, that human love has limits. He comes to recognize, for example, that although his compassion and concern for the half-breeds led him to get them a better deal for their furs, it also meant that they had more money for drinking. In the confession he is struck by the good will of souls and the inexhaustible sum of goodness on earth, yet it is not enough, "for it did not succeed in changing the world." To the parishioners of the Water Hen gathered in the Tousignants' parlor, he preaches a sermon on love, comparing human souls to birds, some flying higher than others. Men and women must free themselves from the mud of human passions he says, from anger, lust, pride, and other such things in order to fly like the lark in the pure light of heaven. The priest finds his analogy in watching a prairie chickens' ball, and the novel ends fittingly with the parishioners at a dance at the half-breeds' and the old priest watching over his flock. *Where Nests the Water Hen* celebrates the power of human love, but acknowledges as well its earthly, finite nature.

Gabrielle Roy's third novel, *Alexandre Chenevert, caissier* (1954), published in English as *The Cashier*, returns the reader to the trials and complexities of life in a modern city. *The Cashier* is Gabrielle Roy's most complex novel philosophically. It is on one level an essay on the human condition which explores the nature of such elusive goals as happiness and love and probes the enigma of human suffering. The book's protagonist, Alexandre Chenevert, a middle-aged bank teller, is a man subject to the miseries of a frail, nervous body and tormented by the desire to understand better the nature and purpose of human existence. On a significant level he is a modern Everyman, a minor white-collar worker submerged in the tedious paperwork of modern civilization. The doctor he visits thinks "his name, indeed, is legion" and sees the life of Alexandre and his fellows as a modern version of slavery:

Every morning at a set hour he walked down a thousand staircases at once, running from every corner of the city toward bulging streetcars. He crowded into them by the hundreds and thousands. From tram to tram, from street to street, you could see him standing in public conveyances, his hands slipped through leather straps, his arms stretched in a curious likeness to a prisoner at the whipping post.[7]

[7] *The Cashier*, trans. Harry L. Binsse (Toronto: McClelland and Stewart, 1963), p. 102. All references are to this edition.

Chenevert's work is dehumanizing; he spends his life in a teller's cage in a day-long battle to keep his columns of figures straight. At noon he stands in a long anonymous line to procure his lunch. Like thousands of others, he is an insignificant denizen of the modern city, his nerves acerbated by the noise of factories and transportation systems, his health eroded by the pollution in the air.

But Gabrielle Roy's purpose at the same time is, as one critic has rightly noted, to show what is precious and unique in this seemingly anonymous individual, to create sympathy for the misanthropic bank teller who is heir to all the ills of spirit and flesh.[8] That sympathy is aroused in the reader by the moral rectitude of Chenevert's conscious design for living and by the correspondent intensity of his suffering. Much of part 1 follows a day in Chenevert's working life; it begins with his sleepless night in which he is tormented alternately by the drift of current events (the development of the atomic bomb, famine in India, earthquakes, rumors of war) and by his own physical miseries—heartburn, headaches, and insomnia. During the day he is overcome by fatigue as a result of not sleeping during the night and becomes irascible and absent-minded; his concern for humanity in general finds no practical application, and the reader becomes aware of Chenevert's immense loneliness. After he makes an error at the bank, he is persuaded to see a doctor to obtain relief from insomnia. Doctor Hudon tells Chenevert that he thinks and worries too much, that he should relax and enjoy life more, perhaps take up bowling. But Chenevert impatiently rejects this advice, for he believes thinking "the only activity that matters." He believes the chief purpose in living is to think, to solve the riddle of existence.

Nonetheless, in part 2 Chenevert goes on a vacation, without his wife, to a lake in the wilderness north of Montreal. Immediately the natural world speaks to him of the vanity of human strivings. He is soothed by the indifference of nature and recognizes the transient physical basis of his own existence. Sitting by the lake, he asks, "Was he himself anything more than one of

<hr />

[8] W. C. Lougheed, introduction to *The Cashier* (Toronto: McClelland and Stewart, 1963).

these green and supple reeds?" In touch with his physical being, at last he is able to sleep. The next day, "the most beautiful day of his life," he retraces in his actions and thoughts no less than the evolutionary history of humankind and comes to recognize the worth of human strivings and inventions: the fire and matches that keep him warm, the snug little cabin that keeps out the rain, the good food and drink from places as far away as China. The author observes at this time of revelation in Chenevert's life: "Indeed the discovery of the world by a man leaning upon century after century of civilization dazzles the heart" (p. 129).

In retracing human history Chenevert stops at a pastoral vision of what seems to him the ideal life, illustrated by the Le Gardeur family from whom he rents the tiny cabin on Lac Vert. Their self-contained world, with its traditional *habitant* farm house, livestock, and poultry, its rich fields and well-provisioned larder, is the emblem of rural self-sufficiency. The Le Gardeurs entertain Alexandre for an evening, eat to their "heart's content," and assure their guest that they are happy with their lives. Chenevert believes this to be "the most beautiful avowal he ever had received in all his life," and he tries to communicate his vision of human unity and rural happiness by writing a long essay for publication. But no sooner has he found peace in this earthly paradise than he begins to feel bored. Ironically, the peace he has sought is characterized by monotony. His bus trip back to Montreal picks up again the evolutionary progress of the human species. Chenevert leaves the Eden of Lac Vert behind him and resumes the restless course of modern man living in the city. From the bus he sees an electrically wired statue of Christ, a powerful image of humanity's continuous spiritual quest and suffering; and when he alights at the city bus station, he is again the wholly anonymous, alienated man that left ten days before. In Montreal his vision of the good life is gone.

Part 3 describes the suffering and death of Chenevert and focuses on the difficult questions of love, happiness, and human misery, as the little cashier makes his final accounts with this world that has so puzzled him. When Chenevert goes to the hospital, his body filled with cancer, he comes to grasp briefly some of the sad truths about human existence. In the hospital, a once-longed-for refuge from the harrassments of his every day life, he envies those who are still going about their business of a wintry night: "He wanted to be back in the cage." Man is so constructed, the author sadly observes, that he only enjoys things once they are gone. Happiness is always just missed, and one is left with regrets. Chief among those regrets for Chenevert is "not to have loved enough when it was time for love." He does, however, enjoy a few days of happiness when his family and his acquaintances from the bank come to see him before his death. His abstract vision at the lake of human brotherhood, expressed in the idea of human progress and the relationship of goods and services, is replaced by an immediate and concrete expression of good will. Ironically, it is his imminent death which brings people together, and he wonders whether perhaps God permits suffering because it creates a universal bond among men.[9] *The Cashier* is a bleak portrait of twentieth-century humanity, alienated by the indifference of technological society, overwhelmed by global problems beyond its control. At the same time, the story of the little cashier, who in spite of his narrow circumstances attempts to understand the mystery and the paradoxes of living, is a poignant testament to the heroism of the human spirit.

Two of Gabrielle Roy's most accomplished books are collections of autobiographical sketches from her Manitoba childhood. In *Rue Deschambault* (1955), translated as *Street of Riches*, the eighteen episodes are bound together by the presence of the girl, Christine, from whose point of view the stories are told. The author's purpose is to recapture the joys of childhood, and one of the ways she does this is by almost entirely eliminating awareness of time. Although time does underline the structural arrangement of the stories (the narrator is a small child at the beginning and a teacher with her first school at the close), it plays no causal role within the stories or in their relationship to each other. Rather, it is the timeless world of childhood—an eternal summer—that the author has created in these lyrical and beautifully wrought vignettes from the past.

[9] Paul Socken traces this theme in his essay "'Le pays de l'amour' in the Works of Gabrielle Roy," *Revue de l'Université d'Ottawa* 46, no. 3 (Summer 1976): 309–23. See also John J. Murphy's "Alexandre Chenevert: Gabrielle Roy's Crucified Canadian," *Queen's Quarterly* 72 (Summer 1965): 334–46.

These sketches might be called songs of innocence because, as in Blake's poems, there are ironies present for the adult reader to recognize. When Christine's uncle talks about a honeymoon as the beginning of marriage when all is beautiful, Christine innocently inquires, "Later on does it become less beautiful?," causing the adults to reflect on life's disappointments and the fragility of human relationships. And again, thinking about love, Christine compares the dutiful relationship of her parents, where tenderness is expressed by anxiousness, to the happiness of the Italian next door who "carried his love upon his countenance like a sun." Christine reflects wistfully that such a wonderful form of love must be "a product of Italy" and not attainable in Canada. But the author's belief that childhood innocence is a lasting source of happiness is insisted upon in the last episode, "To Earn My Living. . . ." Here the narrator must go out into the world to work, but as a teacher she happily finds herself "as though cut off from the rest of the world in the warm little schoolhouse." Outside a snowstorm is sweeping down over the prairies, but Christine reflects, "I was living through one of the rarest happinesses of my life. Was not all the world a child? Were we not at the day's morning?" [10]

Gabrielle Roy, however, did not write only songs of innocence about her past; the four stories about Christine that comprise *La route d'Altamont* (1966), in English *The Road past Altamont*, are songs of experience obsessed with the passage of time, with life's mutability, and the incompleteness of human relationships. In each of the four stories there is a fundamental tension between seeing life as a linear journey and as a circle that completes itself. The first two stories examine this theme in the relationship of the very young to the very old. In "My Almighty Grandmother" Christine at first sees her grandmother, who makes her a beautiful rag doll out of some scrap materials, as a godlike figure, a creator. But when the old woman comes to live with Christine's parents, she becomes helpless and childlike. In "The Old Man and the Child" the little girl takes a trip to Lake Winnipeg with a kindly

---

[10] *Street of Riches*, trans. Harry L. Binsse (Toronto: McClelland and Stewart, 1967), p. 158. In *Gabrielle Roy* (Montreal: Fides, 1975) François Ricard views as central to Roy's writing the attempt to recreate the world she knew as a child.

old neighbor, Monsieur Saint-Hilaire, who makes the girl feel they are on a great adventure, like the explorer La Vérendrye. But when the old man falls asleep in a restaurant, his dentures slipping out of his mouth and his hand dangling down like a dead thing, she is frightened by his old age and his helplessness. In both stories the reader is aware that the old people are nearing death and that their lives have involved them on a long journey both literally and metaphorically. Christine's grandmother was made to leave Quebec as a young woman when she married, and she looks back on her pioneer life in Manitoba as a long exile. Monsieur Saint-Hilaire has come from France and is still preparing himself for one final journey: without understanding that he is nearing the end of his life, Christine sees him "walking all alone in the twilight, as if he were looking for someone."

But the special event celebrated in these stories is the coming together of the very young and the very old. As she becomes forgetful and no longer able to knit, the grandmother talks about goblins tangling her wool at night. Christine's mother explains that childhood beliefs are often reborn in extreme old age, and Christine is puzzled by the way "one spoke at once of old age and of second childhood." To be close to her grandmother the little girl shows her photographs from her youth. The proximity of childhood and old age is described more philosophically by Monsieur Saint-Hilaire, who says to Christine as they contemplate the convergence of sky and lake on the horizon: "Perhaps everything finally forms a great circle, the end and the beginning coming together."[11] Between the two there is still life's journey to be made, and there is a bleak foreshadowing of the transient, sometimes sordid condition of adult life in the third story, "The Move," in which Christine watches a poor family move house. Here Christine becomes aware for the first time of separation and the emotions of guilt and sorrow.

The fourth story, titled "The Road past Altamont," returns to the theme of youth and age with the sad recognition that during life the generations never really come together, that time always

[11] *The Road past Altamont*, trans. Joyce Marshall (Toronto: McClelland and Stewart, 1966), p. 68. All references are to this edition.

remains the condition of awareness and understanding. In this story Christine as an adult takes her mother on a drive through the Pembina Mountains, which make the older woman feel she has been transported back to the hills of her childhood in Quebec. She wishes she could talk to her dead mother (Christine's grandmother), for she now understands how homesick she felt and why she became bitter towards life. She tells Christine that she feels the grandmother lives on inside her ("We give birth in turn to the one who gave us birth when finally, sooner or later, we draw her into our self" [p. 129]). She says in what is perhaps the fundamental recognition of the story: "We come together. . . . We always do finally come together, but so late!" Christine does not yet understand what this experience means (to rediscover one's childhood or to draw close to one's family), for she is anxious to leave her mother and study abroad. But, ironically, this is the very truth about life which her life abroad brings her to recognize.

The Road past Altamont belongs to that body of writing loosely described as wisdom literature. The theme of life as a long journey which in the end describes a circle brings to mind the book of Ecclesiastes and that elemental passage about sun and wind and the earth beginning, "One generation passeth away, and another generation cometh. . . . Unto the place from whence the rivers come, thither they return again." The mystery of change and permanence, of life's passage through time, not only haunts the relationships of the characters but is mirrored in the prairie landscape they inhabit:

These roads in the depths of rural Manitoba, which I had taken to save time, as a short cut to the highway, we call section roads, and there are no other roads like them for going farther and nowhere. . . . I see once more their silent meeting under that enigmatic sky; the wind, lightly playing with them, raises dust from their surfaces and makes it turn in a lasso. I recall their soundless greeting, their astonishment at coming together and parting again so soon—and for what destination? For of whence they have come and where they are going they never say a word. [p. 113–14]

Both *Street of Riches* and *The Road past Altamont* introduce the theme of the artist and her relationship to the world. In "The

Voice of the Pools" the singing of the frogs in April (a cry of distress and a cry of triumph) mysteriously awakens in Christine the desire to be a writer. Her mother does not encourage this ambition, for she sees the writer as a divided person, torn by the desire to live and by the need to stand apart and reflect on life in order to write about it: "Is it not like cutting yourself in two, as it were— one half trying to live, the other watching, weighing?" (p. 132). She seems to recognize that it is a terribly lonely occupation. "To write . . . is this not, finally, to be far from others . . . to be all alone, poor child?" But at the same time, Christine feels that writing is the most perfect communication possible. Of a book's hold over the reader she says, "Is there any possession equal to this one?" Is there "a more perfect understanding?" The older Christine in "The Road past Altamont" recognizes the truth of her mother's words because as a writer she has become withdrawn from life, "a watcher over thoughts and human beings" (p. 133). She also recognizes that there is a sad personal motive underlying her desire to be a writer. She had always wanted to do something important with her life as a recompense to her parents. She had been a late, unwanted child, "a child of duty," as her mother would say of other families where a woman already overburdened had just brought another child into the world. The feelings of the unwanted child are described in *Street of Riches*, where the aged father calls Christine his "Petite Misère" (little unhappy one). She believes herself to be unloved, but at the same time is full of gratitude and has a powerful desire to repay those who have been kindly and have cared for her. Her tribute or recompense, however, comes too late. Christine's mother dies before the young woman has made a name for herself (as Gabrielle Roy's mother died before seeing the dedication in *The Tin Flute*), and there is the haunting realization that while art can bring awareness, it can never restore life.

In *The Hidden Mountain* (*La montagne secrète*, 1961), the story of a trapper-painter from the Northwest Territories who eventually studies art in Paris, Gabrielle Roy makes some revealing observations on the artist's struggles with technique. Pierre Cadorai, the artist-protagonist, finds that the most difficult things to portray were yet the simplest: water, fire, the sky. He experiences his highest moments of inspiration when he comes upon a snowcapped mountain in the remote regions of the Ungava Peninsula. He falls on his knees in reverence, for to him the mountain is a subject of worship as the Madonna and child were for Renaissance painters. His problem is how to capture the splendor and magnificence of the mountain on canvas. The author observes: "Who has not dreamed, on a single canvas, within a single book, to include all one's experience, all one's love, and thus fulfil the infinite hope, the infinite expectation, of men!" When Pierre realizes that he cannot put the whole mountain in a single canvas, he makes instead a series of small pictures, each concerned with one facet of the mountain, each at a different time of day: "And these, taken all together, would be the Resplendent One."

Here, in effect, Gabrielle Roy describes her own impressionistic technique as a writer, which is to eschew drama, the novel constructed like a play with a unified plot, in favor of fiction made up of a series of episodes and characters, the cumulative effect of which is the experience of life itself. Here Gabrielle Roy also reveals her affinity with Willa Cather, an author she admires greatly. There are similarities in the content of their work because they both grew up in the vast, lonely spaces of the prairie. More important, they share a Virgilian perspective on life's brevity, and Cather's example may have helped Gabrielle Roy to find the appropriate forms for her fiction. *The Cashier*, for example, is not unlike Cather's study of middle age and attendant death in *The Professor's House*. Like Cather, Roy places in the middle of her sober narrative about modern urban life a pastoral interlude which returns the protagonist to nature and a simpler mode of existence. The story of Father Joseph-Marie in part 3 of *Water Hen* recalls *Death Comes for the Archbishop*; both narratives about pioneer priests are told in a flat, nonlinear manner in accordance with a view of life that transcends time and place. But in her episodic memory books, *Street of Riches* and *The Road past Altamont*, we are especially reminded of Cather's ideal of the "unfurnished novel" where "the inexplicable presence of the thing not named" gives high quality to art.

All of Gabrielle Roy's books since *The Hidden Mountain* are written in episodic form. *La rivière sans repos* (1970), translated into English as *Windflower*, is the story of an Eskimo girl raped by an American soldier. Her story, which centers on the raising of her blond, blue-eyed son, is told in loosely connected episodes which continue after the boy has grown up and run away from the Eskimo world. *Cet été qui chantait* (1972), with the English title *Enchanted Summer*, is a series of nature sketches from rural Quebec; *Un jardin au bout du monde* (1975), published in English as *Garden in the Wind*, is a collection of four stories that reveal the vastness and solitude of the prairies; and *Ces enfants de ma vie* (1977), translated as *Children of My Heart*, is a group of sketches from the author's days as a schoolteacher in Manitoba. Episodic narration is the formal essence of Gabrielle Roy's art, for in all her writing she views life in the context of time's passage and the inevitable dissolution of all things in it. If there is protest in her art, it is against the fate of all humankind, that each individual life must come to an end.

Pierre's art teacher in Paris says that the subject of a work is merely an excuse to define an inner resonance with the universe. In Gabrielle Roy's fiction that resonance is manifest as a sad refrain on life's brevity and on its condition of suffering. One is made to listen in her fiction to the wind sighing, to rivers murmuring "with ancient sorrows." Like her artist hero in *The Hidden Mountain*, Gabrielle Roy is drawn to "the solitary, lonely, abandoned side of things," especially to the bleak, disheartening north country. But there are affirmations in her fiction as well, more vivid and lasting because made at such great cost: a garden of flowers in the northern prairie wind, an oil painting from the Ungava region, a new baby after a long and hazardous journey. The instinct in human beings to create hints at something potentially great in human nature. But most important is the capacity to feel tenderness and sympathy towards one's fellow human beings. In Gabrielle Roy's fiction there is a melancholy, best rendered by the Latin *lacrimae rerum*, but there is also a quiet joy in the redeeming power of compassion and love.

Selected Writings

Bonheur d'occasion. Montreal: Société des éditions Pascal, 1945. English translation, *The Tin Flute*, by Hannah Josephson (Toronto: Mc-

Clelland and Stewart, 1947). Reprint, New Canadian Library, no. 5 (Toronto: McClelland and Stewart, 1958).

La petite poule d'eau. Montreal: Beauchemin, 1950. English translation, *Where Nests the Water Hen*, by Harry L. Binsse (Toronto: McClelland and Stewart, 1951). Reprint, New Canadian Library, no. 25 (Toronto: McClelland and Stewart, 1961).

Alexandre Chenevert, caissier. Montreal: Beauchemin, 1954. English translation, *The Cashier*, by Harry L. Binsse (Toronto: McClelland and Stewart, 1955). Reprint, New Canadian Library, no. 40 (Toronto: McClelland and Stewart, 1963).

Rue Deschambault. Montreal: Beauchemin, 1955. English translation, *Street of Riches*, by Harry L. Binsse (Toronto: McClelland and Stewart, 1957). Reprint, New Canadian Library, no. 56 (Toronto: McClelland and Stewart, 1967).

La montagne secrète. Montreal: Beauchemin, 1961. English translation, *The Hidden Mountain*, by Harry L. Binsse (Toronto: McClelland and Stewart, 1962). Reprint, New Canadian Library, no. 109 (Toronto: McClelland and Stewart, 1974).

La route d'Altamont. Montreal: Éditions HMH, Coll. L'Arbre, no. 10, 1966. English translation, *The Road past Altamont*, by Joyce Marshall (Toronto: McClelland and Stewart, 1966). Reprint, New Canadian Library, no. 129 (Toronto: McClelland and Stewart, 1976).

La rivière sans repos. Montreal: Beauchemin, 1970. English translation, *Windflower*, by Joyce Marshall (Toronto: McClelland and Stewart, 1970). Reprint, New Canadian Library, no. 120 (Toronto: McClelland and Stewart, 1975).

Cet été qui chantait. Quebec and Montreal: Les Éditions françaises, 1972. English translation, *Enchanted Summer*, by Alan Brown, (Toronto: McClelland and Stewart, 1976).

Un jardin au bout du monde. Montreal: Beauchemin, 1975. English translation, *Garden in the Wind*, by Alan Brown (Toronto: McClelland and Stewart, 1977).

Ces enfants de ma vie. Ottawa: Stanké, 1977. English translation, *Children of My Heart*, by Alan Brown (Toronto: McClelland and Stewart, 1979).

A. M. Klein

A. M. Klein was one of the young Montreal poets associated with A. J. M. Smith and F. R. Scott who, in the late twenties, started publishing poetry influenced by modernism. For Klein this cosmopolitanism was a natural direction to follow, since in his poetry he would become the voice for three separate cultural traditions: Jewish, English, and French-Canadian. But it was also the path that described an increasing alienation from his family's religious and cultural traditions and which culminated in isolation and madness. Klein is Canada's poet of despair, unhappiness that he termed "stark infelicity." Essentially a pastoral poet in search of a lost Eden, Klein laments the loss of a more perfect world in various ways: in the distance he feels from his father and his orthodox faith, in his preoccupation with social injustice, in the isolation of the artist, and in his intimations of encroaching insanity. All of this remarkable poet's work is marked by the voice of the alien.

A brief summary of Klein's life reflects the cultural dispersion he was subjected to as a twentieth-century Jew. He was born in Montreal in 1909 to Jewish emigrants from Russia and was educated in both Hebrew and English schools. He took a bachelor of arts at McGill University, but subsequently went to the French Université de Montreal, where he studied law. Through his background and education he was adept in five languages: English, French, Yiddish, Hebrew, and Latin. He was called to the bar in 1933 and practiced law in Montreal until his early retirement in 1954; during that period he published five books of verse and prose, edited the *Canadian Jewish Chronicle*, and took an active part in the Co-operative Commonwealth Federation party (forerunner of the New Democratic party) and its struggle to alleviate the poverty of the French-Canadian working class. From 1945 to

1947 he was a part-time lecturer in the English department at McGill University. His passionate interest in Zionism resulted in a trip to Israel which gave rise to *The Second Scroll*, a parable combining prose and poetry, about a spiritual journey to the Promised Land. In the mid-1950s Klein suffered a nervous breakdown and lived in seclusion with his wife and family until his death in 1972.

Klein's early poems were collected in *Hath Not a Jew* (1940) and published in New York by Behrman's Jewish Book House. The publisher and the title of the book (from *Merchant of Venice*: "Hath not a Jew eyes? hath not a Jew hands?") indicate the poet's initial identification with a specific cultural tradition. Klein speaks first as a Jew, but he chose to write his poetry in English rather than Yiddish or Hebrew. The choice of language involves a fundamental tension in Klein's poetry between the emotional claims of his religious culture and the intellectual need to view it objectively from a distance. Language (the voice of another people) is one of the strategies Klein uses to achieve that distance.

Klein was raised in the orthodox faith, and his parents hoped he would enter the rabbinate. One of his first instincts as a poet is to celebrate his cultural heritage, but his desire to be a voice for his people is complicated by loss of religious faith. As a student, sensitive to the philosophical and artistic tenor of his age, Klein found himself doubting his father's strict religious beliefs. In "Childe Harold's Pilgrimage" he describes himself as disinherited, "cut off without a penny's worth of faith." The feeling that he has betrayed his father and his heritage is implicit in a poem like "Heirloom," in which he describes his family's humble means and legacy of belief:

> My father bequeathed me no wide estates;
> No keys and ledgers were my heritage;
> Only some holy books with *yahrzeit* dates
> Writ mournfully upon a blank front page.[1]

He is brought to tears when he finds in the pages of these books a white hair fallen from his father's beard. The poet's position is

---

[1] *The Collected Poems of A. M. Klein*, comp. with an introduction by Miriam Waddington (Toronto: McGraw-Hill Ryerson, 1974), p. 113. All quotations of Klein's poetry are from this text.

that of the alien, and the language of his poems, not his father's tongue, is an emblem of his exile.

But search for self and God remain the vital center of Klein's work. In abandoning the strict orthodoxy of his father's faith, Klein looks to Spinoza, the seventeenth-century Dutch philosopher who turned away from the synagogue to formulate an all-embracing pantheism. In "Out of the Pulver and the Polished Lens," a series of nine loosely related poems, Klein exonerates Spinoza as a lapsed Jew by showing how he transcended the limitations of theological dogma and found God in nature and a life of devotion. The first poem describes Spinoza's excommunication by the "paunchy sons of Abraham." The second one recalls the tragedy of Uriel de Costa, a Portuguese heretic who shot himself before his case was brought before the Jewish communal court. Klein sees his own position writ large in these dramatic accounts of loss of faith. He returns to the story of Spinoza, who rejects institutionalized religion where "Jehovah is factotum of the rabbis" and "synods tell God to be or not to be." Forsaking the "abracadabra of the synagogue," Spinoza fulfills his passion for God by turning to nature and the workings of the universe, where he is "utterly vanquished by a star" and by the miracle of a bird's song. He fits his own psalm to this new vision of God's immanence in the universe:

> Lord, accept my hallelujahs; look not askance at these my petty words; unto perfection a fragment makes its prayer.
>
> For thou art the world, and I am part thereof; thou art the blossom and I its fluttering petal.
>
> I behold thee in all things, and in all things: lo, it is myself; I look into the pupil of thine eye, it is my very countenance I see.
>
> . . . .
>
> The wind through the almond-trees spreads the fragrance of thy robes; the turtle-dove twittering utters diminutives of thy love; at the rising of the sun I behold thy countenance.

The ninth and concluding poem in the series contrasts Spinoza's life of devotion and praise to that of the false nineteenth-century Messiah who "took to himself the Torah for a wife" and became a tyrannical lawmaker. Klein urges the reader to remember instead Spinoza, who transcended theological dogma:

> Think of Spinoza, . . .
> Plucking his tulips in the Holland sun,
> Remembering the thought of the Adored,
> Spinoza, gathering flowers for the One,
> The ever-unwedded lover of the Lord.

Taken as a whole, "Out of the Pulver and the Polished Lens" is one of Klein's most accomplished pieces, written in a variety of forms, including rhyming couplets, blank verse, prose, and the breathing line of the psalm. The title refers to Spinoza's occupation as a lens grinder but, more important, suggests the new vision he was creating of "the infinitesimal and infinite." Klein embraced Spinoza's basic premise, namely that everything is part of the Deity, with genuine intellectual excitement, for Spinoza's philosophy allowed him to believe that there was a divine principle in the universe. The influence of Spinoza's thought surfaces in much of Klein's work, even in writings heavily colored by despair.[2]

Although Klein could not affirm the beliefs of his people in his poetry, he could write about his culture. One of his purposes in using English is to address the non-Jewish world and demonstrate the truth of Shylock's contention that the Jews share a common humanity with the rest of humankind and are heirs to a noble tradition. Much of that tradition is biblical and accessible, a fundamental part of Christianity and Western civilization. The darker, more obscure side is the long history of persecution and pogroms which Klein works into his "Design for Medieval Tapestry." The poem, in ten sequences, begins by describing the primal instinct of fear that is a perpetual touchstone of existence for the Jew. There are noises in the night ("Somewhere a hungry muzzle rooted. . . . A clawed mouse squeaked"), and the Jews, like hunted animals, fear for their lives:

> Was it a provost seeking Jews?
> The Hebrews shivered; their teeth rattled;
> Their beards glittered with gelid dews.

Like a Brueghel painting, the poem portrays the familiar scenes

[2] See Gretl Fischer, "Religious Philosophy in the Writings of A. M. Klein," in *The A. M. Klein Symposium*, ed. with an introduction by Seymour Mayne (Ottawa: University of Ottawa Press, 1975), pp. 37–45.

from medieval Jewish life: a religious hermit preaching that Jews should be drowned, soldiers vaunting the cross as a sword, the ghetto where Jews live next to brothels, peasants staring at Jews for signs of the devil's mark. The rabbis interpret the Jews' lot as the just exercise of God's wrath ("His punishment / Is most desirable. The flesh and Jacob / Implores the scourge. For this was Israel meant"). But a contrary voice is raised, that of Klein the doubter, who asserts simply "that pain doth render flesh most sore and hectic":

> That lance-point prick; that scorched bones hiss;
> That thumbscrews agonize, and that a martyr
> Is mad if he considers these things bliss.

But the poem ends with the picture of a burgher sleeping beside his wife and dreaming "of human venery, and Hebrew quarry":

> There will be Jews, dead, moribund and gory;
> There will be booty; there will be dark maids,
> And there will be a right good spicy story.

Klein's countervision to the history of Jewish persecution and antidote for his personal loss of faith is the Zionist dream of the Promised Land, the political prospect of a peaceful life in the new Israel. The poems describing the return to Israel are written in a pastoral, idealized mode. They do not describe the dry, rocky terrain of the Middle East, but celebrate the mythic return to a garden and green pastures. "The Still Small Voice" presents that vision as rebirth:

> The candles splutter; and the kettle hums;
> The heirloomed clock enumerates the tribes,
> Upon the wine-stained table-cloth lie crumbs
> Of *matzoh* whose wide scattering describes
> Jews driven in far lands upon this earth.

> The kettle hums; the candles splutter; and
> Winds whispering from shutters tell re-birth
> Of beauty rising in an eastern land,
> Of paschal sheep driven in cloudy droves;
> Of almond-blossoms colouring the breeze;
> Of vineyards upon verdant terraces;
> Of golden globes in orient orange-groves.

> And those assembled at the table dream
> Of small schemes that an April wind doth scheme,
> And cry from out the sleep assailing them:
> *Jerusalem, next year! Next year, Jerusalem!*

The details in the first stanza (the candles, the heirloom clock, the wine-stained table-cloth) suggest the fulfillment of a filial promise. In the second poem from the group "Sonnets Semitic" the recovery of Israel assumes the shape of a marriage vow:

> At last, my bride, in our estate you'll wear
> Sweet orange-blossoms in an orange grove.
> There will be white doves fluttering in the air,
> And in the meadows our contented drove,
> Sheep on the hills, and in the trees, my love,
> There will be sparrows twittering *Mazel Tov.*

The range of themes and the affirmative vision of the new Israel disappear from Klein's second published collection, titled simply *Poems* (1944). His personal exile from the Eden of his father's faith left him vulnerable to a vision of a fallen world with all its injustices and cruelties. The full impact of what was happening to the Jewry of Europe was being felt by the poet, whose chief emotions in this collection are doubt and despair. The longest part of the book is a grouping of thirty-six poems titled "The Psalter of Avram Haktani," the title being a play on the name *Klein*, since in Hebrew *haktani*, like the German word *klein*, is the word for small. The first psalm sets the negative tone for the whole collection. The voice of prophecy and vision has disappeared from Israel—

> Where in these dubious days shall I take counsel?
> Who is there to resolve the dark, the doubt?

In psalm 3 the poet tries to escape his sense of responsibility and despair by wishing he didn't belong to the human race:

> Would that the Lord had made me, in place of man-child,
>   beast!
> Far easier is the oxen's yoke than the weight of thought,
> Lighter the harness than the harnessed heart!

In these poems Klein accuses God of betrayal and indifference, watching unmoved while the Germans exterminate the Jews. In psalm 6, "Upon the Heavenly Scarp," he writes:

> The Lord looked down, and saw the cattle-cars:
> Men ululating to a frozen land.
> He saw a man tear at his flogged scars,
> And saw a babe look for its blown-off hand.

The angels weep, but God says nothing, as he sends the angel of Sodom to scourge the land. In the most intense psalm of the collection the poet blasphemously proposes to replace God's inadequate system of justice with his own:

> One day the signal shall be given me;
> I shall break in and enter heaven, and,
> Remembering who, below, held upper hand,
> And who was trodden into misery, —
> I shall seek out the abominable scales
> On which the heavenly justice is mis-weighed.
> I know I am no master of the trade,
> Can neither mend nor make, clumsy with nails,
> No artisan, —yet am I so forespoken,
> Determined so against the automaton,
> That I must tamper with it, tree and token,
> Break bolts, undo its markings, one by one,
> And leave those scales so gloriously broken,
> That ever thereafter justice shall be done!

The fullest expression of the poet's doubt and despair comes in another poem titled "Rabbi Yom-Tob of Mayence Petitions His God." To the petitioner "there is no sign upon the skies, . . . no Marvel to which to raise the eyes." Here Klein abandons the pantheism of Spinoza as well and asserts a mechanistic, unintelligent universe.

> Who hails the cloud for love, must heed
> Only the taciturn cloud in speed, —
> Who climbs upon the golden stair
> Of the sun goes blinded by the glare;
> Who counts the stars, will ever find
> More stars in the sky than in his mind.

In such a world the tragedy of the Jews has no compensations, no meaning.

Although Desmond Pacey is correct when he writes that Klein is essentially a psalmist, a lyric poet of praise and lamentation,[3] his assessment overlooks the fact that he also wrote on occasion in a satirical vein in order to express his anger at human injustice and cruelty. In the 1930s it was the economic depression which elicited Klein's anger, and he responded with a series of radical poems consistent with the revolutionary temper of that period. Probably the best of these is a piece titled "The Soiree of Velvel Kleinburger," which describes the poverty of a worker in Montreal's garment industry. Velvel's response to poverty is to go whoring and gambling and to dream of a materialistic utopia symbolized by a plump wife, a Rolls-Royce, and a chauffeur. He has no plans for actively participating in a social revolution to better his condition. The poem is written in the ironical mode of T. S. Eliot's satires, and certain lines such as "My life lies on a tray of cigarette-butts" and aphoristic couplets such as "For I have heard these things from teachers / With dirty beards and hungry features" are direct echoes from the author of "Prufrock." But the humanist's dismay at poverty becomes the satirist's cry of moral outrage when Klein realizes the extent of the holocaust in Europe. Klein's third book of poetry is a long satire in heroic couplets titled *The Hitleriad* (1944). It is not a very successful work, perhaps because, as critics have suggested, Klein did not have a profound understanding of either Hitler or the nature of evil. He sees the Führer as something subhuman, a freak or moron, and believes that his demise will usher in a messianic era.[4] But least successful of all is the poem's form; for in the twentieth century the heroic couplet in the manner of Pope is incapable of treating a subject so important and so terrifying; instead, it renders it slightly comic, trivial.

One is surprised coming to Klein's fourth and final book of poetry, *The Rocking Chair* (1948), because it is so different from the volumes that preceded it. He has moved away completely from his Jewish themes, exchanging the imaginary geography of the

[3] Desmond Pacey, "A. M. Klein," in *Ten Canadian Poets* (Toronto: Ryerson Press, 1958), pp. 254–92.

[4] See Tom Marshall, introduction to *A. M. Klein* (Toronto: Ryerson Press, 1970), p. xiii.

Promised Land for the concrete realities of French Canada, particularly the immediate world of Montreal. Perhaps even more startling is the radical change in Klein's language and verse forms. The poet Miriam Waddington has rightly observed that in *The Rocking Chair* Klein gives up archaic language and Elizabethan rhetoric in favor of a rich use of metaphor. Klein, says Waddington, was no longer so interested in evoking the past as he was eager to discover new realities and meanings through the metaphorical possibilities of language.[5] Klein has turned away from the influence of the Elizabethans and T. S. Eliot and turned to poets like Hopkins and Auden for models, although perhaps the strongest influence comes from James Joyce, a writer Klein studied and admired enormously.

There are a number of continuing concerns: there is still the poet's pleasure in tradition, his nostalgia for childhood, his biting observations on politics, his sympathy for the poor and oppressed. Critics have frequently observed that what Klein has done is to extend his sympathy for his own minority people to that of the French in English-dominated Canada, that his appreciation of French-Canadian life is rooted in the vulnerability of his own culture. In some of the poems such as "The Rocking Chair," "The Spinning Wheel," and "The Sugaring" Klein celebrates in verse certain folk customs associated specifically with rural Quebec. "The Sugaring," for example, describes the tapping of maple trees in early spring and the making of maple syrup. But these poems also search out a symbolic dimension in their subjects. Thus the rocking chair, with its pendulum movement, conveys the mood and static pace of life in the country, while the spinning wheel, a quaint antique from feudal times, suggests a more insidious legacy from the past—taxes and fees that are a continuation of the corvée. "The Sugaring" is an elaborate metaphor identifying the maple trees with the saints of the church:

> Starved, scarred, lenten, amidst ash of air,
> roped and rough-shirted, the maples in the unsheltered grove
> after their fasts and freezings stir.

---

[5] Miriam Waddington, *A. M. Klein* (Montreal: McGill-Queen's University Press, 1970), p. 130.

When the trees are tapped, they are likened to saints being tortured for their faith:

> The saints bleed down their sides!
> And look! men catch this juice of their agonized prime
> to boil in kettles the sap of seraphim!

From this sacrifice comes the sweetness of inspiration and renewed faith. Of particular interest here is the way Klein through
the maple tree metaphor makes religion and culture an organic
extension of the landscape.

There are other Catholic poems such as "The Cripples" and
"For the Sisters of the Hotel Dieu" in which Klein shows the
sympathetic capacity of his imagination to appreciate an alien
people and culture. In "The Cripples" the poet envies those peni-
tents who come to Saint Joseph's Oratory on crutches and in
wheelchairs because they at least still believe in God:

> And I who in my own faith once had faith like this,
> but have not now, am crippled more than they.

Bereft of religion, the poet feels akin to the remnants of the Iroquois tribe whom he describes in "Indian Reservation: Caughna-
waga" as ghosts living in a crypt. The Indians were once a living
part of the landscape like the animals, but they have been vanquished by "better hunters," and are kept on the reserve, a "grassy
ghetto" where they make curios (sweetgrass baskets, beaded shoes)
like "fauna in a museum." With the word *ghetto* Klein draws an
analogy between the plight of the Indian and his own race.

A few of the poems are overtly political in content. Racism is
the theme of "Political Meeting," where in a schoolroom a
French-Canadian politician harangues his audience against con-
scription during the war. The poem concludes with the ominous
lines "in the darkness rises / the body-odour of race." There is a
similarly sinister glimpse of politics in "Monsieur Gaston," where
a local ne'er-do-well rises to a position of power in a corrupt political system. But the tone of the collection as a whole is lyrical
rather than critical. There are a number of poems about
Montreal which celebrate the life of the city in its different seasons. In "Pastoral of the City Streets" it is the nostalgic setting of
childhood summers; in "The Mountain" the park is the place of

first love. Klein's love of language and his affection for the place of his birth merge in the bilingual poem "Montreal," which describes the growth and features of the city in a language shared by both English and French.

In "Portrait of the Poet as Landscape" Klein says the poet creates and takes possession of the world through language, words giving the items of experience their form: "Until it has been praised by the language of the poet, that part / has not been." There is a group of poems—"Grain Elevator," "Frigidaire," "Lone Bather," and others—whose purpose is to describe very ordinary items of experience in such a way that one sees them afresh, not limited by the familiar categories of perception, but in terms of new relationships and new ideas. Klein's linguistic virtuosity, particularly his use of extended metaphors and puns, is the medium of creation. The central metaphor in "Frigidaire" is the description of the refrigerator in terms of a Laurentian village in winter where all the products of the landscape are stored. The grain elevator in the poem of that title assumes many primordial forms, leviathan, lost ark, river cliff as its venerable function as container of life is considered. The metaphors and the alliteration extend our perception of the elevator's purpose and function, giving it mythic proportions:

> O prison of prairies, ship in whose galleys roll
> sunshines like so many shaven heads,
> waiting the bushel-burst out of the beachhead bastille!

In the passage quoted the elevator is like a ship and the prairie a sea; or again it is like a prison with its prisoners of wheat. In the third line, release for the pent-up grain is orchestrated by the explosive *b* sounds as it moves towards its destiny as bread and new life. "Lone Bather" is another poem in which language effects a series of transformations, this time revealing the protean marvel of the human body and its identity with other forms of life. The man in the swimming pool "lets go his manshape" to become various forms—bird, plant, dolphin—as he sports in the water. Even the separate parts of his body are seen in terms of other forms: "His thighs are a shoal of fishes," and his toes move lazily "the eight reins of his ponies." The language in all these poems is that of discovery, of potentialities and new forms. This, says Klein, is the poet's function.

But "Portrait of the Poet as Landscape," which dominates this collection and is often regarded as the most accomplished single poem by a Canadian, lacks the optimism implied by this vision of the poet's craft. It is a lengthy and often harrowing reflection on the nature and status of the poet in society. In the first section the poet appears to be dead—certainly, there is little evidence of his existence—but in the second section it is asserted that he is not dead, but simply ignored, considered unimportant by his society. Although he lives with his wife and family in a respectable neighborhood, he is essentially alone, sustained only by his love of language and verse. In the third stanza he admits that he has his counterparts, fellow poets in other cities, but he avoids their company, for invariably they are egotists, perverted by their obsessions and full of treacheries:

> O schizoid solitudes! O purities
> curdling upon themselves! Who live for themselves,
> or for each other, but for nobody else;
> desire affection, private and public loves;
> are friendly, and then quarrel and surmise
> the secret perversions of each other's lives.

In the fourth section he finds himself living a double life playing the role of father and husband, but in his thoughts living wholly apart from family and society. In the fifth section he asks himself why he is a poet and realizes that it is not for fame or pleasure that he writes, but for peace of mind. It is unhappiness, insomnia of the spirit, which forces him to express himself; and so in the sixth section he fulfills the creative urge by forging his own world through language. The poet's task is to create new forms, to make art serve as a sixth sense. His function is meaningful, but he will remain anonymous, like a structurally significant but unnoticed feature of the landscape. "Portrait of the Poet as Landscape" is a picture of the artist as an introvert, an alien and ghostly creature who writes to relieve his anxieties, to escape his "stark infelicity." The bleakness of the portrait, however, is a measure of its relentless honesty. *The Rocking Chair* is Klein's masterwork and was honored fittingly with the Governor General's Award for 1948.

One of the principal themes in Klein's poems before the war was the anticipation of the Messiah. It is most dramatically envisioned in "Ballad for Unfortunate Ones," where the beggars, cripples, and blind men are made whole by the miraculous advent. The theme is part of Klein's socialist ideology, for the Messiah will only come "when mighty man grants mean man brother's care." It is also part of his personal quest for an emotional substitute for his father and his father's faith.

In *The Second Scroll* (1951), the messianic theme takes on this more secular, personal form as Melech Davidson, a Canadian journalist, makes a trip to Israel in search of his missing uncle. *The Second Scroll* with its single action and brevity is accurately termed a novella; its symbolic, poetic character is emphasized by a number of poems and dramatic scenes which are appended in a glossary to amplify the main text. The best description of the book is that given by Leon Edel, who likens it to Conrad's *Heart of Darkness*, for it is similarly a journey story in which the narrator slowly accumulates impressions and bits of information as he moves closer to an encounter with a fabulous figure.[6] As a child the narrator had often heard his uncle Melech praised as a devout Talmudic scholar; he also vividly remembers the day when his parents denounced the very same man for abandoning his religious studies and becoming a communist in Eastern Europe. A letter from the uncle recanting his Marxist philosophy arrives just as the narrator sets out for Israel on a literary assignment. The letter in which he tells about his experiences enhances his legendary, larger-than-life character: in a Polish pogrom he was supposed to have been killed but miraculously escaped; a Nazi firing squad massacres all the inhabitants of a Jewish village, but Melech crawls out unscathed from under the heap of dead bodies.

On his journey to Israel the narrator tries to find his uncle, but is always too late; the latter has moved on to a new location. The journalist finds in Rome that his uncle for a time was involved with Christianity, in Casablanca that he had been leader of a Jewish ghetto protest movement. When he finally catches up with him in Israel, he has just been killed in an Arab border raid.

[6]Leon Edel, "Marginal Keri and Textual Chetiv: The Mythic Novel of A. M. Klein," in *The A. M. Klein Symposium*, p. 75.

From the viewpoint of the narrator his search is a quest on a psychological level for a father figure, which on a spiritual level is a quest for the Messiah and ultimately God.

The book is also structured as a modern parable of the Wandering Jew in search of Zion. As Desmond Pacey has written, Uncle Melech is not so much a character as "a symbol of the modern Jewish soul, of the Jewish mind at its most intelligent, scholarly, persecuted, tempted by rival ideologies, but finally returning to the ancestral home and ancestral faith."[7] One of the central questions that Melech Davidson struggles with is the existence of evil in the world and its bearing on man's relationship to God.[8] The closest he comes to understanding this ancient theological dilemma is in the extraordinary essay he composes on viewing the paintings of the Sistine Chapel. In the scenes from Genesis he believes Michelangelo projected no less than the whole course of human history, with God repeatedly rescuing man when he is most lost. Evil is part of human experience, but if one can see the whole picture, one sees that out of evil eventually comes good, that ultimately man is rescued and proves divine. This theme is borne home by the image in Klein's narrative of smoke billowing over Europe from the incinerators of the concentration camps. For the Jews it was, as in the biblical days of the Exodus, their cloud by day and their pillar of fire by night. This sense of human history as revelation and destiny rather than endless cycles is reinforced by Klein's poem "Autobiographical," which serves as a gloss to the narrator's childhood. The poet remembers the sights and sounds of his childhood in the Jewish ghetto of Montreal in order to envision once again the fabled city, the New Jerusalem. The poem is at once nostalgic and visionary.

But the optimism of Klein's last book is not the final imprint this writer's life and work leaves on the reader. Klein was only forty-five when a breakdown forced his permanent retirement and silenced his pen. This personal tragedy was not unanticipated in his work. The fourth section of "Portrait of the Poet as Land-

---

[7] Pacey, "A. M. Klein," p. 289.

[8] See M. W. Steinberg, introduction to *The Second Scroll* (Toronto: McClelland and Stewart, 1961).

scape" describes the severe alienation of the artist living in his "schizoid solitudes" and laments his introversion and loneliness. There are poems which deal more directly with the fear of encroaching madness. One of these is psalm 22, "A Prayer of Abraham against Madness," in which he writes:

> O, I have seen these touched ones—
> Their fallow looks, their barren eyes—
> For whom have perished all the suns
> And vanished all fertilities;
> Who, docile, sit within their cells
> Like weeds, within a stagnant pool.

There is another poem, "Ballad of the Nursery Rhymes," in which Klein describes the destruction of the world and the madness of the last survivor. But the apprehension of personal tragedy is most directly and hauntingly rendered in "A Psalm of Abraham of That Which Was Visited upon Him," a poem published only two years before Klein's complete breakdown. It is one of his last public communications and takes the reader to the brink of those "schizoid solitudes" from which the poet never returned.

> A prowler in the mansion of my blood!
> I have not seen him, but I know his sign.
> Sometimes I know him meddling with my food,
> Or in the cellar, poisoning my wines, —
>
> Yet face to face with him I never come;
> But by a footprint, by a book misplaced,
> Or by the imprint of any inky thumb,
> Or by the day's meal, a strange new taste,
>
> I know that he has broached my household peace,
> I know that somehow he has let him in.
> Shall I fling open a window and shout Police!
> I dare not. He is of my kith and kin.

Selected Writings

Hath Not a Jew. New York: Behrman's Jewish Book House, 1940.

Poems. Philadelphia: Jewish Publishing Society, 1944.

Hitleriad. New York: New Directions, 1944.

The Rocking Chair and Other Poems. Toronto: Ryerson Press, 1948.

The Second Scroll. New York: Knopf, 1951. Reprint, New Canadian Library, no. 22 (Toronto: McClelland and Stewart, 1961).

The Collected Poems of A. M. Klein. Compiled with an introduction by Miriam Waddington. Toronto: McGraw-Hill Ryerson, 1974.

Irving Layton

During World War II Canadian poetry was revitalized with the appearance in Montreal of two new journals: *Preview*, established by the English poet, Patrick Anderson, and *First Statement*, published by John Sutherland and subtitled A *Magazine for Young Canadian Writers*. What distinguished the new publications and their writers was that they were urban-centered, concerned with Canada as a society rather than a landscape. Moreover, they held fervently that poetry must play a decisive role in the social struggle. P. K. Page, perhaps the most gifted of the new poets contributing to *Preview*, spoke out against the narrowness of traditional Canadian subject matter (the wilderness theme that preoccupied the Confederation poets, Pratt, and Smith) and urged that writers take stock, not of nature, but of human society: "If [the poet] will hitch-hike to the towns and identify himself with people, forget for awhile the country . . . he may find his age and consequently his belief."[1] In her poetry Page approaches social statement through her sympathetic perception of the lives of others: the nerve-taut daily routine of stenographers, the white inferno of the workers in a salt mine. *Preview* was the more academic of the two journals, supported by poets with English university backgrounds who were inspired by the work of Auden and Spender. *First Statement* shared similar social principles with *Preview*, but was more proletarian in origin and dedicated specifically to providing a forum of expression for Canadian writers. It absorbed *Preview* in 1946, and with the merger Sutherland renamed the journal *Northern Review*. Its principal poets were Raymond Souster, Louis Dudek, and Irving Layton, the last emerging as one of Canada's major literary talents.

[1] P. K. Page, *Preview* (October 1942).

Notoriety is the special trademark of Irving Layton, the embattled poet from the slums of Montreal. Exuberant, quarrelsome, determinedly out of step with prevailing opinions, Layton is the dominant figure in his generation of poets. Born in Romania in 1912, he grew up in Montreal in a Jewish community that was adjacent to the French working-class area. There his mother supported a large family by keeping a small grocery store. Street-wise and a rebel at school, the boy nonetheless continued his education, taking an undergraduate degree from Montreal's Macdonald College and subsequently studying economics and political theory at McGill University. As a young man he supported himself in a variety of ways, eventually becoming a teacher in a parochial school in Montreal and at Sir George Williams University. From 1960 to 1978 he was professor of English at York University in Toronto.

Layton is one of the country's most prolific poets, with more than thirty collections of verse. His earliest efforts to be published were part of the general ferment that gave birth to the new poetry magazines in Montreal. Layton was John Sutherland's brother-in-law and helped to purchase the press on which *First Statement* was first printed. Layton wrote stories and poems for the magazine and peddled copies from store to store. It was wartime, and publishing poetry was a profitless adventure, but the group of impecunious writers, held together by a strong socialist commitment, struggled on, and the magazine printed some early Layton poems which remain among his best. In 1945 Layton brought out his first collection, *Here and Now*, under the First Statement Press imprint.

In the early 1950s Layton, with fellow poets Louis Dudek and Raymond Souster, founded Contact Press, a cooperative that encouraged and published the works of many younger poets. Layton annually brought out a collection of poems with Contact Press at his own expense until 1956 when, after a Canadian Foundation grant, his book *The Improved Binoculars* was to have been brought out by Ryerson Press in Canada. But Ryerson, the official publisher of the United Church of Canada, balked at what was regarded as Layton's obscene language and removed its name from every copy. Layton railed out at the philistinism and puritanical character of Canadian publishing; the public furor brought him an invitation from McClelland and Stewart to bring out a collection of poems with them. A *Red Carpet for the Sun* appeared in 1959 and won the Governor General's Award for that year. Layton remained with McClelland and Stewart, where his books enjoyed wider sales than the work of any other Canadian poet. In addition to important individual collections such as *Balls for a One-Armed Juggler* (1963), *Lovers and Lesser Men* (1973), and *For My Brother Jesus* (1976), Layton brought out a *Selected Poems* (1969); a 589-page blockbuster, *The Collected Poems of Irving Layton* (1971); and, with New Directions in New York, *The Selected Poems of Irving Layton* (1977), introduced by Hugh Kenner. There was no slackening in either Layton's productivity or his public recognition.

Reading through Layton's work, one feels the presence of almost two separate writers, the noisy social rebel on the one hand, the serious literary craftsman on the other. Layton is so absorbed with the poet as a public figure, a rebel, that Northrop Frye named him "the most outstanding poetic personality in contemporary Canada." Another critic, George Woodcock, cites this fact as the source of a major weakness in Layton's work, that the poet and social rebel are not one and the same.[2] Certainly much of Layton's poetry has to be classed as anecdotal and occasional verse, pieces written to make outspoken comment on the times and to enhance the poet's public personality. In these poems Layton boasts of his feats as a lover:

> Hell, my back's sunburnt
> from so much love-making
> in the open air.[3]

And he also goes to great lengths to describe sexual acts in order to shock and outrage his fellow citizens in what he terms "a cold

---

[2] Northrop Frye, introduction to *Il Freddo Verde Elemento*, in *Irving Layton: The Poet and His Critics*, ed. Seymour Mayne (Toronto: McGraw-Hill Ryerson, 1978), pp. 251–54; George Woodcock, "A Grab at Proteus: Notes on Irving Layton," *Canadian Literature* 28 (Spring 1966): 5–21.

[3] These lines are from "Look, the Lambs Are All around Us," in *The Collected Poems of Irving Layton* (Toronto: McClelland and Stewart, 1971). All further selections of poetry are cited from this same text.

Presbyterian country." Much of his fierce energy in these poems is directed at the "cultivated bourgeois" who likes poetry but would prefer a poet like Layton dead before enjoying his verse. Indeed, Layton's egotism and his literary feuds have prevented many Canadians from appreciating his better poems. Layton directs a special contempt at his fellow poets who, he says in "The Modern Poet," have grown insipid in the twentieth century:

> Since Eliot set the fashion
> Our poets grow tame;
> They are quite without passion
> They live without blame
> Like a respectable dame.

In "Prologue to the Long Pea Shooter" he specifically names a number of Canadian poets for whom he has no respect, making them the subjects of a lengthy piece of doggerel:

> . . . write as bleakly in a pinch
> As Livesay, Smith, and Robert Finch;
> And be admired for a brand-new pot
> If you're as empty as Marriott.

The unfortunate part is that this kind of verse is neither witty nor in any way significant. As a young man Layton labeled himself a Marxist, but political and social commitment have always been secondary to his self-appointed role of social outcast and prophet and his cult of individuality.

Although Layton's self-dramatization has resulted in a large amount of second-rate verse, he is at the same time a serious poet of amazing energy and range. His hatred for conformist society and his contempt for what he terms the insipidness of the academic and literary worlds are feelings which also fuel one of the genuine themes of his poetry—universal misanthropy. His hatred of humanity is the Swiftian kind which is aimed at men and women collectively, but which reserves love for individuals. The theme is most broadly stated in an early poem titled "Paraclete." The speaker is someone apart from humankind, an intercessor, who has made a study of the nature of human beings and found nothing but savagery and love of slaughter:

> I have studied history, he said.
> I expect nothing from man

> Save hecatombs.
> C'est son métier. And ferity.

The allusion here is to the Holocaust, when six million Jews were put to death in Europe during the Second World War. The image recurs with haunting frequency throughout Layton's work. For the poet there is something perverse in being human:

> It is life itself offends this queer beast
> And fills him with mysterious unease;
> Consequently only half-movements
> Delight him—writhings, tortured spasms
>
> Or whatever can stir his derision
> By defect or ungainliness

The human impulse to kill and the fascination with the grotesque inspire in the speaker of the poem outrage and contempt, and he turns away, saying in the last line, "Let the gods who made him, pity him." In "The Improved Binoculars" the poet's rejection of humanity becomes an apocalyptic vision where he sees a city in flames and the people rushing to save themselves. But what appalls the poet is the fact that the people nevertheless enjoy seeing their fellow citizens suffer:

> And the rest of the populace, their mouths
> distorted by an unusual gladness, bawled thanks
> to this comely and ravaging ally, asking
>
> Only for more light with which to see
> their neighbour's destruction.

Horrified by this vision of human depravity, the poet keeps himself apart from society. This isolation inspires in him a compassionate identification with the innocent creatures of the world that have suffered and died at human hands. Layton's poetry is filled with images of suffering animals and tortured insects. Ironically, their slaughter is a paradigm of humanity's fate. One of Layton's best known poems, "The Bull Calf," describes the routine killing of a young animal on a dairy farm where there is no use or profit in raising a bull calf. However, the intense feelings of the poet witnessing the slaughter give the scene a tragic dimension. The poet joys in the promised strength and pride of the young animal, in the miracle of all living things. But the calf is soon dealt a fatal blow, and the poet's horror and compassion are beautifully etched in those lines describing its death:

> Struck
> the bull calf drew in his thin forelegs
> as if gathering strength for a mad rush . . .
> tottered . . . raised his darkening eyes to us,
> and I saw that we were at the far end
> of his frightened look, growing smaller and smaller

The calf's body is dumped into a pit, while the poet turns away from the scene and weeps. Margaret Atwood in *Survival* cites this poem as a striking instance of the peculiarly Canadian capacity to identify with suffering animals.[4]

In another well-known poem, "Cain," the poet is himself the instrument of death, taking his son's air rifle and for sport killing a frog. In this piece the poet is implicated in the cruelty of human beings that he rages against in other poems. His guilt is measured by the pathos of the frog's death: after he has been hit, his spring is a "miserable flop, the thrust all gone / Out of his legs," and he is described "throwing out his sensitive pianist's / Hands as a dwarf might or a helpless child." Again the death of an innocent creature is associated with human tragedy, this time with the expiring of Lear and Oedipus. The frog's fragile body makes the poet rage against all mortal things, against the brevity and the meaninglessness of existence. The dead frog, described as a "retired oldster" and as a "dead leaper, Chaplin-footed," becomes a symbol of humanity and its equally "absurd" fate.

> O Egypt, marbled Greece, resplendent Rome,
> did you also finally perish from a small bore
> In your back you could not scratch? And would
> Your mouths open ghostily, gasping out
> Among the murky reeds, the hidden frogs,
> We climb with crushed spines toward the heavens?

The poet's wanton cruelty in killing the frog becomes a joke played against himself, for the dead creature makes him reflect grimly on his own death. In the final stanza the frog on his back,

---

[4] Margaret Atwood, *Survival* (Toronto: Anansi Press, 1972), p. 77.

"one delicate / Hand on his belly, and his white shirt front / Spotless," resembles a stage entertainer who is laughing at a joke the poet cannot quite hear.

Misanthropic poems about human depravity and the absurdity of existence are balanced by poems which present strong, positive feelings for specific individuals. Invariably, those individuals are women. In "Berry Picking" the poet explores the tender relation of husband and wife who are temporarily separated by physical distance and by a misunderstanding. The poem is both an apology for an unspecified offense ("I only vex and perplex her") and a statement of love for the woman's integrity and quiet dignity. The contrite poet is awed by her easy relationship with the children who surround her with their laughter and by her relationship with the natural world where she gathers wild berries:

> So I envy the berries she puts in her mouth.
> The red and succulent juice that stains her lips;
> I shall never taste that good to her, nor will they
> Displease her with a thousand barbarous jests.
>
> How they lie easily for her hand to take,
> Part of the unoffending world that is hers;
> Here beyond complexity she stands and stares
> And leans her marvellous head as if for answers.

The woman's simplicity and her honesty ("one for whom yes is always yes") make the poet not only regret his offending behavior but cause him to question the nature of his craft, which he now deems childish and deceitful. Layton is a romantic poet, and his ego and craft are central concerns to much of his work. The poem concludes in a romantic confession whose rhetoric embraces the tradition of English love poetry as far back as Shakespeare:

> No more the easy soul my childish craft deceives
> Nor the simpler one for whom yes is always yes;
> No, now her voice comes to me from a far way off
> Though her lips are redder than the raspberries.

One of Layton's most anthologized poems is an elegy written on the death of his mother, "Keine Lazarovitch 1870–1959." In a preface to *A Red Carpet for the Sun* Layton sketched a portrait of his mother and father which serves as a gloss on the poem and tells us something of his origins as a poet:

My father was an ineffectual visionary; he saw God's footprint in a cloud and lived only for his books and meditations. A small bedroom in a slum tenement, which in the torrid days steamed and blistered and sweated, he converted into a tabernacle for the Lord of Israel. . . . Had my mother been as otherworldly as he was, we should have starved. Luckily for us, she was not; she was tougher than nails, shrewd, indomitable. Moreover, she had a gift for cadenced vituperation; to which, doubtless, I owe my impeccable ear for rhythm.

The poem "Keine Lazarovitch" is written in praise of his mother's powerful personality, her pride, her strong will, her fierce energy. The poem includes several descriptive phrases from the prose sketch. The emphasis in the poetic portrait, however, falls on her voice:

> I thought, quietly circling my grief, of how
> She had loved God but cursed extravagantly his creatures.
>
> For her final mouth was not water but a curse,
> A small black hole, a black rent in the universe,
> Which damned the green earth, stars and trees in its stillness
> And the inescapable lousiness of growing old.

On one level the poet is describing the voice of his own rebellious, misanthropic spirit and ends with his keeping both the old woman and the voice alive.

> O fierce she was, mean and unaccommodating;
> But I think now of the toss of her gold earrings,
> Their proud carnal assertion, and her youngest sings
> While all the rivers of her red veins move into the sea.

The love the poet feels for a woman this time finds consummate expression in the passionate rhetoric of an elegy and makes this one of Layton's most accomplished poems. Here Layton is a rhetorical poet in the good sense, for the stylized rhythms and phrases he uses give heightened significance to the powerful emotions he is expressing.

The energy and will to power that the poet admires so fervently in his mother inspires him conversely with contempt for the meek and faint-hearted. In "For Mao Tse-Tung: A Meditation on Flies and Kings" the "comfortless, vituperative" voice of the mother can be heard in the son's castigation of repressed and conformist societies. Attack on society has always been central to Layton's function as a poet. In his long-time battle with academics, churchmen, and social workers, Layton has written countless occasional poems where the poet appears as satyr, rebel, or inebriate, thumbing his nose at prudery and self-righteousness and shouting angry, contemptuous words at those who would censor his activities. In "For Mao Tse-Tung" he assumes the more sober part of tragic hero who ultimately flees the sterile bonds of society and enters alone into a forest where he has a vision of a noble but lonely death. The poem begins with the speaker's striking out at a halo of tormenting flies, symbol of his critics in society, and he asserts that unlike Jesus or Buddha he will not forgive his enemies. Their way is to offer comfort to "the meek-browed and poor / In their solid tenements," but the speaker sees such people as lowly vegetation tossed about by the sweeping winds. In contrast Mao Tse-Tung wields political power over the masses, and the poet identifies himself with the poet-dictator, saying, "You are as alien as I." Fleeing the meek "in their religious cages," the poet turns to nature ("on this remote and classic lake"), embracing its healthy energy and also embracing death as part of the natural cycle. In contrast to Schiller's "Ode to Joy" with its vision of universal brotherhood in heaven, Layton proposes the ecstasy of the full physical life here on earth.

> Here is ecstasy,
> The sun's outline made lucid
> By each lacustral cloud
> And man naked with mystery.
> They dance best who dance with desire,
> Who lifting feet of fire from fire
> Weave before they lie down
> A red carpet for the sun.

The Heraclitean images of fire and sun which recur frequently in the poems and the theme of nature dying and continually re-creating itself point to the prevailing influence of Nietzsche on Layton. That influence is announced in the title of an early poem, "The Birth of Tragedy," which was also the title of Nietzsche's first book. The title brings together joy and suffering, which Layton sees as inextricably joined in both life and art.[5] Nietzsche asserts in his early writings that in great art there is a powerful dialectic between the Dionysian forces of passion and suffering and the Apollonian forces of order and reason. The struggle is greatest and the work of art most powerful when it takes the fullest account of reality; or to put it another way, artistic control is only significant when the passion dramatized is powerful and threatens destruction. In later writings Nietzsche shifts his focus from art to the process of reality itself, which he finds most significantly expressed in the will to power. He no longer asserts the dialectic between Apollo and Dionysus, but sees nature, or the Dionysian force, as complete—the source and goal of all existence.

In his poem "The Birth of Tragedy" Layton rehearses for himself the same philosophical progression. In the first stanza he identifies himself as the poet who observes and gives order to the activities of both humankind and nature:

> And me happiest when I compose poems.
>> Love, power, the huzza of battle
>> are something, are much;
> yet a poem includes them like a pool
>> water and reflection.
> In me, nature's divided things—
>> tree, mould on tree—
>> have their fruition;
> I am their core. Let them swap,
> bandy, like a flame swerve
> I am their mouth; as a mouth I serve.

But in the second stanza he observes that nature is oblivious to the works of men and women, to the monuments they have created to their gods (the "sensual moth" drops its shadow on the

[5] See Wynne Francis, "Layton and Nietzsche," *Canadian Literature* 67 (Winter 1976): 39–52.

garden of flowering stone). In the third stanza the poet surrenders to a vision of nature forever creating and destroying itself:

> A quiet madman, never far from tears,
>   I lie like a slain thing
>   under the green air the trees
> inhabit, or rest upon a chair
>   towards which the inflammable air
> tumbles on many robins' wings;
>   noting how seasonably
>   leaf and blossom uncurl
> and living things arrange their death
> while someone from afar off
> blows birthday candles for the world.

The reference to the madman recalls Nietzsche's final insanity, but refers more specifically to society's view of the poet who abandons orthodox creeds in order to become one with nature. The "inflammable air" again evokes the Heraclitean principle that all natural process is a form of burning or fire. That idea brings the poem to its climax in the image of the birthday candles for the world, the idea of chronological time giving way to the principle of eternal fire. "The Birth of Tragedy" is a pivotal poem in Layton's work philosophically, defining nature as the center of reality and the will to power and tragic isolation as the poet's relation with society.

The artist's isolation is central to a group of poems in which the poet discusses his role as artist and the question of his survival through art. In a surrealistic poem titled "The Cold Green Element," Death appears to wait for the poet at the end of the garden walk, for "the black-hatted undertaker / who, passing, saw my heart beating in the grass, / is also going there." He tells of a dead poet who has been retrieved from the ocean and hung from the city's gates. The image suggests the poet is a criminal who becomes a public spectacle, yet his status is purely that of a curiosity, for even if his limbs should twitch in the air, there would be no wonder or awe felt; the crowd would idly continue peeling oranges. One of Layton's persistent themes is the poet ignored in his own country. The speaker of the poem turns away from society to nature (embracing the trunk of a tree like a lover), where he is again confronted with death, corruption, and disease. A tree struck by lightning has become a "hunchback with a crown of leaves," and ailments from the labels of medicine bottles are said to have fled to the winds, filling the air with disease and death. His own manhood is spent, and he has a vision of his past as "murdered selves" hanging from the ancient twigs of a catalpa tree. A dog, much like a wolf, howls for the poet's death, and he sees both his life and death as a poet in the haunting surrealistic image of "the worm / who sang for an hour in the throat of a robin." The image contains the cycle of life and death and song, again the Nietzschean idea expressed in "The Birth of Tragedy" that nature is forever creating and destroying itself and that humanity's rage for beauty and order is contained within that cycle. The poem ends, however, with the cries of young boys distracting the poet from his acceptance of his mortality. The sounds of the boys make the poet feel he can be young once more, that he can again be a "swimmer in that cold green element" which is life.

In "Whatever Else Poetry Is Freedom," an enigmatic poem rich in meaning and allusion like the poems of Wallace Stevens, Layton is particularly concerned with the artist's desire for immortality. Poetry is freedom because it allows the artist to develop to his full stature (to walk on stilts), but at the same time he is mortal and foresees his ultimate death and decay in the spectacle of a dead toad on the road. The passing of time (mortality) is measured in the poem by Heraclitean images of fire: when the poet sees the sun reflected in the windshield and fender of a car, it is as if the car were a hearse, reminding him of his own ultimate dissolution. In the center of the poem there is a reference to Canute, the Anglo-Saxon king who tried to hold back the advance of the tide. According to Layton, the king half believed in his power to command the sea, but when the waves came "nuzzling at his feet," he turned the incident into a jest to teach his flatterers that he was not all-powerful. The story in turn earned him a legendary immortality—"Your stave brings resurrection, O aggrievèd king." The poet sees himself driven to similar clownish acts to secure immortality (to escape "the mist" of his finite and temporal being).

If one piece were to be singled out as a masterwork, that piece

in Layton's canon would be "A Tall Man Executes a Jig," a powerful allegory about humankind's response to the mortal condition
and inevitable death.[6] With its central image of a man silhouetted
against the horizon and its essentially philosophical texture, the
poem is not unlike Edward Arlington Robinson's "Man against
the Sky." The title of Layton's poem suggests the fine line between
the activities of living and a dance of death ("Your jig's up," the
man in the poem says to a wounded grass snake). The ultimate
question that the poem raises is whether humanity should attempt to transcend materiality (through religion, art) or whether it
should accept the life processes themselves as the full measure of
existence.

In the first stanza the man, out in a field, spreads his blanket
on the grass and finds himself completely at one with nature,
feeling the pull of the sun in the growing grass and listening to the
sounds of birds and insects. A swarm of blackflies in their frenetic
motion represents the energy of life, but as the man watches the
flies, he begins to separate himself from nature by theorizing,
thinking of life in terms of history (Thucydides) and mathematics
(Euclid). Appropriately, the flies turn against the man and assault
him with their stings. The man stands up, assuming his full physical stature. In the images of Plato and Donatello he also assumes
stature as a rational and imaginative being. But he is still part of
the natural world, a physical being haloed by flies whose condition is without perceivable meaning:

> Yet jig jig jig, the haloing black jots
> Meshed with the wheeling fire of the sun:
> Motion without meaning, disquietude
> Without sense or purpose, ephemerides
> That mottled the resting summer air.

Against this vision of blind, purposeless nature human beings
erect systems of belief and values. The tall man is a creator, a
Nietzschean figure compounded of "ambition, pride, the ecstasy
of sex," whose quest for a significant destiny is made up of Judaic,

---

[6] There is a good discussion of this poem in Patricia Keeney Smith's "Irving Layton
and the Theme of Death," *Canadian Literature* 48 (Spring 1971): 6–15.

classical, and Christian mythology. But in the fourth stanza, when the goal is reached and the hour of revelation is at hand, nothing happens: "The sky darkened. Some birds chirped. Nothing else." Instead the tall man sees at his feet "a violated grass snake that lugged / Its intestine like a small red valise." Instead of discovering in himself divinity, the tall man is confronted in the dying snake with his mortality. This is not the snake in the Garden of Eden whose "vivid tongue . . . flicked in praise of earth" and taught men sensual joy, but rather a "cold-eyed skinflint . . . filled with curses for the earth." Of all the suffering creatures in Layton's poetry, this one poses the most significant relationship for the poet. The tall man weeps while the snake drags itself towards a hedge and dies:

> Backwards it fell into a grassy ditch
> Exposing its underside, white as milk
> And mocked by wisps of hay between its jaws;
> And then it stiffened to its final length.
> But though it opened its thin mouth to scream
> A last silent scream that shook the black sky,
> Adamant and fierce, the tall man did not curse.

The tall man's response is not to curse his condition as a mortal, but to accept it. In the last stanza he lies down again in the grass, this time stretched out beside the snake "in fellowship of death." Again he experiences oneness with nature, inhaling its odors and letting his mind travel back in time to man's evolutionary origins in "caves, mounds, and sunken ledges." In the last lines, instead of a god revealed, the grass snake appears in the heavens:

> Meanwhile the green snake crept upon the sky,
> Huge, his mailed coat glittering with stars that made
> The night bright, and blowing thin wreaths of cloud
> Athwart the moon; and as the weary man
> Stood up, coiled above his head, transforming all.

The vision that transforms all is once again nature, the life force. The image of the snake in the sky deliberately evokes the myth of the Fall in the Old Testament and the evil dragon of the Book of Revelations. These myths and all their artistic elaborations are recalled in order to be rejected. The dead snake, whose image appears across the heavens, represents the wisdom of the earth. The poet appears to be saying that nature is the only reality, the origin and the end of all knowledge and values, the only valid subject of art. "A Tall Man Executes a Jig," with its vivid, unforgettable imagery, is one of the truly remarkable poems in Canadian literature.

One writes of Layton with reservations. The poet's public personality, his egotism and arrogance, obtrude on the reader's appreciation of his work. He is not a technical innovator (one is reminded instead of the work of other poets—Yeats, D. H. Lawrence, Wallace Stevens), and his thinking owes much to the philosophy and writings of Nietzsche. Yet Layton has an ear for the rhetoric and rhythms of great poetry and has produced several pieces that will surely live on. George Woodcock has perhaps summed up Layton best when he writes that he is "a poet in the old romantic sense . . . flamboyant, rowdy, angry, tortured, tender, versatile, voluble, ready for the occasion as well as the inspiration, keeping his hand constantly in, and mingling personal griefs and joys with the themes and visions of human destiny."[7]

Selected Writings

Here and Now. Montreal: First Statement Press, 1945.

Love the Conqueror Worm. Toronto: Contact Press, 1953.

The Cold Green Element. Toronto: Contact Press, 1955.

The Bull Calf and Other Poems. Toronto: Contact Press, 1956.

The Improved Binoculars. Selected poems with an introduction by William Carlos Williams. Highlands, N.C.: Jonathan Williams, 1956.

A Red Carpet for the Sun. Toronto: McClelland and Stewart, 1959.

Balls for a One-Armed Juggler. Toronto: McClelland and Stewart, 1963.

Collected Poems. Toronto: McClelland and Stewart, 1965.

[7] Woodcock, "A Grab at Proteus: Notes on Irving Layton," p. 21.

Periods of the Moon. Toronto: McClelland and Stewart, 1967.

Selected Poems. Edited with a preface by Wynne Francis. Toronto: McClelland and Stewart, 1969.

The Collected Poems of Irving Layton. Toronto: McClelland and Stewart, 1971.

Lovers and Lesser Men. Toronto: McClelland and Stewart, 1973.

The Pole-Vaulter. Toronto: McClelland and Stewart, 1974.

The Unwavering Eye: Selected Poems, 1969–1975. With a foreword by Eli Mandel. Toronto: McClelland and Stewart, 1975.

The Darkening Fire: Selected Poems, 1945–1968. With a preface by Wynne Francis. Toronto: McClelland and Stewart, 1975.

For My Brother Jesus. Toronto: McClelland and Stewart, 1976.

The Uncollected Poems of Irving Layton, 1936–1959. Edited with an afterword by W. David John, preface by Seymour Mayne. Oakville, Ont.: Mosaic Press, Valley Editions, 1976.

The Poems of Irving Layton. Edited with an introduction by Eli Mandel. Toronto: McClelland and Stewart, 1977.

The Selected Poems of Irving Layton. Introduction by Hugh Kenner. New York: New Directions, 1977.

The Covenant. Toronto: McClelland and Stewart, 1977.

The Tightrope Dancer. Toronto: McClelland and Stewart, 1978.

Droppings from Heaven. Toronto: McClelland and Stewart, 1979.

For My Neighbours in Hell. Oakville, Ont.: Mosaic Press, Valley Editions, 1980.

Europe and Other Bad News. Toronto: McClelland and Stewart, 1981.

Robertson Davies

Robertson Davies, essayist, playwright, critic, and novelist, is frequently named Canada's leading man of letters. Born in 1913 in Thamesville, Ontario, where his father (eventually a senator) published the local newspaper, Davies was expensively educated at Upper Canada College, Toronto, and at Queen's University, Kingston, where he was enrolled as a nondegree student because he had not fulfilled the entrance requirements in mathematics. He went on to Balliol College, Oxford, where he received the bachelor of letters degree in 1938 and produced a distinguished thesis, *Shakespeare's Boy Actors*, which was published the following year. He worked for a year at the Old Vic Repertory Theatre, married a girl he had met at Oxford who was also working at the Old Vic, and returned to Canada in 1940 to become literary editor of *Saturday Night*. Two years later he was made editor of the *Peterborough Examiner* and stayed with that paper for more than twenty years, during which time he published eighteen books of his own writings and produced several of his plays. In 1963 he was appointed the first master of Massey College, Toronto, where he taught drama courses for the University of Toronto and continued to write. Davies has attracted public attention throughout his career by his witty, often satiric observations on Canadian life and by his cultivation of a theatrical personality. The high esteem in which this author is held, however, has a more solid foundation in certain philosophical concerns which have informed Davies's writings for many years and which give his work as a whole a coherency of purpose and statement.

A list of Davies's subjects would be almost endless, for he has an insatiable interest in all manner of knowledge and information. In his plays we learn about such curious matters as Bohemian puppetry, jest books, Victorian photography, while in the novels we are made to consider such diverse subjects as hagiography, Jungian psychoanalysis, heraldry, and the stagecraft of the illusionist. What is impressive is the way Davies's out-of-the-way lore is made to yield real knowledge about human life.

Although there is great range and diversity to his interests, certain themes recur consistently in all of Davies's writings. As a Canadian Davies frequently attempts to define the essential character of life in Canada, pointing to those special traits of a people with a northern geography and limited political power. More generally, as a critic of contemporary manners, Davies is concerned with attacking the narrow-mindedness and philistinism of any society hostile to individuality and the imaginative life. In this regard Davies frequently aims his barbs at women, who, in his opinion, often embody the stultifying influences of conformism and self-righteousness. But the serious core of Davies's writing is a concern with the values of the carefully examined life. He has long been fascinated with Jung's theories of wholeness in human personality and with the importance of myth in explaining the patterns of individual lives. Davies has also been much attracted to the Swiss psychologist's idea that evil is an embodiment of the unlived life, those things that an individual has repressed in himself. In Davies's public voice there is an aristocratic disdain for the majority of people, but there is also admiration expressed for the individual who tries to understand his thoughts and feelings fully, who places feeling on the same plane of importance as reason, and whose life's goal is not the pursuit of happiness, but of self-knowledge. Indeed, we might say that the program of all of Davies's writing is the search for wisdom.

Davies's development as a writer began with the creation of Samuel Marchbanks, an irascible Johnsonian eccentric, whose scathing opinions on humankind were first voiced in the columns of the *Peterborough Examiner*. In 1947 Davies assembled the sketches in book form as *The Diary of Samuel Marchbanks*. The book's success resulted in a sequel, *The Table Talk of Samuel Marchbanks* (1949), and twenty years later *Samuel Marchbanks' Almanack* (1967). Marchbanks is a crusty old bachelor who lives alone in Skunk's Misery, Ontario, from which vantage point he passes judgment on society in general and on Canadians in particular. With typical comic acerbity he observes: "Most Canadians dislike and mistrust any great show of cheerfulness. If a man were to sing in the street he would probably end up in jail." Marchbanks believes Canadians are essentially puritans who frown on pleasure in any form. A Canadian woman, he says, "is a dowdy and unappetizing mammal, who is much given to Culture and Good Works, but derives no sinful satisfaction from either," while "the Canadian male is so hounded by taxes and the rigors of our climate that he is lucky to be alive," much less have sex appeal. It is the uncertainty of the weather, says Marchbanks, which "makes Canadians the morose, haunted, apprehensive people they are." Ibsen's plays, he adds, reflect the Canadian spirit admirably, a favorite observation by Davies over the years. Marchbanks's own life as a Canadian is dramatized in his winter-long battle with his furnace and his struggle in summer with the weeds in his garden. Marchbanks is an admirer of eccentric individuality; he rails against the present, with its ideals of conformity and machine-age efficiency. He claims to be a democrat, but admits: "The idea that a gang of anybodies may override the opinion of one expert is preposterous nonsense. Only individuals think, gangs merely throb." It has been suggested that Marchbanks's exaggerated and often outrageous observations represent a parody of Davies himself—his own iconoclastic spirit, arrogant misanthropy, and antifeminist feelings.[1] The suggestion is fitting, for Davies comes to assert in his later critical writings that fictional characters often represent something the author has been forced to suppress in himself.[2] The Marchbanks books are often reminiscent of Davies's favorite Canadian author, Stephen Leacock. They are sometimes ponderous and sometimes trivial, but for Davies they represent an important apprenticeship with the techniques of humor.

The second phase in Davies's development saw him turn to the theatre as a vehicle for comedy and for presenting his ideas and social comments. In the years 1947–54 he wrote and produced

[1] Elspeth Buitenhuis, *Robertson Davies* (Toronto: Forum House, 1972), p. 16.

[2] See the essay "Phantasmagoria and Dream Grotto," in *One Half of Robertson Davies* (Toronto: Macmillan, 1977), pp. 201–22.

more than a dozen plays, several of them for the Peterborough Little Theatre. The published plays include *Overlaid* (1948), *Eros at Breakfast and Other Plays* (1949), *Fortune, My Foe* (1949), *At My Heart's Core* (1950), and *A Jig for the Gypsy* (1954). The subjects and settings of these plays vary greatly—*Fortune, My Foe* is about an immigrant from Prague who wants to start a puppet theatre in Canada, while *A Jig for the Gypsy* deals with politics and magic in nineteenth-century Wales—but a constant theme in the plays, indeed in all of Davies's writings, is the importance of art to civilization. Perhaps the liveliest and most amusing treatment of this theme is in the brief, one-act play *Overlaid*. Here Pop, an old Canadian farmer, and his middle-aged daughter, Ethel, argue as to how Pop should spend a $1,200 windfall from a paid-up insurance policy. Pop, who describes himself as "the Bohemian set of Smith township, all in one man," dreams of going on a spree in New York City, where he would enjoy a gourmet dinner, sit in the front row at the Metropolitan Opera, and wind up at a night club show, perhaps giving fifty dollars for the stripper's brassiere. When his daughter, however, is persuaded to confide her inner dream of spending the money on a huge granite tombstone that would give solidity and dignity to the family name, Pop yields to what he calls her "power of goodness" and gives her the money. Pop's love of theatre and opera and his dream of a good time is "overlaid" by the tombstone; Davies wants the audience to view this very Canadian symbol of "goodness" in a negative light.

The conflict between the world of imagination and a sober, utilitarian environment is strongly emphasized in *At My Heart's Core*, which is set in the backwoods society of Upper Canada in 1837. The central characters include the Strickland sisters—Catherine Parr Traill and Susanna Moodie—who were willing to sacrifice personal needs and comforts in order to achieve certain cultural goals. The play, however, develops another theme, one that becomes of central importance in Davies's later works. As in *Overlaid*, the central characters (the Strickland sisters and a third pioneer woman, Frances Stewart) are each brought to confess their innermost dreams. Mrs. Stewart admits a romantic regret for an aristocratic social life that she lost when she rejected a suitor in Ireland, Mrs. Traill admits an ambition to become an acknowledged botanist, and Mrs. Moodie confesses her desire to be a famous writer. Cantwell, the man who elicits these confidences, does so in order to betray the women publicly and revenge himself on their "tight, snug, unapproachable little society," from which he and his wife are excluded. One of the minor characters in the play calls Cantwell the devil, pointing to an important idea in Davies's writing—namely, that we identify as evil any embodiment or open expression of our secret longings. To the three women in the play Cantwell is the devil incarnate because he has successfully tempted them to give voice to their repressed thoughts and wishes. In addition he has stolen their peace of mind by making them feel that their dreams can perhaps be realized. Davies's early plays are fascinating to read in the light of his later fictions, for one can trace in embryo the development of certain ideas that were to gain importance as he continued to write. But the plays are not wholly satisfying in themselves because characters are always secondary to ideas and remain very much one-dimensional types.

The third phase in Davies's work was the writing of three related novels about the social, moral, and artistic life of a small Ontario city called Salterton. These novels, published in the 1950s, are essentially comic and contain many lively and entertaining scenes, but like the early plays suffer from flatness of characterization. The plot of *Tempest-tost* (1951) turns on an outdoor production of Shakespeare's *Tempest* by Salterton's little theatre group, a plot rich in comic ironies because Shakespeare's play is served up in a bumbling amateur production. Davies's chief purpose in the novel is to satirize the cultural immaturity of Canada, where aesthetic standards must take second place to the ambitions and narrow-minded prejudices of the people. For example, the puritanical chairwoman of the theatre group is opposed to casting a suitably statuesque girl as Juno because the girl is said to be "an awful one for the boys." The man who will play Gonzalo is a mathematician with no real use for literature or any art form, and the play's Ferdinand is a man more interested in wiring the stage than in acting.

In *Leaven of Malice* (1954) Davies continues to make fun of Canadian provincialism, but in this deftly plotted comedy he probes that more serious theme—the nature and operation of evil. The plot turns on the repercussions which ensue when a false engagement announcement is placed in the Salterton newspaper. This bit of malice works in the community to bring all the major characters into a series of conflicts with each other. In accord with Davies's idea that evil is actually an expression of one's suppressed fears and wishes, the characters in the novel are shown to be freed by the false announcement and its implications. Solly Bridgetower, the young man named as the future groom, is tied to his domineering mother and actually does dream of being free to marry and live his own life. Similarly, Pearl Vambrace, the girl named as the bride, is in thrall to her father's possessive nature. Although the couple scarcely know each other when the announcement appears, they do in fact become engaged when the novel closes.

A *Mixture of Frailties* (1958), the third and most ambitious novel in the Salterton trilogy, is a study of the development of an artist, a *Künstlerroman*. Although the novel begins and ends in Salterton and continually refers to its values, its focus is on Monica Gall, a young Salterton woman sent to England to train as an opera singer. Monica seems an unlikely heroine because of her family's working-class background and fundamentalist religion. The special interest of the novel, however, is the relationship between the artist and her life, how she gradually substitutes the universal values of art for the specific and limited values of her Salterton background. One of the most difficult questions for this girl who once sang with the Heart and Hope Gospel Quartet is that of religion; the strict beliefs of the little gospel church have no points of reference for Monica outside Salterton. But she finds both a religious and an aesthetic creed in the Welsh concept of *hiraeth*, a longing of the spirit for what is unattainable in this world, a longing which paradoxically gives life meaning and purpose. This idea reconciles her to her family, for she recognizes that they too in their limited way have yearned for the unattainable. In spite of its important themes, the novel is not wholly successful. The farcical tone of the Salterton scenes does not mesh with the serious portrait of the artist. The Canadian setting is the world of childhood and comedy, while England and Europe are the place of art, education, and wisdom. Unfortunately, Monica's consciousness does not comprehend and integrate both worlds fully.

In A *Mixture of Frailties* Monica's mentor, Sir Benedict, describes the theme of a certain opera as "the metamorphosis of physical man into spiritual man." This summary describes exactly the intent and achievement of *Fifth Business* (1970), an expansive and complex book which has been a bestseller and may be Davies's masterwork. The first of a trilogy of novels whose principal characters originate in the small Ontario town of Deptford, *Fifth Business* takes the form of a long letter written by a retired schoolteacher, Dunstan Ramsay, who is intent on revealing to the headmaster of the school that he is not the colorless person his colleagues always assumed him to be, that his life on the contrary has been wide-ranging and eventful. The letter is prompted by a patronizing "Farewell" published in the *College Chronicle* which makes Ramsay appear "a typical old schoolmaster doddering into retirement with tears in his eyes and a drop hanging from his nose."[3] His life has been far from conventional: badly wounded in the First World War, Ramsay was awarded a Victoria Cross, has lived with a wooden leg, and remained unmarried. His special field of interest as a history teacher has been hagiography; he has spent his summers traveling in Europe researching the lives of the saints and has written articles of substance published by the Jesuits in the *Analecta bollandiana*. He has also kept the company of a group of circus performers who play an important part in his life.

But the unifying thread has been a lifetime involvement with two characters from his childhood, Boy Staunton and Mary Dempster. In the novel's opening scene, Ramsay, a boy of ten, ducks to avoid a snowball (containing a stone) thrown at him by his friend and rival, Boy Staunton. The snowball instead strikes pregnant Mary Dempster, the Baptist preacher's wife, who falls, gives birth to a son, Paul, prematurely, and is said to have been made "simple" by the accident. All through his life Ramsay is trapped in a guilty relationship with Boy, Mary Dempster, and

[3] *Fifth Business* (New York: Signet Classics, 1971). All references are to this edition.

Paul, and it is the novel's special purpose to show how Dunstan comes to terms with his feelings of guilt and becomes a well-balanced individual at last.

The problems of tone and point of view that seriously mar *A Mixture of Frailties* are solved in *Fifth Business* by Davies's choice of Dunstan Ramsay as first-person narrator. In the earlier novel the characterization of Monica Gall is not large enough to unite the serious episodes concerning her development as an artist and the farcical treatment of Salterton. But Dunstan Ramsay is a narrator whose sensibility, similar to the author's, includes both satirical delight in the foibles of human nature and religious awe at the unfathomable mysteries of human experience. *Fifth Business* accordingly is a hybrid of unlikely literary modes—satire and romance. Such writing is not easily done, because the author is working with forms of experience that are poles apart. A romance portrays a hero's quest for some kind of ideal, while satire focuses on the incongruities that exist between a professed ideal and what actually happens. But satirical romance describes exactly the double nature of this book and its hero, and one of the most impressive feats in *Fifth Business* is the way Davies indulges the satirist's delight in human folly without ever destroying the solemn, religious mood of the hero's romantic quest.

Dunstan Ramsay's lifetime pursuit is to understand the relation of history to myth. History is made up of ordinary, everyday events, and this is the part of life that Ramsay views satirically. His tongue-in-cheek, sometimes cynical view of life begins with a portrait of Deptford, the small town of his birth. He tells us that the town with a population of only five hundred has five churches of various degrees of solvency and fervor, two doctors, one of whom is rather clever in real estate, a dentist whom he describes as "a wretch without manual skill," and a veterinarian "who drank but could rise to an occasion." The only survivor of the town's first family, Ramsay relates, is a demented old woman who periodically escapes her nurse-housekeeper, rushes outside, and throws herself down in the road, "raising a cloud of dust like a hen having a dirt-bath, shouting loudly, 'Christian men, come and help me!'" (p. 16) Davies's comic treatment of small town life is sometimes in the best vein of Stephen Leacock's buffoonery. Such is the account of the suicide of a dishonest lawyer who had a passion for hunting:

The police and the coroner and everybody else implicated took every precaution that the truth about Orph should not leak out. And so, of course, the truth did leak out . . . [but] the story given to the public was that Orph, who had handled guns all his life, had been cleaning a cocked and loaded shotgun and had unaccountably got the end of the barrel into his mouth, which had so much astonished him that he inadvertently trod on the trigger and blew the top of his head off. Accidental death, as clearly as any coroner ever saw it. [p. 145]

A much harsher form of satirical humor accompanies Ramsay's account of Boy Staunton's life. Where Ramsay is a man of thought who lets fate or destiny guide him, Boy is an active, success-oriented man, a shaper of history who by the end of the novel has built up an empire in the sugar business and is about to be made lieutenant governor of Ontario. As young men, Ramsay and Staunton are rivals for the hand of Leola Cruickshank, but Boy wins her. Ramsay, on the sidelines, watches the poor girl fail to keep pace with Boy's ideal of smartness and sophistication in a woman. She labors at lessons in bridge, Mah-Jongg, golf, and tennis and tries to read Book-of-the-Month selections, "but nothing made any impression on her, and bewilderment and a sense of failure had begun to possess her." When she goes shopping, she comes back with what Boy calls "another god-damn Mary Pickford rig-out," and if he took her shopping in Paris, "the session often ended in tears, because he sided with the clever shopwomen against his indecisive wife, who always forgot her painfully acquired French as soon as she was confronted with a living French creature" (p. 137). After Leola's decline and death, Boy marries an ambitious feminist, Denyse Hornick. Davies's fondness for satirizing women assumes a particularly cruel aspect in the hilarious portrait of Denyse's teen-age daughter Lorene:

Adolescence was well advanced in Lorene, and she had large, hard breasts that popped out so close under her chin that she seemed to have no neck. Her body was heavy and short, and her physical coordination was so poor that she tended to knock things off tables that were quite a distance from her. She had bad vision and wore thick spectacles. She already gave rich promise of superfluous hair and sweated under the least stress. Her laugh was loud and frequent, and when she let it loose, spittle ran down her chin, which she sucked back with a blush. Unkind people said she was a half-wit, but that was untrue; she went to a special boarding-school where her teachers had put her in the Opportunity Class, as being more suited to her powers than the undemanding academic curriculum, and she was learning to cook and sew quite nicely. [p. 213]

The satire of Boy's life has a deadly serious purpose, which is to reveal the tragic limits of the unexamined life. Boy's unthinking pursuit of wealth and power leaves him empty and depressed, and at the end of the novel his death is the fulfillment of a deep wish.

Dunstan Ramsay's lifelong quest to understand the nature of goodness is initiated by his guilty involvement in the accident to Mrs. Dempster. Raised a Scottish Presbyterian with the Calvinist conviction that human nature is fallen and depraved, young Ramsay feels he committed a "mountainous crime" when he ducked the snowball that injured Mrs. Dempster. In spite of her simple mind, Mrs. Dempster appears to Ramsay to be a saint, a woman "who lived by a light that arose from within" (p. 48). He believes that during her life she performs three miracles, each of which effects a man's salvation. She gives herself to the tramp, Surgeoner, in the town gravel pit; she raises Ramsay's brother, Willie, from the dead; and she appears to Ramsay himself as a Madonna on the battlefield at Passchendaele. In her roles as prostitute, healer, and mother of Christ, she is associated with the three Marys of the New Testament, assuming a mythic status in Ramsay's life. His search for the type of Passchendaele Madonna and his study of the saints' lives stem from his romantic idealization of Mrs. Dempster. His quest to understand her becomes a quest to understand himself.[4]

Ramsay has two mentors who help him on the road to gaining self-knowledge. In his association with the Jesuits of the Bollandist society, he comes to know and admire an elderly, somewhat theatrical, priest by the name of Padre Blazon, whom he questions on the perplexing matter of his personal saint, Mary Dempster. In Deptford, Father Reagen had given Ramsay a theological

[4] Elspeth Buitenhuis, *Robertson Davies*, p. 67.

answer and advised that she was likely a "fool-saint," someone who seems full of holiness and love but whose virtue, because it is without intelligence or purpose, comes to nothing. Padre Blazon, on the other hand, gives a psychological answer to Ramsay's question:

Turn your mind to the real problem. . . . who is she in your personal world? What figure is she in your personal mythology? If she appeared to save you on the battlefied, as you say, it has just as much to do with you as it has with her—much more probably. Lots of men have visions of their mothers in time of danger. Why not you? Why was it this woman? [p. 159]

In fact, early in life Ramsay had rejected his hardheaded, domineering mother, and from the time as a boy when he watches Mrs. Dempster nursing Paul at her breast until the end of her life, when as her guardian he makes her funeral arrangements, he plays the role of a son to Mary Dempster.

In their conversation Padre Blazon also advises Ramsay that the beginning of wisdom is the union of the body to the spirit. "Forgive yourself," he says, "for being a human creature, Ramezay" (p. 160). This lesson is greatly expanded in Ramsay's encounter with Liesl, a grotesquely ugly woman who travels with Paul Dempster's circus. He is tempted to bed by her, has a fight with her during which he brutally twists her nose, and afterwards feels that "a great cloud . . . has lifted from [his] spirit" (p. 200). Liesl introduces herself to Ramsay as his personal devil with whom he has wrestled and brought about a change in himself. She says, in words that recall Padre Blazon, that she wants him to know he is human and that there is a whole area of his life that he has not yet lived, that out of Calvinist feelings of guilt he has repressed. Finally, she says: "Who are you? Where do you fit into poetry and myth? Do you know who I think you are Ramsay? I think you are Fifth Business" (p. 202), which she explains is a minor but necessary role in European operas—that of the observer who is nonetheless essential to the denouement of the plot.

The wisdom of Padre Blazon, restated more forcefully by Liesl, is consistent with ideas that Davies has put forth repeatedly in public lectures. In a speech to the Ontario Welfare Council entitled "Preaching Selfishness," Davies told an audience of social workers that they must give some thought to helping themselves as well as others and that the most important question to ask is, "Who am I?" When speaking to university graduates at convocations he urges young people of an intellectual bias not to neglect their feelings. The thing we come most to fear in life is those feelings we have repressed, the portion of our life that remains unlived.[5]

Critics have shown that Davies has been strongly influenced by the ideas of Carl Jung, that Dunstan Ramsay's search for self-knowledge is very similar to Jung's process of individuation whereby a man or woman achieves a feeling of wholeness.[6] The people in Ramsay's life all have a significant role to play in the structure of his personality and in the delving of his unconscious. Mrs. Dempster is Ramsay's anima, his ideal image of woman, while Boy Staunton is his shadow, the dark, repressed side of his self. As Ramsay probes the realm of the unconscious that is master of his fate, he comes to recognize other archetypal figures that are important to his life: the Sleeping Princess (Leola Cruickshank), the Magician (Paul Dempster), the witch or she-devil (Liesl), the Wise Old Counselor (Padre Blazon). He also perceives that during his life he has undergone significant transformations.[7] As a young man his loss of consciousness in battle and the destruction of his identity tag are a kind of death. Dunstable, the name he was christened with, is altered to Dunstan by the nurse in the hospital, and he is symbolically reborn. At the same time, he learns that his parents have died, and he becomes devoted to Mary Dempster and his study of the saints. Dunstan, fittingly, is the name of a saint who resists temptation in the form of a woman by twisting her nose. The encounter with Liesl, who

---

[5] See *One Half of Robertson Davies*: "Preaching Selfishness," pp. 69–74; "The Deadliest of the Sins," pp. 62–68; and "Gleams and Glooms," pp. 223–47.

[6] See Gordon Roper, "Robertson Davies' *Fifth Business* and 'That Old Fantastical Duke of Dark Corners, C. G. Jung,'" *Journal of Canadian Fiction* 1, no. 1 (Fall 1972), pp. 33–39. See also David Webster, "Uncanny Correspondence: Synchronicity in *Fifth Business* and *The Manticore*," *Journal of Canadian Fiction* 3, no. 3 (Fall 1974), pp. 52–56; and Marilyn Chapman, "Female Archetypes in *Fifth Business*," *Canadian Literature* 80 (Spring 1979): 31–36.

[7] See Barry Wood, "Magic, Myth and Metaphor in *Fifth Business*," *Critique* 19, no. 2 (1977), pp. 23–32.

forces Ramsay to recognize the makeup of his personal mythology and his public role as Fifth Business,[8] parallels the saint's story and marks Ramsay's entry into his age of wisdom.

The popular and critical success of *Fifth Business* encouraged Davies to explore the Deptford material in two more novels. *The Manticore* (1972) is narrated by Boy Staunton's son, David, who has had a nervous breakdown after his father's death and is undergoing therapy at the Jungian Institute in Zurich. David examines his life chronologically so that a completely different perspective is taken on many of the events narrated by Ramsay in *Fifth Business*. The novel, however, focuses on David's breakdown and the process of establishing a meaningful pattern for his life again. The process includes crawling with Liesl into the womblike depths of a cave where bears were once worshipped, such that David is reunited with his infancy and animal nature, both associated with a teddy bear that quelled his fears of the dark as a child.[9] *World of Wonders* (1975) is the story of Paul Dempster, known professionally as Magnus Eisengrim, and the consequences of the snowball thrown at the beginning of *Fifth Business* are viewed from yet another perspective. Magnus, now in his sixties, is a world-celebrated magician, and Ramsay, as a historian, is making a record of his life which includes not only Paul Dempster's own account of his transformation into Eisengrim but the thoughts and reactions of important admirers such as the Swedish film director Jurgen Lind and the members of his film crew. Fascinating though they are, neither *The Manticore* nor *World of Wonders* is as successful as the first volume in the trilogy. The problem is that the wealth of information about Jungian analysis and the stagecraft of magic is not wholly integrated with the central character studies in these novels; it is interesting material, but not given the fully developed dramatic purpose that the study of the saints' lives is given in *Fifth Business*.

[8] Carole Gerson's essay, "Dunstan Ramsay's Personal Mythology," *Essays on Canadian Writing* 6 (Spring 1977): 100–108, argues that Christian, Jungian, and Freudian elements all converge in a complex pattern of anality, misogyny, and repression—the real subtext of Ramsay's autobiography.

[9] Those interested in Jungian theory as fictionalized in *The Manticore* should read Patricia Monk's "Psychology and Myth in *The Manticore*," *Studies in Canadian Literature* 2 (Winter 1977): 69–81.

210

Davies's principal weakness in his plays and his novels is that Shavian propensity to explain his ideas at length rather than dramatize them fully through character and action. In *Fifth Business* both Padre Blazon and Liesl are splendid charcterizations, but their conversations with Ramsay have a homiletic cast. The nature of Jungian analysis and the importance of magic are subjects presented even more clinically in the subsequent novels. However, to cite this flaw in Davies's writing is also to draw attention to his strength, which is that he is a writer with important ideas for us to consider. Davies's ideas have international origins and universal application, but as a comic writer Davies approaches humor in a peculiarly Canadian way. He sees satire, not as an agent to destroy the formal structures of society, but as a means of changing society for the better—as a leavening agent (to use one of his favorite metaphors) in creating a better and wiser world. The realm of wisdom is always Davies's vision and goal.

Selected Writings

The Diary of Samuel Marchbanks. Toronto: Clarke, Irwin, 1947. Reprint, paperback (Toronto: Clarke, Irwin, 1966).

Overlaid: A Comedy. Toronto: Samuel French, 1948.

Eros at Breakfast and Other Plays. Toronto: Clarke, Irwin, 1949.

The Table Talk of Samuel Marchbanks. Toronto: Clarke, Irwin, 1949. Reprint, paperback (Toronto: Clarke, Irwin, 1967).

At My Heart's Core. Toronto: Clarke, Irwin, 1950.

Tempest-tost. Toronto: Clarke, Irwin, 1951. Reprint, paperback (New York: Penguin Books, 1980).

Leaven of Malice. Toronto: Clarke, Irwin, 1954. Reprint, paperback (New York: Penguin Books, 1980).

A Mixture of Frailties. Toronto: Macmillan, 1958. Reprint, paperback (New York: Penguin Books, 1980).

A Voice from the Attic. Toronto: McClelland and Stewart, 1960. Essays.

Samuel Marchbanks' Almanack. Toronto: McClelland and Stewart, 1967.

Fifth Business. Toronto: Macmillan, 1970. Reprint, paperback (Markham, Ont.: Penguin Books, 1977; New York: Signet Classics, 1971).

The Manticore. Toronto: Macmillan, 1972. Reprint, paperback (Markham, Ont.: Penguin Books, 1976).

World of Wonders. Toronto: Macmillan, 1975. Reprint, paperback (Markham, Ont.: Penguin Books, 1977).

One Half of Robertson Davies. Toronto: Macmillan, 1977. Essays.

The Rebel Angels. Toronto: Macmillan, 1981.

Margaret Avison

The author of three slim volumes of verse, Margaret Avison is known to readers of poetry as Canada's most intellectual and deliberate writer. She was born in Galt, Ontario, in 1918, but, as a minister's daughter, grew up in different parts of the country, including western Canada. She began writing poetry while she was a student at the University of Toronto in the late 1930s, and her early pieces were of such high quality that A. J. M. Smith included a selection of her work in his 1943 anthology, *The Book of Canadian Poetry*. Subsequent poems appeared occasionally in *Canadian Forum*, *Contemporary Verse*, and American magazines such as *Kenyon Review*, *Poetry* (Chicago), and Cid Corman's *Origin*. But Miss Avison is not a prolific poet; her first book, *Winter Sun*, did not appear until 1960. Its importance to Canadian literature was recognized by a Governor General's Award. Her second collection, *The Dumbfounding*, was published in 1966 and signaled an important change in both her life and her poetry—the central theme of the book is the author's active commitment to Christianity. A third collection, *Sunblue*, was published by a small Maritime Press in 1978. Margaret Avison worked at secretarial and library posts and lectured at Scarborough College, University of Toronto. In 1968, as an active Christian, she became a social worker for the Presbyterian Church Mission in Toronto and a secretary for the Canadian office of a Southeast Asia mission. The intellectual demands she puts on her reader, the richness of metaphor in her verse, and the anomaly of her Christian philosophy in the twentieth century make her one of the most challenging and important writers in Canadian literature.

Margaret Avison's reputation as a difficult poet derives from her belief that poetry represents a fresh seeing and recreating of the world. She believes that a poem should defamiliarize the world for the reader, that it should present a world that is newly perceived rather than known according to familiar categories of perception. She deplores the passivity of our imaginations and insists that we begin to see the multidimensional reality that lies beneath the familiar surface of physical things and events. Her poetic credo is stated most directly in the sonnet "Snow":

> Nobody stuffs the world in at your eyes.
> The optic heart must venture: a jail-break
> And re-creation. Sedges and wild rice
> Chase rivery pewter. The astonished cinders quake
> With rhizomes. All ways through the electric air
> Trundle candy-bright disks; they are desolate
> Toys if the soul's gates seal, and cannot bear,
> Must shudder under, creation's unseen freight.
> But soft, there is snow's legend: colour of mourning
> Along the yellow Yangtze where the wheel
> Spins an indifferent stasis that's death's warning.
> Asters of tumbled quietness reveal
> Their petals. Suffering this starry blur
> The rest may ring your change, sad listener.[1]

The imagination, writes Avison, must venture forth on its own and explore the many shapes and meanings which remain unrevealed by our sense perceptions.[2] Her term for the imagination, "the optic heart," stands exactly on the borderline between what is perceived and what is felt. With the optic heart one experiences other patterns to reality, where the four elements assume new relationships and interpenetrate each other. Thus the water grasses seem to chase the river, whose water in turn is like molten pewter; the volcanic soil ("astonished cinders") erupts with plant life

---

[1] Most of the poems quoted can be found in Avison's first two collections, *Winter Sun* (Toronto: University of Toronto Press, 1960) and *The Dumbfounding* (New York: W. W. Norton, 1966); rpt. in one volume, *Winter Sun / The Dumbfounding* (Toronto: McClelland and Stewart, 1982). "The Butterfly" can be found in *The Oxford Book of Canadian Verse*, ed. A. J. M. Smith (Toronto: Oxford University Press, 1960); "Perspective," "The Iconoclasts," and "The Local and the Lakefront" appear in *Poetry of Mid-Century, 1940–1960*, ed. Milton Wilson (Toronto: McClelland and Stewart, 1964).

[2] My reading of Avison's poetry is indebted to Ernest Redekop's *Margaret Avison* (Toronto: Copp Clark, 1970).

("Rhizomes"), while the air is charged with fire. The pleasures ("the toys") of this larger perception are lost if we do not use our imaginations to explore "creation's unseen freight." In the sestet Avison argues that snow is instructive: it is seasonal death, and in China, where the wheel spins signifying spiritual death through mechanical routine, it is fittingly the color of mourning; but it contains all colors, and the snowflakes are likened to multi-colored asters. When snow is perceived in terms of colors and shapes ("petals"), then the reader's blurry vision will be altered and he or she will begin to see the rest of the world imaginatively.

In "Perspective" Avison writes about the physical restraints on human vision which limit our apprehension of the world around us. She argues that there is something false in linear perspective because it diminishes what in reality does not diminish at all. She says, "Your seeing is diseased / that cripples space." Linear perception puts humanity at the center of the world, which is perhaps necessary, but it also distances and lessens the reality of that world. She asks the reader how accurate his vision is:

> Do you miss the impact of that fierce
> Raw boulder five miles off? You are not pierced
> By that great spear of grass on the horizon?

She refers the reader to the painter Andrea Mantegna, who transcends the spatial limits of linear perspective by keeping figures in the background as intensely defined as those in the foreground. In "Butterfly Bones: or Sonnet against Sonnets" Avison argues that our perception of the world must not be limited by the ordinary conventions of seeing and articulating. Butterflies in museums are really skeletons that only dimly suggest the reality of the insects' lives:

> What law and wonder the museum spectres
> bespeak is cryptic for the shivery wings,
> the world cut-diamond-eyed, those eyes' reflectors,
> or herbal grass, sunned motes, fierce listening.

Similarly, there are sonnets, she says, which "move towards final stiffness," describing the world as it is conventionally perceived without provoking new awareness in the reader.

Avison is concerned to create relationships in language that will force new perceptions. One of her favorite techniques is to merge disparate sensory perceptions so that the world is perceived as tactile and aural as well as visual, kinetic as well as static. In an impressionistic celebration of spring titled "Easter" Avison describes the pangs of birth in terms of a musical note that threads through the landscape:

> After the blur of doves the milky air
> Lulls, and listens, and there
> Is the sorrow of all fullness.
> But on the hillside the frail tremulo
> Of a new dayspring, eggshell and lilac, wanders
> through the drenched quiet branches.

A more disorienting technique involves radical shifts in point of view during the course of a poem. To free the reader from the laws of linear perspective, Avison changes the viewpoint so that the subject of the poem is considered from numerous angles in space and time. That seems to be the central idea behind "From a Provincial," which moves from the narrator looking at some postcards in time present to some midges gathered in the light of Milton's candle to a group of centurions making camp for Caesar in ancient Gaul. We are all provincials in that we are limited by the geography and the society in which we live, but the paradox is that we are not very alert to the country or the age in which we live ("Part of the strangeness is / Knowing the landscape"). A shift in perspective creates an awareness of the here and now.

Avison is described as a rigorously intellectual poet, but the ideas in her poems are always rendered as things for the senses to perceive and feel. Thus in "Snow" the multidimensional nature of reality is rendered in a series of images which yoke together unlikely experiences—"rivery pewter"—reversing our perceptual expectations. The concrete, sensory bias of her epistemological concerns is reflected when she refers to "the mind's eyes" and "the mind's ears." To probe further the complex nature of reality Avison uses those resources of language favored by the Metaphysical poets—puns, paradoxes, and irony.[3] There is a pun fun-

---

[3] See the chapter on Avison titled "The Mind's Eyes (I's) (Ice): The Poetry of Margaret Avison," in William H. New's *Articulating West: Essays on Purpose and Form in Modern Canadian Literature* (Toronto: New Press, 1972), pp. 234–58.

damental to her poetry in her use of the word *sense*, which denotes both the physical perceptions and the intellect, that is, meaning. The first line of "Mordent for a Melody" is a brilliant instance of Avison's linguistic dexterity. "Horsepower crops Araby for pasture" carries at least three simultaneous meanings which displace each other and create a quickly shifting temporal perspective. The line reads: the horse finds pasture in Arabia, or the motor gets oil in Arabia, and from these two readings emerges an ironic third possibility—the motor displaces the horse (the Arabian) and puts it out to pasture. Avison sees the world as constantly changing and uses puns and paradoxes to break down our fixed categories of perception and the ironies they give rise to. The sonnet "Tennis" is an example of an extended use of puns piled one on top of another.

> Service is joy, to see or swing. Allow
> All tumult to subside. Then tensest winds
> Buffet, brace, viol and sweeping bow.
> Courts are for love and volley. No one minds
> The cruel ellipse of service and return,
> Dancing white galliardes at tape or net
> Till point, on the wire's tip, or the long burn-
> ing arc to nethercourt marks game and set.
> Purpose apart, perched like an umpire, dozes,
> Dreams golden balls whirring through indigo.
> Clay blurs the whitewash but day still encloses
> The albinos, bonded in their flick and flow.
> Playing in musicked gravity, the pair
> Score liquid Euclids in foolscaps of air.

During the course of the poem the tennis match becomes a musical performance, a courtship, a fight, a formal dance, a mathematical exercise. Again what the poem embodies is the liberating of perception—that first step so that the individual ultimately can live in a world of his or her own ordering.

Several of Margaret Avison's poems are concerned with the inhuman structures people create because of limited perception. The cities in these poems, with their towering office buildings and lonely rooming houses, threaten to extinguish the human spirit. In "All Fool's Eve," a poem similar to T. S. Eliot's "Preludes," the city is associated with death: a sunset is described as "crumbling ash" that "leaves the west chill," and the city itself is described as "funeral bare." At night it is haunted by its own reflection in the glass towers. The urban world embodies for Avison, as it did for the Romantic poets, the fading of creative perception. Wordsworth's image of the prisonhouse closing in about the child is evoked in Avison's image of children "roundeyed, caught by a cold magic, / Fading of glory." The idea of humanity making its own prison in which to live is reinforced by the image of the monkeys shivering in their cement-floored garden at the zoo. At the end of the poem "Doors slam" and "lights snap," restoring the prose of night. In "Civility a Bogey" civilization is judged false because, in the words of the poem, it brings bulls into a china shop. The bulls are the big office buildings and corporations they represent; the china shop is Avison's image of an ideal city structure which effects the refinement of the human spirit through the arts.

In "The Local and the Lakefront" human perception is shown to be distorted by the clutter on the physical landscape. A sunset viewed from a Toronto bus station parodies romantic yearning:

> the sunset
> blurges through rain and all
> man tinfoil, man sheetlead
> shines, angled all awry,
> a hoaxing hallelujah.

Like Emerson, the Canadian poet also sees human perception cluttered with the freight of the past and the trappings of other cultures: "Exporters. Glutting us / with Danish spoons / and aum." The human soul becomes a commercial item, and at the beginning of "Intra-Political" the poet asks,

> Who are we here?
> boxed, bottled, barrelled
> in rows?
> Comestibles with the trick
> of turning grocer, shoplifter
> or warehouse trucker . . .

The hope expressed is that some day, through fresh seeing, we will "unbox ourselves," put aside "the buying, selling, trucking,

packaging of mudcakes," and eat from a "transfiguring board."
Humankind renewing itself is imaged in the concluding stanza of
"Far off from University," where the city landscape is likened to a
babe feeding from the mothering dawn:

> breast bared for its blind suckling
> a more than mother leaned, drew breath, tendering.
> Cement and weeds, sky, all-night diner, flesh,
> gathered as being; fumbling, fed.

There is seeming nostalgia for the country and for a rural past in
Avison's city poems, but Avison is not a nature poet; hers is a
Blakean nostalgia rather for the child's more creative vision asso-
ciated with pastoral rather than urban existence.

The artist must play a part in the transfiguring of human existence. That role, says Avison in "The Iconoclasts," is to explore
the world in search of a new order, but the quest is likely to seem
futile and backward. Retreat from familiar forms of civilized life
involves the artist in a return to a more brutal, primitive reality.
Thus the dervish on the steppes replaces the reason and order of
Roman civilization, and the Viking leaves his ordered society for
the chaos of the sea in order to discover Vinland. The poet asks
whether Archibald Lampman's prowling in the Gatineau Hills
and northern rivers could not be compared to the cavemen who
left behind their bone heaps, furs, and murals to move into the
sun. The artist's dangerous and unfamiliar route is imaged in the
deadly rapids and whirlpool of "The Swimmer's Moment." In this
allegorical poem Avison states that most people turn back when
the chance comes to venture forth and change the world:

> For everyone
> The swimmer's moment at the whirlpool comes,
> But many at that moment will not say
> "This is the whirlpool, then."

Those who turn back save themselves from danger, but they
become "bland-blank faces," like the comestibles in "Intra-
Political" that are "boxed, bottled, barrelled in rows." Of those
who heed the call of the imagination and venture into the whirlpool, many are lost (are defeated, go mad, die), but one or two—
the great inventors and artists—will pass through the whirlpool

unharmed and will see a new world in "the silver reaches of the estuary" that lies beyond. Only from that vantage point can the world be seen anew.

The impact of the artist on a mechanistic order is the subject of a poem curiously titled "Meeting Together of Poles and Latitudes (In Prospect)." In the first two stanzas Avison contrasts those who act with those who imagine. The men and women of action, who force their way through the world,

> Taste the bitter morning, and have at it—
> Thresh, knead, dam, weld,
> Wave baton, force
> Marches through squirming bogs . . .

These people, the poet says, seldom encounter those "who are flung off," the seemingly passive people who live by their imaginations. The latter gaze at the vapor trails made by active men and play with things (mathematics, telephone wires) that practical people use. But in the third and concluding stanza the poet contemplates what the result of their meeting might be:

> When they approach each other
> The place is an astonishment:
> Runways shudder with little planes
> Practising folk-dance steps or
> Playing hornet,
> Sky makes its ample ruling
> Clear as a primary child's exercise-book
> In somebody else's language.

In this newly imagined place there are still airplanes, but their flight forms artistic patterns on the runways and in the sky. The world is transformed into an artistic rather than purely mechanistic form. The two kinds of people are both necessary but what is most important is their meeting.

In early poems and in *Winter Sun* Avison frequently speculates on the purpose of life. In "The Butterfly" (1943) there is the image of a purposeless void which will eventually swallow the beautiful insect:

I remember it, glued to the grit of that rain-strewn beach
that glowered around it, swallowed its startled design
in the larger iridescence of unstrung dark.

The same sense of brevity and bewilderment to life is voiced in "Apocalyptic?," where we live "in sparrow time" and make but one arc under the sky. Existence as "sparrow time" in an "unstrung dark" is connected in some poems with images of contemporary life as a wasteland. In "Not the Sweet Cicely of Gerardes Herball" the gardens are weedless, not from cultivation, "but from / sour unfructifying November gutters," and the landscapes in these poems repeatedly suffer "estrangements from the sun." In "Grammarian on a Lakefront Park Bench" the poet describes her own life as "choked day, swollen to almost total swamp." These poems in *Winter Sun* suggest an urban sensibility being strangled by the rigid mechanistic forms of industrial life and desperately in search of a faith or belief that will daily redeem one's temporal existence. The search for a sign is rendered in "To Professor X, Year Y," where a crowd is gathered in the civic square, but no one can explain why the people are milling there. In "Voluptuaries and Others" she writes about a kind of illumination—a lighting up of one obscure corner of the terrain that nonetheless signals an advance.

In these poems the imagination of the artist comes closest to effecting that advance. But in a letter to Lawrence M. Jones, Margaret Avison writes that on 4 January 1963 she experienced a religious awakening which for the first time made Christ a reality to her. She explains that as a minister's daughter she always "had the will to be good," but this new experience was "getting to be where Christ's suffering goes, terribly on," getting to know him at last as "sovereign, forgiving, forceful of life." She looks back on her work and regrets that she had "cut off his way by honoring the artist" and describes her past as a "long wilful detour into darkness."[4] The result of that experience in her poetry is a collection of lyrics which are among the finest religious poems written in the twentieth century.

[4] See Lawrence M. Jones, "A Core of Brilliance: Margaret Avison's Achievement," *Canadian Literature* 38 (Autumn 1969): 50–57.

A group of these poems in *The Dumbfounding* describe, in the manner of Donne, Herbert, and particularly Gerard Manley Hopkins, the personal, exhilarating experience of knowing Christ.[5] The actual experience of rebirth is recorded in the poem titled "Person." The poet imagines herself enclosed in a tomb:

> Beneath
> steel tiers, all walled, I lay
> barred, every way.

In her prison the poet has felt cut off from God because of the distance and sovereignty implied in the concept "*I am.*" But then the poet realizes for the first time that Jesus was a person, that his humanity is in fact the door to what is divine:

> "I am." The door
> was flesh; was there.

And what brings humankind and God together finally is love:

> But such
> is love, the captive may
> in blindness find the way:
>
> In all his heaviness, he passes *through.*

In the final stanza of this poem she describes herself as one of God's flock "drenched with Being and created new."

The moment of realizing Christ's love is for Avison "the dumbfounding." The poem with that title describes different scenes from Christ's life on earth—his walking on water, healing a blind man, his death and resurrection. Those who have awakened to Christ's presence experience great joy, but in the last stanza the poet reminds the listener that the beginning of new life is through mortification and self-renunciation, following Christ

> through the garden to
> trash, rubble, hill,
> where, the outcast's outcast, you
> sound dark's uttermost, strangely light-brimming, until
> time be full.

[5] There is a good article by George Bowering on this aspect of Avison's poetry: "Avison's Imitations of Christ the Artist," *Canadian Literature* 54 (Autumn 1972): 56–69.

Margaret Avison's religious experience leads in two directions—to compassion for her fellow human beings expressed through Christian service, and to a poetry which reveals the ongoing divine essence in all things. In "Searching and Sounding," a dramatic poem in which she tries to discover the full measure of Christ's intent for her life, she acknowledges that Christ is not to be found in the beauty of summer fields, but in the slums of the city ministering to the wretched and desperate.

> I look for you
>
> . . . .
>
> and find you here
> in the sour air
> of a morning-after rooming-house hall-bedroom;
> not in Gethsemane's grass, perfumed with prayer,
> but here,
> seeking to cool the gray-stubbled cheek
>   and the filth-choked throat
>   and the scalding self-loathing heart.

The poet at first runs from this vision, but finally submits because the essence of Christ revealed to her is not a statue to be worshipped in a church, but a dimension to humanity that lives on in service. For as she confesses, "I need something human / somebody now, here, with me." The lonely figures that inhabit the city of Avison's poems are viewed with compassion. In "July Man," Avison the social worker describes a forlorn tramp on a park bench ("in the sorrow / of the last rubbydub swig, the searing, and / stone-jar solitude lost") who nonetheless still feels something of the miracle of being alive.

The ongoing miracle of life, as revealed by Christ, is expressed by Avison in a poetic technique which renders the impact of the world through the senses. One thinks of Hopkins and his concept of inscape, for Avison too tries to render what is being experienced from inside and with physical stress. She still writes poems about ways of perceiving reality, but the meaning of Christ (as companion and all-encompassing) informs that perception with unity and immediacy. The poems in Avison's third collection, *Sunblue*, celebrate the physical world as informed by a unifying

224

perception.[6] In "March Morning," for example, the landscape is not only apprehended visually but has texture which suggests taste and silence which suggests sound:

> The diamond-ice-air is ribbon-laced
> with brightness. Peaking wafering snowbanks are
> sun-buttery, stroked by the
> rosey fingertips of young
> tree shadows
> as if for music;
> and all the eyes of God glow, listening.

Perception seems to be infinitely extended: shadows stroke snow-banks as if making music, eyes are said to listen. In the last section of the poem a boy takes off his jacket in the sun and breathes "crocus-fresh breadwarm / Being." What Avison is describing is life lived in the presence of divinity.

The unity this vision confers is expressed by Avison's favorite poetic techniques—puns, paradoxes, oxymorons. Thus in "Hid Life," a poem about apples left on the tree in winter, she describes the fruit hanging "in a stick-dry, snow-dusty / network of branches / against lamb's wool and pastel blue of sky" and asks, as she contemplates the sodden fruit, "Is the weight only / a waiting?" The rotting fruit, with its Christian association with death, contains the seeds of new life and forms part of the poet's ongoing experience of rebirth and fresh seeing.

Although Margaret Avison's poems are remarkable for their intellectual austerity and their expression of religious faith, there are a few poems which speak more simply and directly to the reader while also forming a bond with the great lyric poems of the twentieth century. "New Year's Poem" and "A Nameless One" are particularly fine examples—in both poems thought and feeling are perfectly balanced and given flawless expression.

"New Year's Poem" is, obliquely, an elegy written in memory of Anne, mentioned briefly at the middle point of the poem. In the first part the narrator looks about a room that has been the scene of a Christmas party, a room that recently "brimmed / with perfumes, furs, and black-and-silver / Crisscross of seasonal con-

[6] *Sunblue* (Hantsport, Nova Scotia: Lancelot Press, 1978).

versation." But the thought of Anne brings to the narrator images of winter and death, and "the stiff grave / Where so little can contain." The juxtaposition of the Christmas party and the grave swept by winter wind produces in the narrator a consoling reflection:

> Gentle and just pleasure
> It is, being human, to have won from space
> This unchill, habitable interior
> which mirrors quietly the light
> Of the snow, and the new year.

The poem is pervaded with a quiet sense of loss; the death of a loved one seems to be pivotal. That loss is reflected for the narrator in the barrenness of winter, which seems to embody a truth about the brevity and the bleakness of all human existence. But the narrator staves off despair by reflecting that for a time human beings also know the warmth and hospitable pleasure of a living habitation and look forward to the promise of the new year. There are a unity and balancing of imagery in the poem (the crisscross of party conversation parallels the skull and crossbones marked by the birds in the snow; the circle of furniture in the room is paralleled by the loop of winter wind) and a central paradoxical statement which give the poem the classical perfection of Keats's "Ode on a Grecian Urn."

In "A Nameless One" the poet is less concerned with the poetic values of balance and order than with conveying the nature of something living. The title refers to an insect that spends its brief lifespan in a lodger's second-floor bathroom. It flies up to the ceiling in the morning, at noon stands "still as a constellation of spruce needles," and by four is dead, like wilted cornsilk, on the floor. The life of this insignificant insect makes the narrator intensely aware of place as well as time; the lodger's bathroom is no longer an anonymous room, but a place where a life has been lived. The narrator sees the room "with new eyes," as part of the creation:

> Its insect day
> has threaded a needle
> for me for my eyes dimming

> over rips and tears and
> thin places.

The bathroom is where the insect had its being, and the narrator now sees it as a "room / adequate for one to / be, in." This is a poem about expanding perception, but on another level it is a personal poem as well about loneliness, anonymity, and death. The narrator's awareness of life in place and time is extended, but there is also an emotional identification implicit between poet and insect which gives a rare access to the poet's feelings.

But Margaret Avison is not a confessional poet; her poems, even when describing the natural world, are ever concerned with meaning. In her statements of religious faith she is closely related to the English Metaphysical poets and to Hopkins, but in her epistemological concerns she is allied to a tradition of American writing with its wellspring in Emerson and the Transcendentalists. As a contributor to Cid Corman's *Origin*, she is rightly associated with the tradition of Pound and Williams and Olson and with other contributors to *Origin* such as Robert Creeley and Denise Levertov, although her development has been highly individual. Avison's poems make considerable demands on the reader, but in spite of their difficulty they offer a rare and lasting imaginative experience and are among the best written by a Canadian.

Selected Writings

BOOKS

Winter Sun. Toronto: University of Toronto Press, 1960.

The Dumbfounding. New York: W. W. Norton, 1966.

Sunblue. Hantsport, Nova Scotia: Lancelot Press, 1978.

ANTHOLOGIES CONTAINING OTHER POEMS

The Book of Canadian Poetry. Edited by A. J. M. Smith. Toronto: Gage, 1943.

Other Canadians: An Anthology of the New Poetry in Canada, 1940–1946. Edited by John Sutherland. Montreal: First Statement Press, 1949.

Canadian Anthology. Edited by Carl F. Klinck and Reginald E. Watters. Toronto: Gage, 1956.

The Penguin Book of Canadian Verse. Edited by Ralph Gustafson. Harmondsworth: Penguin Books, 1958.

The Oxford Book of Canadian Verse. Edited by A. J. M. Smith. Toronto: Oxford University Press, 1960.

Poetry 62. Edited by Eli Mandel and Jean-Guy Pilon. Toronto: Ryerson, 1961.

Poetry of Mid-Century, 1940–1960. Edited by Milton Wilson. Toronto: McClelland and Stewart, 1964.

Twentieth-Century Poetry and Poetics. Edited by Gary Geddes. Toronto: Oxford University Press, 1969.

Al Purdy

Although vagabonding about much of the world, Al Purdy is known as the poet of rural Ontario. And just as Ontario is central to any conception of Canada as a nation, so Purdy's work has assumed a central position of importance in the growing body of Canadian poetry since the Second World War. One of the distinctive features of Purdy's career is that he has both a serious and a popular audience. Lauded by academics as one of the country's most accomplished writers,[1] Purdy has also published his verse in newsstand magazines such as *Maclean's*, *Weekend*, and *Saturday Night*. No other Canadian poet has quite so successfully bridged the span between an intellectual and a popular readership.

Purdy was born in 1918 in Wooler, Ontario, a small farming community very close to Ameliasburg, where he now lives. He began his wandering at the age of sixteen when he dropped out of school to drive a taxi in Trenton. During the depression he rode a freight train to Vancouver and subsequently served with the Royal Canadian Air Force in British Columbia. In 1944, while stationed in Vancouver, he published his first book of poems, *The Enchanted Echo*, at his own expense. It was not, however, until the mid-fifties when Purdy began work as a script writer for the Canadian Broadcasting Corporation that he took his role as poet seriously. Purdy and his wife lived for a time in Montreal, but then moved to Roblin Lake at Ameliasburg, where he built his own home and took up permanent residence in the country of his United Empire Loyalist ancestors. From Ameliasburg, however, he traveled to the Cariboo, Newfoundland, Baffin Island, Cuba, England, Europe, Mexico, and Japan, so that while he is one of

[1] See, for example, the monograph by fellow poet and university professor George Bowering, *Al Purdy* (Toronto: Copp Clark, 1970).

Canada's most local poets, he is at the same time one of the country's most international in scope.

Purdy's popularity with a general readership has much to do with the engaging speaking voice in his poetry—a familiar, self-deprecating voice that combines sober, ecclesiastical truths with a great lust for living. The poet's easygoing personality is always on display in his work—in the colloquial language and broken sentences, and particularly in the openly subjective viewpoint. In "Spring Song," for example, where the middle-aged poet is stretched out on the ground listening to the frogs sing and trying to change the oil in his car, he reflects on the irony of sexual desire in an aging man's body. Sex is one of the most splendid features of being alive, says Purdy, but, alas, a man's sexual capacity wanes with the years. The poem concludes with a comic but at once sober picture of the poet as middle-aged lover:

> Here I am
>   with both hands high
> under the skirts of the world
> trying to figure it out too late for
> someone breathed or sighed or spoke
> and everything rearranged itself
> from is to was.[2]

Purdy features himself repeatedly in comical, self-humiliating situations—for example, caught by dogs with his pants down while relieving himself in the Arctic, or on another occasion trying to trade a poem for a beer in a hotel tavern. In that poem, "At the Quinte Hotel," he describes himself as a "sensitive man," while at the same time he is brawling in the saloon. Purdy's good humor and vitality attract the reader to share in his adventures. But it is the combination of the jocular and the elegiac which gives Purdy's best verse its unique quality.

Beneath the tough, sometimes sardonic exterior of Purdy's verse there is a pervasive sense of human impotence, contingent on the transitory nature of existence.[3] A central theme is continual loss through time, most poignantly struck in the poems

[2] Except where noted, all poems are cited from Al Purdy, *Being Alive: Poems, 1958–78* (Toronto: McClelland and Stewart, 1978).

[3] See John Lye's essay, "The Road to Ameliasburg," *Dalhousie Review* 57 (Summer 1977): 242–53.

Purdy writes about his ancestors and about the Hastings and Prince Edward County region in which his family lived. In "Fathers" he tells us that he was only two years old when his father died.[4] This is not a poem about a man's early tragic death (his father in fact had lived to be sixty), but time as thief is still the poem's theme, for through death the boy is robbed of a vital connection to the world. He looks at old snapshots of his father but cannot actually remember him; he demands more, something tangible from the flesh that gave him life, but nothing is granted. The lament for a father he has never known and the bond to a place marked by the father's absence lie at the heart of Purdy's continual return in fact and in poetry to Ameliasburg; they are central to his romantic preoccupation with the passage of time.

In place of the father, the poet's grandfather assumes a mythic presence, bringing into focus the poet's quest for personal identity and his ambiguous feelings about the country of his ancestors. Out of memories of his grandfather and the legacy of impoverished land the old man once farmed, Purdy has constructed some of his best poems. These are not sentimental poems about heroic pioneer figures or the simple pleasures of country life. The old man as presented in "Elegy for a Grandfather" is not a venerable biblical patriarch, but "a tough big-bellied Pharaoh, with a deck of cards in his pocket," a backwoods farmer and lumberjack "who lived on rotten whiskey / and died of sin and Quaker oats age 90 or so." Home is similarly a rough place; in "My Grandfather's Country" we glimpse a poor region "where failed farms sink back into earth / the clearings join and fences no longer divide." Nonetheless, it is imperative for the poet to establish a vital link with this place and its people. From his grandfather's stories ("My Grandfather Talking—30 Years Ago") and from learning the history of the region (the "Roblin's Mills" poems), the poet fashions a picture of the crude pioneer community with its proprieties and superstitions, its hopes for the future. Placed alongside a later picture of a "defeated" country where the farms return to bush and scrubland, the poetic history of the Belleville region becomes an elegy to human defeat by nature and time. The poet in turn, de-

---

[4]"Fathers" appears in *The Stone Bird* (Toronto: McClelland and Stewart, 1981), p. 85.

spite his hard-nosed veneer, emerges a romantic figure who identifies with the defeated and dispossessed.

Two well-known poems have their origins in Purdy's complex feelings about place. In "The Country North of Belleville" the poet is haunted by the heroic but futile labor of his ancestors to turn a poor, stony land into rich farm country. There is a picturesque beauty to the landscape, especially in autumn when the hills turn red and gold, "yet this is the country of defeat / where Sisyphus rolls a big stone / year after year up the ancient hills." It is a country where the farms are being reclaimed by the forest, where "old fences drift vaguely among the trees" and piles of moss-covered stones have lost their meaning "under the meaningless sky." The poet is uneasy because he has abandoned the struggle of his father and grandfather, thereby in a sense denying them the significance of their lives, although he still feels their claim of loyalty and kinship on him. His alienation is measured at the end of the poem by the fact that when he comes back to the country of his ancestors, he gets lost and must inquire the way from strangers.

"Wilderness Gothic," written after the poet's return to live at Ameliasburg, is set in the same region and is similarly haunted by a sense of the futile endeavors of the past. But here personal loss yields to apocalyptic elegy. The poem's occasion is the repairing of the local church spire; the poet is watching from across Roblin Lake. The man hammering in the sky recalls Icarus and the futility of repeated efforts to transcend the human condition. In a brief middle stanza describing the yellow fields of August and the death of three young birds on the highway, the poet reminds us that there is only one ultimate reality—finite matter subject to the inexorable laws of decay and death. In the nineteenth century his ancestors attempted to escape that reality through their religious beliefs. He sees them, however, as victims of "an age and a faith in transition." They brought their customs and beliefs from the old country, but the niceties of Victorian life did not accord with the physical reality of the wilderness. The lives of the settlers became drudgery, their religion superstition. The poem destroys the myth of the heroic and devout pioneer, and as it closes, we wonder, with the narrator, whether the workman should bother to make his repairs on the church spire. The poet says, "Perhaps he will fall." The melancholy pervading both of these poems is tempered by the poet's casual, offhand manner. There is a wry humor, for example, when he speculates on the workman's situation: "his volunteer time and labour donated to God, / minus sick benefits of course on a non-union job." This colloquial matter-of-factness in the speaker's voice effectively offsets the potential sentimentality in the poem.

The speaker's wry but forthright voice has affinities with the tone of the narrator in William Carlos Williams's poetry. Williams's influence was not really felt in Canada until the 1950s, which were the formative period in Purdy's career. In form Purdy's verse often resembles Williams's; they both write characteristically short poems with open lines and almost no punctuation. And in tone there is a similarity of effect created by the colloquial language and the deliberately antipoetic stance the writers take toward their craft. Both view the poem as structured around a process of discovery or celebration.[5] In "Trees at the Arctic Circle" and "Arctic Rhododendrons," Purdy attempts to reveal the essence of the northern vegetation, a process which includes rejecting his own initial assumptions and expectations. His scorn for the dwarf ground willows becomes admiration when he realizes their roots touch the permafrost, that they are nourished by death; and he admonishes himself by saying that to take away the dignity of any living thing is to make life itself trivial. "Arctic Rhododendrons" records his surprise at the unexpected beauty of the miniature shrubs when they are in bloom. Purdy's feeling for the particulars of the arctic landscape constitutes another significant link with the American poet. As George Bowering has pointed out, Purdy in the 1950s began to underscore the necessity and importance of locale. In *Paterson* Williams wrote, "To make a start / out of particulars / and make them general," and this is echoed when Purdy says he will "find a story in every rock / Along

[5] In *Butterfly on Rock: A Study of Themes and Images in Canadian Literature* (Toronto: University of Toronto Press, 1970), pp. 169–71, D. G. Jones locates the meaning of Purdy's poems in the tone of the talk and the gathering of detail, not in conclusions.

the Fraser, write everything, / Perhaps not well."[6] Purdy's Roblin Lake poems fulfill that objective and belong, like Pound's *Cantos* and Williams's *Paterson*, to a modern tradition of personal epics where history must be rediscovered and values renewed.

Purdy's debt to Williams, however, is of a general nature. His elegiac themes mark him uniquely from most of his contemporaries. The subject matter of Purdy's poems often suggests the likelihood of an angry writer whose theme will be social and political injustices. "Transient," one of Purdy's regularly anthologized pieces, recounts the experience of bumming his way to Vancouver during the depression, and with its familiar picture of the bread lines, Indian prostitutes, men begging for cigarettes, one expects the narrator of the poem to be angry and embittered that the social and political systems of the thirties were permitted to exist. But, instead, there is a romantic nostalgia in the poem for the time of youth and a belief that the experience has made him physically one with the country through which he has traveled. The poem concludes with three flashbacks in time enclosed by the weary recognition that one constantly grows older. What is lamented is not social injustice but the inexorable passage of time.

There is no rebellion in Purdy's verse, no striking out against corrupt political leaders; instead, Purdy explores his fascination with strong men such as Che Guevara or John Kennedy who in his personal mythology play the part of father substitutes and have their archetype in his grandfather. In an elegy, "For Robert Kennedy," he says there are public men who become "large as mountains or the endless forests / in the love men bear them," but they die, such solid things "turn misty," and humanity continues its search "to find the one man." Purdy does not see Christ as fulfilling that quest, because he views the promise of immortality for the individual as an illusion; thus symbolically the man repairing the church spire must fall. But at the same time, Purdy does not rail out at Christianity as a hollow institution; he allows a man or woman any belief that will give life meaning.

Purdy's travels in the Arctic have produced a number of poems in which one glimpses something of the white displacement of

[6] See Bowering, *Al Purdy* (Toronto: Copp Clark, 1970), p. 38.

Inuit culture. One of the best of these poems is "Eskimo Graveyard,"[7] which casually records the poet's thoughts as he takes a
walk through a tiny arctic community. He is disturbed by the
body of a dead Eskimo woman who has not been buried because
the gravel at the graveyard is needed to build a schoolhouse.
What disturbs the poet is not the indignity perpetrated on the old
woman or her people, but the fact that she is dead and will be
forgotten and that the little community will in all likelihood completely disappear some day. It is the long perspective on life's ultimate meaninglessness that preoccupies him. At the end of the
poem the white tents of the community, visited regularly by government airplanes, are compared to glowing swans. The myth of
Leda impregnated by Zeus in the form of a swan is evoked. One
of the children of that union was Pollux, who loved deeply his
mortal brother Castor. The narrator of the poem, however, is
skeptical that such brotherly love will be born from the contact of
white and Eskimo people; the community will simply die out.
The same elegiac reflection on the transience of life informs "Lament for the Dorsets," a poem about a group of giant Eskimos
who mysteriously disappeared in the fourteenth century.

The vision which permeates all of Purdy's poetry is that human
life is tragically short and, within the general cosmic framework,
without significance. In an earlier period a number of Purdy's
poems would be said to belong to the graveyard school of poetry,
their vision of universal death and decay is so pervasive. The
creatures of nature whose lives are often quickly extinguished are
presented as emblems of life's cruel brevity. In "Skeleton by an
Old Cedar" and "Starlings," the poet reminds us that birds, seemingly so removed from the cares of the world, are ultimately
"wrestled to earth . . . by death." He then describes their corpses
swarming with ants and maggots and submicroscopic organisms
which "hold high revels / . . . and fester onward in the condition
which is life." Human existence is equally fugitive: in the remains
of an Indian village the poet imagines the green growth of spring
pressing on "femurs, vertebrae, and delicate / belled skulls of
children," while in the local poolroom he becomes aware of the

---

[7] "Eskimo Graveyard" is published in *North of Summer* (Toronto: McClelland and
Stewart, 1967), p. 26.

old men, retired railway brakemen, and ex-soldiers, full of senile statistics and yearning for their youth in "the time of death." "Evergreen Cemetery" places the poet in the middle of his own mortal condition. The uneasiness he feels in the cemetery, surrounded by his dead ancestors, is not really mitigated by the honesty that death forces on him. He is filled with despair to think all human aspirations end in damp ground and says, "If that's being human it's best done with." But the fact that individual life is short and without unique purpose cannot completely effect a permanent despair; the poet recognizes in this same poem that the sunlight in the graveyard also illuminates elsewhere the beauty of a girl's skin, and the evergreens growing on graves also grow on the mountains he loves to climb. Life is perhaps only a joke (there is a startling rictus grin in the image of the poet's dying mother, who has stuffed her false teeth up her rectum), but it is to be enjoyed, and the poem concludes with the speaker hurrying out of the cemetery "before the gates close."

Purdy's quest, as one critic has correctly suggested, is to find a "basis for man's transcendence of his own earthly life, without ceasing to embrace it."[8] He does this in two important ways: first, by viewing time as psychological as well as scientific, thus allowing for the continuous reality of the past in the present and future, and second by searching for mythic and historical roots so that one's individual experiences can be seen as part of a timeless continuum. In several poems he reminds us that the mental faculty frees humankind from the confines of biology and scientific time. In "House Guest" he shows how a man is always integrating two forms of time. While the poet and his visitor discuss the importance of various aspects of human history and culture—Jews in the Negev, the Celtic invasion of Britain, Peking Man, the Bible as mythic literature—they also contend over the best way to make their coffee, pound nails, cook eggs.

In "Cariboo Horses," one of Purdy's most popular poems, physical time (or time present) is a gray morning at 100 Mile House, a town in the interior of British Columbia, where the

[8]This thesis is put forth by Ofelia Cohn-Sfetcu in "The Privilege of Finding an Opening in the Past: Al Purdy and the Tree of Experience," *Queen's Quarterly* 83 (Summer 1976): 262–69.

poet sees the cowboys coming into town to pick up supplies at the grocers. They tie up their horses outside the tavern alongside "jeeps and fords and chevvys." The scene is commonplace in a small western town in the 1950s, but for the poet it evokes a panorama of history wherein horses have played a vital role in human affairs. He recalls first the Indians of the Cariboo region who hunted on horseback, then reaching further in place and time brings to memory earlier species of horse—the mulelike kiang used to haul stone in the building of the pyramids, the onager, a wild ass used for hunting in Asia, and the quagga, an extinct species related to the zebra. In time present in the little British Columbia town the poet sees "only horses," but by evoking history (mental time), the scene comes alive with the potency of the past and the splendid tradition of man's relationship to horses. There is a characteristic elegiac note in the fact that the horse, like its primitive ancestors, is slowly moving towards extinction, the combustion engine having replaced horse power.

On a personal level Purdy is naturally concerned with individual survival. The hard biological reality of existence is that the individual possesses neither stability nor permanence. However, if he sees himself as part of the continuing flow of humanity and his work as a link in the great chain of human endeavor, then he transcends his mortal time-bound existence. This points up for Purdy the importance of ancestors and community and sharpens the loss of a father he knew only through old photographs and anecdotes. In the poems about his grandfather and about the community around Roblin's Mill, he states directly his belief that his predecessors have not vanished from the earth but that they continue on in him both physically and spiritually. "In the Dream of Myself" welcomes the idea that the nature and experiences of one's ancestors predetermine much that characterizes the individual's life:

> father and grandfathers are here
> grandmothers and mother
> farmers and horsebreakers
> tangled in my flesh
> who built my strength for a journey
> Their old habits with rifle and cradle

their ways of listening
these made me lefthanded
inclined me to baldness at fifty

In "Elegy for a Grandfather" the poet conceives of himself as a reincarnation of his grandfather, so that the dialogue in "My Grandfather Talking—30 Years Ago" is in fact between the old man and his younger self. The poet becomes acutely and satisfyingly aware that "what happened still happens"; he asserts in "Roblin's Mills (1)" "that one can hear the voices of the old ones on the party line sometimes before the number is dialed, that a lump in one's throat is "the Adam's apple" of one's ancestors.

Purdy's vision of human history, however, is not a static one. Essences remain, but forms change. The poet humorously recognizes in "House Guest" that his own bad temper of a morning rehearses human evolution from snarling ape to Homo sapiens. The most dramatic interpolation of mental and scientific time ("time that tick tocks always in my body") and the long view of human history is found in "The Beavers of Renfrew," a masterly poem about the place of humankind in the universe. The physical time of the poem (time present) finds the narrator listening to his neighbor, old Jake Loney, working with a chainsaw cutting down trees for firewood, and later observing the beavers working around their earthen dams at night. Observing the creatures of nature "at peace with themselves," at one with their watery environment, he exclaims:

I wonder what screwed-up philosophy,
what claim to a god's indulgence
made men decide their own importance?

Standing in the moonlight, he envisions a time in the mythic past when human beings, a biological accident, were inferior to the animals who helped them to survive. This part of the poem reads like an Indian legend told to explain the creation of the world and humankind's place in it. The water and the land creatures make an agreement to arrest their evolutionary development, to stay completely still, which allowed the human species to catch up to them. But humanity, says the poet, has forgotten the secret of staying still and being at peace with itself and the world, and the poem ends with the speaker the next day puzzling his neighbor by asking whether humankind should not "make a left turn in / time and just stay here / . . . instead of going on to the planets." The poet wonders whether men and women should not stop and enjoy the world that they live in so comfortably rather than press on to conquer new worlds. Humanity's unique capacity to survey and understand the history of the species allows it to transcend individual existence, but does not ensure that it will continue to enjoy this special position in the universe. But the story of humankind is not over, and Purdy's poems correspondingly evade clearly articulated conclusions.

Selected Writings

The Enchanted Echo. Vancouver: Clark & Stuart, 1944.

Pressed on Sand. Toronto: Ryerson, 1955.

Emu, Remember! Fredericton: Fiddlehead Poetry Books, 1956.

The Crafte So Longe to Lerne. Toronto: Ryerson, 1959.

The Blur in Between. Toronto: Emblem Books, 1962.

Poems for all the Annettes. Toronto: Contact, 1962.

The Cariboo Horses. Toronto: McClelland and Stewart, 1965.

North of Summer. Toronto: McClelland and Stewart, 1967.

Wild Grape Wine. Toronto: McClelland and Stewart, 1968.

Love in a Burning Building. Toronto: McClelland and Stewart, 1970.

Hiroshima Poems. Trumansburg, Ont.: Crossing Press, 1972.

Selected Poems. Toronto: McClelland and Stewart, 1972.

On the Bearpaw Sea. Burnaby, B.C.: Blackfish Press, 1973.

Sex and Death. Toronto: McClelland and Stewart, 1973.

In Search of Owen Roblin. Toronto: McClelland and Stewart, 1974.

The Poems of Al Purdy. Toronto: McClelland and Stewart, 1976.

Sundance at Dusk. Toronto: McClelland and Stewart, 1976.

At Marsport Drugstore. Sutton West, Ont.: Paget Press, 1977.

No Other Country. Toronto: McClelland and Stewart, 1977.

A *Handful of Earth*. Coatsworth, Ont.: Black Moss Press, 1977.

Being Alive: Poems, 1958–78. Toronto: McClelland and Stewart, 1978.

The Stone Bird. Toronto: McClelland and Stewart, 1981.

Margaret Laurence

One can trace the development of Canadian poetry with reference to succeeding groups of writers who reacted against the values of previous generations and forged new literary goals. One thinks of the Confederation poets, the Montreal poets of the *McGill Fortnightly Review*, the World War II poets of *Preview* and *First Statement*, and of the special climate they created for such major talents as Pratt, Birney, Layton, and Purdy. But until very recently there has been no sense of a developing tradition among Canadian fiction writers. In discussing the Canadian novel one moves from one isolated instance of achievement to another, with great gaps in between. In the first half of this century certain writers and fictions stand out as historically important: Grove created the first body of realistic prairie fiction; in *As for Me and My House* Ross composed a powerful study of the depression; and Hugh MacLennan in *Barometer Rising* (1941) and *Two Solitudes* (1945) wrote the first novels about Canada's sense of developing nationhood. There were also fine novels from Ethel Wilson, Robertson Davies, and Mordecai Richler, but these books and their authors do not describe anything like a line of descent. Perhaps this is because Canadian novelists tended to see themselves in relation to novelists and publishers outside the country, or perhaps because there were not issues large enough to bring writers together.

The first writer to create a feeling of tradition among Canadian novelists is Margaret Laurence. In an introduction to Sinclair Ross's *The Lamp at Noon and Other Stories* she writes that reading the novel *As for Me and My House* at the age of eighteen "had an enormous impact on me, for it seemed the only completely genuine one I had ever read about my own people, my

own place, my own time."[1] This is one of the first instances of a Canadian novelist acknowledging the influence of an earlier Canadian writer. A letter to Ethel Wilson in praise of *The Innocent Traveller*, written while Laurence was at work on *The Stone Angel* (both novels are about old women) also reveals her concern with literary ancestors.[2]

No Canadian writer has enjoyed as great a degree of popular and critical success as Laurence herself. Born Jean Margaret Wemyss in Neepawa, Manitoba, in 1926, she grew up in that town as an orphan cared for by her mother's family. She was educated at the University of Manitoba and began work on a newspaper in Winnipeg. Marriage to Jack Laurence, an engineer, took her in 1950 to Africa, where she started to write fiction while raising a family. Her first book, *A Tree for Poverty* (1954), was an edition of Somali poetry and prose that she translated into English. *This Side Jordan* was published in 1960 and won the Beta Sigma Phi prize for the best first novel by a Canadian. This was followed by a book of short stories, *The Tomorrow-Tamer*, published in 1963. Both books are set in Ghana during the approach of independence and reveal the traumatic effects of emerging nationhood on both Africans and anxious Europeans. In 1963 Margaret Laurence also published a travel memoir, *The Prophet's Camel Bell*, which describes her two years in Somaliland.[3]

Laurence's renown, however, rests, not with her African books, but with a series of five novels all set in part in the fictional prairie town of Manawaka. The first of these, *The Stone Angel* (1964), about a ninety-year-old woman recalling a turbulent life as she approaches death, is frequently considered the best. *A Jest of God* (1966), about an unmarried schoolteacher, was made into a successful movie, *Rachel, Rachel*. *A Jest of God* also won Margaret Laurence her first Governor General's Award for fiction. *The*

[1] Introduction to Sinclair Ross, *The Lamp at Noon and Other Stories* (Toronto: McClelland and Stewart, 1968), p. 7.

[2] Laurence to Wilson, Ethel Wilson Papers, Special Collections, University of British Columbia Library.

[3] In "Margaret Laurence's Early Writings: 'a world in which others have to be respected,'" *Journal of Canadian Studies* 13, no. 3 (Fall 1978), pp. 13–18, Patricia Morley sees Africa as a "catalyst and crucible for much of Laurence's work." Morley is also the author of *Margaret Laurence* (Boston: Twayne, 1982).

Fire-Dwellers, the story of a middle-aged housewife, is set mostly in Vancouver and is the least successful of the series. A *Bird in the House* (1970), a group of autobiographical stories about a writer growing up on the prairies, establishes Manawaka as the fictional counterpart to Laurence's hometown of Neepawa. *The Diviners* (1974), an ambitious *Künstlerroman* which stayed at the top of the best-selling lists for sixty consecutive weeks, won for the author a second Governor General's Award. The good sale of her fiction allowed Margaret Laurence, divorced from her husband, to work independently as a writer. Her adopted Lakefield, Ontario, home is an area where many Canadian writers, including the Strickland sisters, Archibald Lampman, and the poet Isabella Valancy Crawford, lived before.

Margaret Laurence's popularity rests squarely on her power to create character. In twentieth-century literature, where characterization is often secondary to symbolism and myth or to the technical matters of storytelling, whether stream-of-consciousness or the self-reflexive process of storytelling itself, Margaret Laurence's fictions stand out for their unforgettable portraits of women wrestling with their personal demons, striving through self-examination to find meaningful patterns to their lives.[4] The author has said in an interview: "I don't think I have ever written anything in which the main character hasn't been in my mind for at least several years, sometimes many years."[5] In turn those characters, after the novel is written, remain indelibly fixed in the mind of the reader.

The Stone Angel is the story of Hagar Shipley, a proud, embittered, but frightened old woman who at the age of ninety still struggles to maintain her independence. She lives with her son Marvin and his wife in Vancouver, but she is ailing, almost bedridden, and they are resolved to put her in a nursing home. After they take her for a preliminary visit to Silverthreads, she escapes from them and makes her way to a deserted fish cannery up the coast where for two days she is closer than ever before to the es-

[4] See Nancy Bailey, "Margaret Laurence, Carl Jung, and the Manawaka Women," *Studies in Canadian Literature* 2, no. 2 (Summer 1977): 306–21.

[5] See Clara Thomas, *The Manawaka World of Margaret Laurence* (Toronto: McClelland and Stewart, 1976), p. 60.

sentials of existence—nature, silence, her own thoughts and feelings. When she is discovered, she is taken to a hospital, where she dies. The linear plot is simple and straightforward, but the story moves on two levels; the greater part of the novel consists of Hagar's memories of her rebellious youth in Manawaka, her failed marriage to an improvident, uncouth farmer, Bram Shipley, and her haphazard raising of her two sons, John and Marvin. The shifts in time between past and present flow naturally from the thought processes of an old person living largely in the past; only the chronological arrangement of the flashbacks reminds us of the artist's manipulation of the story.

In Margaret Laurence's fiction biblical references are an important touchstone in the creation of character and development of theme.[6] Hagar's name recalls the wife of Abraham in the Old Testament, the bondswoman who was replaced by Sarah and sent out with her son into the desert wilderness. The biblical allusion establishes Laurence's heroine as a wanderer who, at the same time, is, not free, but a captive to some overpowering force. Another religious image that defines the heroine is the stone angel over her mother's grave in the Manawaka cemetery; it stands over the prairie wilderness with sightless eyes, for the carver left the eyeballs blank. Hagar's father erected the stone angel, not as an emblem of love for the dead woman, but out of pride, to proclaim his dynasty in the new land.

The captive exile, blind to herself and to the needs of others, is a fitting description of Hagar. Laurence has conceived of her heroine as a tragic figure, a woman who knowingly brings about her own unhappiness. Her great flaw is her pride, her instinct to rebel, summed up in her adoption of the battle cry of the Currie clan, "Gainsay Who Dare." Her stubborn refusal to yield to the wishes of others proves as destructive to herself as to those around her. Her old age is a purgatory in which she is tormented by her memories of a wasted and unhappy life. For the reader her life

[6] See Sandra Djwa, "False Gods and the True Covenant: Thematic Continuity between Margaret Laurence and Sinclair Ross," *Journal of Canadian Fiction* 1, no. 4 (Fall 1972), pp. 43–50; and Frank Pesando's "In a Timeless Land: The Use of Apocalyptic Mythology in the Writings of Margaret Laurence," *Journal of Canadian Fiction* 2, no. 1 (Winter 1973), pp. 53–58.

unfolds in a series of scenes in which she obstinately held herself apart from others, refusing to give or accept love. When in youth her brother is dying, for example, she refuses to comfort him by pretending to be their mother. She marries Bram Shipley in order to defy her father's wishes, but her pride won't let her accept her husband's unambitious way of life or take pleasure in their marriage relationship. Similarly, she betrays her two sons by trying to shape them according to her ambitions and by never openly expressing her love for them. A large portion of Hagar's unhappiness is in her inability to communicate freely to others, although there are times when she feels sorely pressed to do so.

Hagar's tragedy is not wholly individual, but is tied to the time and place in which she lived. As a girl growing up, Margaret Laurence had felt oppressed by the presence in the house of her grandfather, a severe, uncommunicative man in his eighties whose word was law. The author has said that *The Stone Angel* was an attempt to understand her grandparents' generation, those rugged pioneers who had to repress their every emotion in order to survive and ultimately prevail in a bleak and hostile land. Laurence has written "how difficult they were to live with, how authoritarian, how unbending, how afraid to show love, many of them, and how willing to show anger."[7] Hagar is one of their company, for she resembles in both appearance and deed her pioneer father, Jason Currie, who with the stone angel proclaimed his dynasty like a "fledgling pharoah in an uncouth land." Although she is never religious, she has the puritan's instinct to deny herself those very things she wishes; in old age she considers herself "unregenerate," and in accordance with her Calvinist heritage she is haunted by guilt.

The Stone Angel is not a religious novel, but there is a pattern of redemption working to bring the heroine peace before she dies. The pattern is set in motion for Hagar by the very act of remembering and acknowledging her failure in all the roles that life has cast her in. That process comes to a climax when she takes refuge in the fish cannery and is joined by Murray F. Lees. As Laurence's biographer and critic, Clara Thomas, suggests, Lees's

---

[7] Laurence, *Heart of a Stranger* (Toronto: McClelland and Stewart, 1976), p. 16.

function in the novel is analogous to the Fool's during King Lear's agony on the heath.[8] Lees lives with the guilt of the death of his son who was burned in a fire at home while his parents attended a religious revival meeting. When Lees tells his painful story, he brings Hagar to confront once again the most difficult part of her life's story—her responsibility for the death of her favorite son, John. At the end of her confession her mind clouds over, but later in the hospital we realize she has been freed from the past. Her moment of self-knowledge comes when the clergyman sings "Old Hundred" with its theme of praise and rejoicing. She says to herself "I must always, always, have wanted that—simply to rejoice," and asks, "How is it I never could?" The fault in part stemmed from her society, where all emotions "were forced to a standstill by some brake of proper appearances," but they were deeply personal as well:

Pride was my wilderness, and the demon that led me there was fear. I was alone, never anything else, and never free, for I carried my chains within me, and they spread out from me and shackled all I touched.[9]

By this point in the narrative, Laurence's ugly, evil-tempered old woman has the full sympathy and admiration of the reader. She lives long enough to perform what she calls two "truly free acts." One is to fetch a bedpan for the girl in the room with her, the other is to tell Marvin that he was "the better son." Both are acts of charity, not committed out of daring or defiance, but out of love and compassion. She dies holding a glass of water, a symbol of redemption and life.

The vitality and authenticity of Laurence's narratives derive from her skillful use of first-person narrators. Hagar's rebellious, carping nature is perfectly captured by the tone of cruel mockery with which she speaks of others and by an irony that she turns on herself and her own ambitions. Near the very beginning of the novel, when Hagar describes the stone angel on her mother's grave, she recalls another grave with its inscription invoking eternal rest for one Regina Weese:

[8] Thomas, *The Manawaka World of Margaret Laurence*, p. 71.

[9] All references are to the Bantam-Seal edition of *The Stone Angel* (Toronto: McClelland and Stewart, 1978), p. 261.

So much for sad Regina, now forgotten in Manawaka—as I, Hagar, am doubtless forgotten. And yet I always felt she had only herself to blame, for she was a flimsy, gutless creature, bland as egg custard, caring with martyred devotion for an ungrateful, fox-voiced mother year in and year out. When Regina died, from some obscure and maidenly disorder, the old disreputable lady rose from sick-smelling sheets and lived, to the despair of her married sons, another full ten years. No need to say God rest *her* soul, for she must be laughing spitefully in hell, while virginal Regina sighs in heaven. [p. 2]

The passage is humorous with its earthy, biting imagery and its observation on life's ironies. But what is crystallized in this passage is a psychological dilemma fundamental to the novel and to all of Laurence's writing, namely the tyranny of one generation over the next. The voice in Laurence's novels is always that of the oppressed individual seeking freedom.

That is nowhere more true than in her second Manawaka novel, A *Jest of God*, the story of a spinster schoolteacher who lives with her widowed mother. The portrait of Rachel Cameron is almost a casebook study of an "old maid" obsessed by her fears and inhibitions. It is a vividly realized but claustrophobic novel, narrated by a woman on the edge of hysteria; the effect, as Clara Thomas puts it, is "like one long, barely controlled scream."[10] Rachel's life, conducted always under the watchword of "proper appearances," is exceedingly narrow. She is isolated from most human contact by the bond of duty to her mother.[11] Mrs. Cameron is a frail but vain little woman whose tyranny over her daughter ranges from sharp censure of her activities to pathetic intimations of her own death. Rachel's only diversion beyond teaching school is a casual acquaintance with Hector Jonas, who took over her father's undertaking business, and a friendship with Calla, a fellow teacher and repressed lesbian whose life is devoted to fundamentalist religion.

Rachel's life is informed by a powerful need to have children. Her name like Hagar's is biblically symbolic; she mourns for the children that she has never had. At school her frustrated desire

[10] Thomas, *The Manawaka World of Margaret Laurence*, p. 71.

[11] See C. M. McLay, "Every Man Is an Island: Isolation in A *Jest of God*," *Canadian Literature* 50 (Autumn 1971): 57–68.

emerges in an overwhelming affection for one of the boys, Jimmy Doherty; but she must repress that instinct, for she knows that it will hurt the boy and he in turn would hate her:

What might happen, if ever he or any of them discovered how I value him? They would torment me, certainly, but this is nothing to the way they would torment him. The old words for it, the child's phrase—it's so cheap, so cold and full of loathing. . . . But James would be cruel, too, if he knew. He'd find some means of being scathing. He'd have to, out of some need to protect himself against me. [12]

Rachel cannot help compare her narrow existence to that of her sister Stacey, married with four children and living in Vancouver. When her father died, Rachel had come back to Manawaka to teach and look after her mother.

The plot of A Jest of God describes a brief affair Rachel has during the summer holiday with Nick Kazlik, a teacher from Winnipeg staying at his father's farm near Manawaka. Rachel's need for love is so strong that she overcomes all her fears and self-doubts and enters a passionate physical relationship with Nick, hoping that she will become pregnant.

"If I had a child, I would like it to be yours." This seems so unforced that I feel he must see it the way I do. And so restrained, as well, when I might have torn at him—*Give me my children.* [p. 181]

But Nick withdraws from the relationship when Rachel confesses her desire for children. Ironically, this man who might have delivered Rachel from the tyranny of her mother and her own inhibitions is similarly bound to his parents. He is fettered by his brother's death and his guilty refusal to carry on his father's farm. He shows Rachel a snapshot of a boy, which she concludes is his son, but is actually of himself. Both Rachel and Nick are trapped by their need to seek out and establish their own identity in relation to their parents.

But Rachel believes for a time that she has become pregnant and undergoes a desperate struggle deciding whether to accept or reject the child—a conflict waged between her deepest needs and

---

[12] A Jest of God (Toronto: McClelland and Stewart, 1977), p. 7. All references are to this Bantam-Seal edition.

desire and her instinct for social self-preservation. The growth
within her proves to be a benign tumor, but the struggle she en-
dures has a powerfully liberating effect. As she comes out of the
anesthetic after the operation, she says, "I am the mother now."
Her words make no sense to the nurse in attendance, but they
signify her emergence as an adult, no longer wholly dependent
on her mother. Her liberation is marked by her leaving Manawaka; in spite of her mother's tears and threats, Rachel accepts a
teaching position in Vancouver. She takes her mother with her to
the coast, thinking of her now as her "elderly child."

Rachel is not a tragic figure like Hagar, who was the knowing,
willful agent of her own thwarted existence; rather, she is an
ironic figure like Eliot's Prufrock, repressed and self-conscious.
The closing lines of the novel direct us to the same achievement
of self-knowledge and wry self-acceptance that Eliot gives to his
protagonist:

I will walk by myself on the shore of the sea and look at the freegulls
flying. I will grow too orderly, plumping up the chesterfield cushions
just-so before I go to bed. I will rage in my insomnia like a prophetess. I
will take care to remember a vitamin pill each morning with my breakfast. I will be afraid. Sometimes I will feel light-hearted, sometimes
light-headed. I may sing aloud, even in the dark. I will ask myself if I am
going mad, but if I do, I won't know it. [p. 246]

The Fire-Dwellers, a novel about Rachel's older sister, Stacey,
is Laurence's portrait of the contemporary housewife and mother.
Stacey is the opposite of her sister, uninhibited, gregarious, "with
some guts and some humour." [13] Her dilemma is not in coming to
terms with herself so much as in accepting a world which she perceives as increasingly chaotic and threatening. In Stacey's hectic
urban existence there are accidents and suicides, and from the
media comes a steady barrage of reports on war and potential
global disaster—the world on the brink. She experiences the vulnerability of being human in relation to her children, whom she
wishes to protect from the violence of the world.

The title of the novel specifies her dilemma on several levels.

---

[13] Margaret Laurence to Joan Hind-Smith. See Hind-Smith, *Three Voices* (Toronto: Clarke Irwin, 1975), p. 44.

With the nursery rhyme "Ladybird, ladybird / Fly away home" running through her head as she falls asleep, she dreams of her children caught in a fire: "Only this one can she take with her, away from the crackling smoke, back to the dream world. She must not look to see which one."[14] Stacey reacts to the pressures of the twentieth century with a sense of imminent apocalypse and conflagration, a vision not only created by the media but supported by the immediate volcanic setting of her home on the west coast. The title also directs us to a central strand in the plot, which concerns Stacey's brief love affair with a young artist, Luke Venturi. With her Calvinist background from Manawaka, she sees herself as a guilty creature consumed with the fires of lust, like Saint Augustine when he went to Carthage. The title reaches even further back, evoking the Heraclitean idea of all things on fire, constantly changing. Stacey is approaching her fortieth birthday, another dimension to her crisis of consciousness, and is preoccupied with time and being mortal.

Technically *The Fire-Dwellers* is one of Laurence's most ambitious works. She uses a combination of first- and third-person narration in order to portray both the external contemporary urban world and its effect on one of its inhabitants. The satirical contemporaneity of the book, however, is also part of its weakness as a fiction; one suspects that, as time passes, Stacey's faddish existence (her banana diets, esoteric self-improvement courses) will become dated like the lives of the characters in Sinclair Lewis's fiction. What will endure is her struggle to accept a threatening world and be at home in it. She comes to this acceptance through her long-suffering husband, Mac, who carries on with an unrewarding job because he holds seriously his responsibility to provide for his family. Stacey reflects in her wryly exaggerated manner:

When we've got all four kids through university or launched somewhere, and Mac retires and is so thin you have to look twice to see him and I'm so portly I can hardly waddle, we can go to Acapulco and do the Mexican hat dance. I can't stand it. I cannot. I can't take it. Yeh, I can, though. By God, I can, if I set my mind to it. [p. 260]

[14] *The Fire-Dwellers* (Toronto: McClelland and Stewart, 1978), p. 25. All references are to this Bantam-Seal edition.

While Margaret Laurence was writing novels, she was also producing a number of short stories that appeared in a variety of magazines including *Chatelaine*, *Saturday Evening Post*, and the *Atlantic Advocate*. Eight of these stories, all about a young girl named Vanessa MacLeod growing up in Manawaka, were collected into one volume and published under the title *A Bird in the House*. Laurence calls these stories "fictionalized autobiography," written in order to exorcise the powerful demons of her own past, particularly the figure of her grandfather who had inspired in her so much bitterness while growing up.

I came to write about my own background out of a desire—a personal desire—to come to terms with what I will call my ancestral past. . . . I recall [my grandfather] as a man impossible to please, and I recall myself rebelling desperately against this hard, harsh sort of personality. . . . Only after I had finished writing these short stories did I begin to realize that, although I had detested him, I had come to some kind of terms with him.[15]

Ironically, the grandfather is the hero in *A Bird in the House*. In Canadian literature Grandfather Connor is the most powerfully realized portrait of the patriarchal pioneer, the self-made man. He is proud, tough, self-disciplined, and demands obedience from others. In Laurence's imaginative world he is the archetypal parental figure who inspires fear, guilt, and rebellion in her heroines. In the same interview already quoted, Laurence describes her grandfather as "a very strong, authoritarian old man— I never remember him as anything but an old man. He seemed to be as old as God right from the moment I first had a memory of him." In the cycle of stories, Laurence gives the grandfather figure exactly the mythic proportions of the Old Testament God, exacting obedience and respect from the members of his family, but never showing them love. The only emotion he exhibits is anger. To the young Vanessa the old man's angry refusal to help his ne'er-do-well brother Dan and his rude, peremptory treatment of his youngest daughter's "gentlemen callers" seem outrageous. But from the outset the portrait of the grandfather is a complex one,

[15] Clara Thomas, "A Conversation with Margaret Laurence and Irving Layton," *Journal of Canadian Fiction* 1, no. 1 (Winter 1972), pp. 65–69.

for we are made to realize that the old man's concept of an authoritarian, patriarchal society was one that was valid for his generation. He plays a role, wears a mask, which Vanessa only sees through once—when she finds her grandfather crying after his wife's death. But as he grows very old and Vanessa begins to mature herself, she sees him in more human terms. There is, however, a final showdown between the old man and his granddaughter when, during the war, she comes home late one night with a young man from the air force. The grandfather not only reprimands them for being out late but surmises that the young man is already married. Eventually the old man's guess proves correct. It is infuriating to the girl that he is right, but it is also the author's way of accrediting him with wisdom. When he dies, the members of the family reflect on his life—his coming from Ontario to Manitoba by steamer, his walking from Winnipeg to Manawaka, earning his way by shoeing horses, building up his house and business by long years of hard work—but they cannot cry. They are just amazed that he is gone:

I was not sorry that he was dead. I was only surprised. Perhaps I had really imagined that he was immortal. Perhaps he even was immortal, in ways which it would take me half a lifetime to comprehend.[16]

Years after, Vanessa realizes the extent of that immortality. She herself has become like her grandfather: "I had feared and fought the old man, yet he proclaimed himself in my veins."

In *The Diviners*, Laurence's fifth Manawaka book, the heroine's feelings of outrage and defiance are no longer directed against a specific parental figure, but against society as a whole. Laurence expands the scope of her imaginative rebellion by making her heroine, Morag Gunn, an orphan, one of the country's dispossessed. She is raised by an indigent garbage collector and his wife and befriended by the town's family of Metis outcasts. Growing up in Manawaka is a long struggle with poverty and social prejudice. The woman who emerges becomes a writer who, in exorcising the demons of her personal past, exposes the sorrows and injustices of the whole country.

[16] *A Bird in the House* (Toronto: McClelland and Stewart, 1979), p. 177. All references are to the Bantam-Seal edition.

In the earlier novels, Laurence's characters are so vigorously drawn that they are etched in one's memory as fixed types: the querulous old woman, the neurotic spinster, the bitchy, restless housewife. Their psychological immediacy is so great that they seem like casebook studies. In *The Diviners*, however, the author seems to approach human personality as a mystery, with no easy psychological explanation. Likely this is owing to the fact that *The Diviners* is an artist's story, a *Künstlerroman*, and that in creating a character close to herself (though not in the historical, strictly autobiographical sense) Laurence cannot so easily understand and explain her actions. Much of the narrative consists of Morag's memories and her simultaneous questioning of their authenticity. For example, remembering the dog that slept on her bed when she was a very small child and thinking how calm and tolerant her mother was, she suddenly breaks in on herself and asks whether she is not creating scenes and characters instead of remembering them. Similarly, in this novel Laurence calls the writer's facile assumptions about his work into question:

The river was the colour of liquid bronze this morning, the sun catching it. Could that be right? No. Who has ever seen liquid bronze? Not Morag, certainly. Probably no one could catch the river's colour even with paints, much less words. A daft profession. Wordsmith. Liar, more likely. Weaving fabrications. Yet, with typical ambiguity, convinced that fiction was more true than fact. Or that fact was in fact fiction.[17]

The novel follows the familiar pattern of the *Künstlerroman*: childhood memories, the struggles of a sensitive adolescent against the misunderstanding and bourgeois attitudes of a small town, the excitement of university, the failure of marriage, apprenticeship in exile, and the slow, difficult process of self-discovery through art. But Morag in the present is not simply the successful writer looking back with satisfaction over the long, hard climb to success; rather, she is still struggling to see the meaningful patterns to her existence, still divining (as the title suggests) to know herself and understand her relations with others, particularly her grown daughter. The mystery of self suggests

[17] *The Diviners* (Toronto: McClelland and Stewart, 1979), p. 25. All references are to the Bantam-Seal edition.

the mystery of others, and in this novel Margaret Laurence has given us some unforgettable, haunting characterizations. One remembers Christie and Prin, the poor couple who raise Morag; Christie, the garbage collector, who has the romantic pride and the imagination to create a world of the spirit greater than Manawaka could ever aspire to; dull-witted Prin who grows every year fatter and more childlike until she eventually disappears inside her voluminous body. They are not analyzed or explained (we do not know what makes Christie rage against the night, or what makes Prin retreat from the world); rather, they are presented to us in the fullness of living, inexplicable and inviolable. Similarly, Jules Tonnerre, Morag's Metis lover from Manawaka who slowly destroys himself, cannot be explained in terms of his background. Any such attempt would be trite, an ethnic cliché; the mystery of existence is too great. We are also given glimpses of Manawaka townspeople from other books—the Camerons, MacLeods, Kazliks—which give them new dimensions as characters.

The techniques in the novel enhance this recognition of the unknowable.[18] Where in the earlier novels the characters analyzed their thoughts and actions in interior monologues, Morag in *The Diviners* is much of the time remembering the past, but always unsure that she has seized on its import. The novel opens with the description of a series of photographs, "snapshots," from Morag's earliest childhood. There is an opacity in such images, and Morag resists the temptation to interpret them for fear of deceiving herself. In sorting out her memories from the pictures, she reflects, "I don't even know how much of that memory really happened and how much of it I embroidered later on." The "Memorybank Movie" continues this technique of presentation rather than explanation in the novel. Meaning as such is recognized to be mythic and fragmented and is reflected in the importance of songs, mottoes, tales.

The Diviners, with its sentimental and cynical heroine, has much of the appeal of Laurence's earlier novels, but the impasse

---

[18] There is a good discussion of form and technique in *The Diviners* and of the creative process as subject in Ildikó de Papp Carrington's "'Tales in the Telling': *The Diviners* as Fiction about Fiction," *Essays on Canadian Writing* 9 (Winter 1977–78): 154–69.

reached here in understanding character and the implicit questioning of art itself, its efficacy, its values, makes this a more complex book than those written before. Fittingly, after its publication Laurence foreswore writing another novel.

Selected Writings

This Side Jordan. London: Macmillan, 1960. Reprint, New Canadian Library, no. 126 (Toronto: McClelland and Stewart, 1976).

The Tomorrow-Tamer. London: Macmillan, 1963. Reprint, New Canadian Library, no. 70 (Toronto: McClelland and Stewart, 1970).

The Prophet's Camel Bell. Toronto: McClelland and Stewart, 1963.

The Stone Angel. Toronto: McClelland and Stewart, 1964. Reprint, New Canadian Library, no. 59 (Toronto: McClelland and Stewart, 1968), and Bantam-Seal Book (1978).

A Jest of God. Toronto: McClelland and Stewart, 1966. Reprint, New Canadian Library, no. 111 (Toronto: McClelland and Stewart, 1974), and Bantam-Seal Book (1977).

The Fire-Dwellers. Toronto: McClelland and Stewart, 1969. Reprint, New Canadian Library, no. 87 (Toronto: McClelland and Stewart, 1973), and Bantam-Seal Book (1978).

A Bird in the House. Toronto: McClelland and Stewart, 1970. Reprint, New Canadian Library, no. 96 (Toronto: McClelland and Stewart, 1974), and Bantam-Seal Book (1978).

The Diviners. Toronto: McClelland and Stewart, 1974. Reprint, Bantam-Seal Book (Toronto: McClelland and Stewart, 1979).

Alice Munro

In the 1970s all areas of Canadian writing were stimulated by a renaissance of interest in literature and culture, but probably the greatest amount of attention in this decade was focused on Canada's women writers, a conjunction of feminist literary interest and the intriguing fact that a disproportionately large number of Canada's best writers have from the outset been women. Such accomplished writers as Dorothy Livesay, Margaret Laurence, and Gabrielle Roy have enjoyed a high profile. To their ranks have been added Margaret Atwood, who in both verse and fiction documents the contemporary power struggle between the sexes; Marian Engel, whose novel, *Bear*, probes the nature of female sexuality, and Jane Rule, who describes relationships between women with insight and sensitivity.

But from among the many women writers who were published and enjoyed critical success in the 1970s, Alice Munro has emerged as the most accomplished artist. Her reputation as one of Canada's best writers was not easily achieved. She was born Alice Laidlaw in 1931 and brought up near Wingham, Ontario, a rural community not far from Lake Huron. Her childhood was spent on an impoverished farm, where her father raised silver foxes and her mother fought a losing battle with Parkinson's Disease. She attended the University of Western Ontario for two years, then married and moved with her husband to British Columbia, where the latter worked first for the T. Eaton Company in Vancouver, then later opened a successful bookstore in Victoria. She had begun writing and publishing short stories at the university, but while she raised a family of three daughters, her work progressed very slowly, stories appearing occasionally in *Canadian Forum*, *Chatelaine*, and the *Tamarack Review*. She drew very little public attention, and even when her first collection of

stories, *Dance of the Happy Shades* (1968), won the Governor General's Award, she remained an obscure figure in the Canadian literary scene. However, when her second book, *Lives of Girls and Women*, was published in 1971, the literary climate had changed, and although she had been publishing fiction for nearly twenty years, Alice Munro was hailed an important new talent. Another collection of stories, *Something I've Been Meaning to Tell You*, appeared in 1974, and a series of connected stories titled *Who Do You Think You Are?* was published in 1978, winning the author another Governor General's Award. A second marriage took Alice Munro back to southwestern Ontario, to write and publish in such prestigious and fashionable magazines as the *New Yorker, Ms.*, and *Redbook*.

One reason for the slow recognition of Alice Munro's work is that she is essentially a short story writer. Although *Lives of Girls and Women* was published as a novel, it was first written and submitted to McGraw-Hill Ryerson as a series of stories which the author later revised in the form of a *Bildungsroman*, a loosely patterned autobiographical novel. *Who Do You Think You Are?* has a similar structure. Alice Munro does not find large narrative structures congenial to her talent; she is the master rather of the compressed tale, the meditation, the brief but penetrating *aperçu*.

But what is most remarkable about Alice Munro's fiction is her style; in her prose the sentences are painstakingly crafted, their effects carefully weighed and balanced. Her writing has been compared to magic realist painting, for she has an extraordinary eye for surface detail, for colors, shapes, textures. She has admitted a particular fondness for the work of American painter Edward Hopper,[1] and in the following paragraph from "Walker Brothers Cowboy" there is a similar accumulation of concrete detail that evokes a specific time and place:

My father and I walk gradually down a long, shabby sort of street, with Silverwoods Ice Cream signs standing on the sidewalk, outside tiny, lighted stores. This is in Tuppertown, an old town on Lake Huron, an

---

[1] See *Eleven Canadian Novelists*, interviewed by Graeme Gibson (Toronto: Anansi Press, 1973), p. 256; and John Metcalf's "A Conversation with Alice Munro," *Journal of Canadian Fiction* 1, no. 4 (Fall 1972), p. 57.

old grain port. The street is shaded, in some places, by maple trees whose roots have cracked and heaved the sidewalk and spread out like crocodiles into the bare yards. People are sitting out, men in shirt-sleeves and undershirts and women in aprons—not people we know but if anybody looks ready to nod and say, "Warm night," my father will nod too and say something the same.[2]

Frequently the narrator in Munro's fiction is a young girl who carefully observes life, not making judgments but noting all the peculiarities in the world around her. That world is authenticated by the small textures, the descriptions of setting, matters of dress, standards of conduct, mannerisms of speech, assumptions, and attitudes which specifically characterized the small Ontario town in the 1940s. There is a documentary quality to the best of Munro's fiction.

Alice Munro's short stories can be divided roughly according to setting, Ontario or British Columbia. Generally the British Columbia stories are not as good as those set in Ontario, where the author's imagination is most firmly rooted. The British Columbia stories are largely satires on contemporary life, particularly those ludicrous aspects of the counterculture in the late 1960s and early 1970s. One thinks here of "Memorial," a funny and sad look at a desperately hip middle-aged couple living in fashionable West Vancouver who, armed with Gestalt, Yoga, and Transcendental Meditation, scarcely experience the death of their eldest son. Some of the British Columbia stories probe intimately into the relationship of a man and wife who have become estranged from each other. In stories like "Material," "Tell Me Yes or No," and especially "The Spanish Lady" a woman reflects on a marriage that has failed, and it is as if in her thoughts she is really communicating with this man for the first time.

"The Spanish Lady" is an excellent example of Munro's superb craftsmanship. Structurally her stories belong to the modernist tradition of storytelling, where seemingly unconnected pieces of narration are juxtaposed in such a way that a new meaning or powerful emotion is evoked. The narrator of this story is returning by train to the west coast and to a marriage that has

[2] *Dance of the Happy Shades* (Toronto: McGraw-Hill Ryerson, 1968), p. 1.

failed. She reflects on her husband's infidelity with a young schoolteacher, a family friend, and relives some of the painful emotions of discovery and betrayal. On the train she is approached by a Rosicrucian who claims that he knew her in another life, that she had been a Spanish lady. When she gets off the train in the half-deserted station at Vancouver, an old man who had been sitting on a bench lets out a cry, staggers, and falls dead on the floor. The onlookers conclude he has died from a heart attack. The narrator's unhappiness is suddenly placed in another context, that of life's brevity. Similarly, the vignette of the Spanish lady loses its romantic quality and becomes a stark image of time and human mortality. The narrator, however, concludes the story by saying she does not understand entirely what it means:

By that cry Hugh, and Margaret, and the Rosicrucian, and I, everybody alive, is pushed back. What we say and feel no longer rings true, it is slightly beside the point. As if we were all wound up a long time ago and were spinning out of control, whirring, making noises, but at a touch could stop, and see each other for the first time, harmless and still. This is a message; I really believe it is; but I don't see how I can deliver it. [3]

The Ontario stories turn back to the country of the author's childhood. Some bring to mind the Southern writers Munro admires, writers like Faulkner, Flannery O'Connor, and Eudora Welty. [4] The narration in these stories reflects the collective viewpoint of the townspeople as they gossip about and mull over in their minds events that have taken place in their part of the country. "Something I've Been Meaning to Tell You" is a particularly good example of this kind of story. We are given fourteen loosely connected scenes from the life of two sisters which we must fit together like the pieces of a puzzle. The one sister, Char, is an aloof, attractive, but incurably romantic woman who has been in love all her life with the town's most dashing and celebrated man, Blaikie Noble. The latter, however, has married and lived away

[3] *Something I've Been Meaning to Tell You* (New York: Signet, 1975), p. 153. All references are to this text.

[4] Metcalf, "A Conversation with Alice Munro," p. 56, and Gibson, *Eleven Canadian Novelists*, p. 248. See also J. R. (Tim) Struthers, "Alice Munro and the American South," in *The Canadian Novel Here and Now*, ed. John Moss (Toronto: N C Press, 1978), pp. 21–33.

from the town for many years, and Char has settled for marriage with an invalid high school teacher. The other sister, Et, has contented herself with the role of old maid and town dressmaker, sharing closely the life of her sister and brother-in-law. But when Blaikie comes back to town a widower, Et decides to change the situation that has existed for so many years. Although the story is light-hearted and entertaining there is a matter-of-factly sinister tone throughout as the bizarre and sometimes grisly accidents of fate that shape human lives are recounted. The story has a Gothic quality, with its decaying mansion, memories of finer days in the town's now dilapidated hotel, rat poison, and mysterious death. "The Time of Death," the story of a nine-year-old country-western singer who scalds her little brother to death, is another story of this kind. It has a more serious purpose, however, for the focus falls on the poverty of the country people and the harshness of the landscape as a way of explaining the grotesque and pathetic events of the story.

In most of her Ontario stories Alice Munro mines her own past, especially adolescence with its disquieting memories of inarticulate, aborted relationships and personal failures. "An Ounce of Cure" tells the story of a teen-age girl who gets drunk while baby-sitting in order to escape the unhappiness of an unrequited love. The memorable moment in this story is not the confrontation between the drunken girl and the couple who employed her for the evening, but the girl's sense of despair sitting in this couple's modern living room, looking out the picture window at the trees tossing in the early winds of spring and feeling that she will never experience happiness. The story "Red Dress—1946" (the title suggests a realist painting) recounts a girl's fears of rejection and failure when she attends a high school dance. The most powerful moment in this story comes at the very end when the girl returns home and through the kitchen window sees her mother sitting up with a cup of tea waiting to hear of her daughter's success at the dance. The girl's precarious struggle for happiness is burdened further by this realization that her mother is seeking compensation for a broken life through her daughter's happiness. Munro makes this statement most effectively through the details of her story—the too frilly red dress that the mother labors so hard to sew in contrast to the faded paisley kimono she wears herself, as she waits for her daughter's return.

These are the carefully observed details which give such authenticity to Munro's masterpiece, *Lives of Girls and Women*, the story of a girl growing up in rural Ontario. One of the reasons the book has enjoyed a well-deserved popularity is that it examines the process of growing up from a specifically female viewpoint. Del Jordan, the heroine, becomes aware at an early age of the socializing process whereby sex distinctions determine her relations to others. She is expected to help her mother in the house, instead of working with her brother and her father in the fox pens; she is expected to be gentle in her behavior, submissive to authority, and modest about her accomplishments. These stereotyped feminine traits are not inconsistent with Del's nature; the difficulty in being a young woman for Del arises over the matter of intelligence. Society honors and respects a boy who shows intellectual promise, but a bright girl is considered suspect. The matter becomes a crisis of identity when she reads a magazine article by a New York psychiatrist who discusses male and female habits of thought:

He said that the differences between the male and female modes of thought were easily illustrated by the thoughts of a boy and girl, sitting on a park bench, looking at the full moon. The boy thinks of the universe, its immensity and mystery; the girl thinks, "I must wash my hair." When I read this I was frantically upset; I had to put the magazine down. It was clear to me at once that I was not thinking as the girl thought; the full moon would never as long as I lived remind me to wash my hair.[5]

She sees another article, "Is Your Problem That You're Trying to Be a Boy?," but asserts that "it had never occurred to me to want to be a boy." The question of sexual identity is not resolved in the course of the novel, but Del's mother, a woman with rudimentary feminist ideals, prophesies that life will some day be very different for women:

There is a change coming I think in the lives of girls and women. Yes. But it is up to us to make it come. All women have had up till now has

[5] *Lives of Girls and Women* (New York: Signet, 1974), p. 150. All references are to this text.

been their connection with men. All we have had. No more lives of our own, really, than domestic animals. [pp. 146–47]

She says that her daughter will want to have children, but warns her that in marriage a woman always gets "the burden." The important thing is for a woman to use her brains, to achieve self-respect. But Del's mother is an eccentric, unpredictable woman, so in the course of the novel Del only listens to her words, does not take them to heart.

The whole novel is structured around a series of dilemmas for the young girl to resolve, dilemmas which chart her growing awareness and initiation into life. That evanescent feeling of a child's happy, uncomplicated existence is captured in a brief opening section, "The Flats Road," which describes the comical, short-lived marriage of the hired hand, Benny. Del enjoys describing the bizarre events that take place on their country road and is not yet embarrassed to accompany her strange mother into town on a shopping expedition. But that mood of childish pleasure in observing with impunity the curious but familiar adult world gives way in section 2, "Heirs of the Living Body," to the terror of participating for the first time in a frightening ritual—a family death. The event is profoundly disturbing to the young girl not only because it raises for the first time the problem of human mortality but also because it forces the girl to choose between two opposing views of life.

One of the fundamental conflicts in the novel is between the two sides of Del's family. Her mother is an eccentric, skeptical woman; hers is a world of endless, unfinished housework, schemes for self-improvement, and lonely philanthropic causes. The members of Del's father's family, in contrast, lead meticulously organized lives; all their attention is on the smooth conduct of their practical affairs. In the first part of "Heirs of the Living Body" Del spends a summer vacation with her father's family, where she observes her Uncle Craig writing a carefully ordered history of the family and another of Wawanash County, where they live. His manuscripts are full of endless factual details (births, deaths, fires, weather reports), all sorted and arranged for inclusion in the book. Del's two great aunts bring the same order to their domestic tasks, completing weekly marathons of scrubbing, hoeing, washing, ironing, baking. There is an intricate formality as well to their social relations; they are polite and deferential in company, all the while lacing their conversation with ironies and sly mockeries. Del's mother, on the other hand, is offensively direct with her opinions, devoid of tact or politeness. There are some brittle comic scenes when the two sides of the family are together:

In my mother's house [my aunts] turned sulky, sly, elderly, eager to take offense. Out of my mother's hearing they were apt to say to me, "Is that the hairbrush you use on your hair? Oh, we thought it was for the dog!" Or, "Is that what you dry your dishes with?" They would bend over the pans, scraping, scraping off every last bit of black that had accumulated since the last time they visited here. [p. 30]

When Aunt Elspeth plays "Road to the Isles" by ear on the piano, Del's mother offers to teach her to read music. "Then you can play really good things," she says. Aunt Elspeth refuses, "with a delicate, unnatural laugh, as if somebody had offered to teach her to play pool."

The divergent family values result in a traumatic confusion for Del when her Uncle Craig suddenly dies. Her mother takes a positive view of death, arguing like a transcendentalist philosopher that a man is part of nature and that when he dies he simply changes form, the composite elements of the body going back to nature to become birds and animals and flowers. She extends her view in the light of an article she has read titled "Heirs of the Living Body," which argues that in the future human parts will be reused and there will no longer be death in the old sense. The aunts do not speculate on the philosophical implications of death, but spend great energy preparing food for the funeral, making sure all the arrangements have been correctly made for this social occasion. Similarly, the townspeople discuss such practical matters as getting the casket through the front door. Neither approach deals with the emotion of grief or the disappearance of Uncle Craig's personality. Neither view placates Del's fear of death, and at the funeral, when her cousin Mary Agnes tries to force her to view the body, she becomes hysterical and bites the girl's arm. She is put in Uncle Craig's office as a punishment and there has a horrific vision of life as a sea of confusion, obscenities, and humiliations of the flesh. This vision of chaos is the reverse of the mystic's vision of order and light, but it represents a direct confrontation with death denied by both the mother's and the aunt's views and allows Del to get through the funeral service. Del does not resolve the question of death, but she is able to survive her first experience of it and takes her place when the mourners file past the casket for a "last look." This section of the novel reminds the reader of James Agee's *A Death in the Family*.

There is much artistry in "Heirs of the Living Body." The death theme is anticipated from the outset by images of time and bodily corruption: for example, there is Uncle Craig with his old photographs of the family, including the picture of himself as a handsome adolescent stretched out on a rug in contrast to the stout old man Del sees, with his square sagging face and blind eye. There is also Del's cousin Mary Agnes, who was "deprived of oxygen in the birth canal," a strange girl with glasses and dusty-looking skin who was once stripped naked by a group of boys and left lying in the mud in the fairgrounds. Mary Agnes takes Del for a walk along the river, where they find a dead cow. Del's instinctive fear of death is expressed in her desire to desecrate the carcass, whereas Mary Agnes calmly touches the eye of the dead animal, thereby associating herself in Del's mind with the physical body, its helplessness and its corruption.

Much of the artistry in this section also stems from its richly comic effects in capturing the attitudes of country people, their ideas and behavior. At the funeral the aunts are overwhelmed, not by their brother's death, but by the size of the crowd at the service. One woman warns the sisters not to "risk" their best china, another is delighted to find with the tea things watermelon-rind pickle, "Uncle Craig's favorite." Even the ills of the physical body are rendered at times with high comic effect in this chapter of the novel. There is the description of Mary Agnes's mother, Aunt Moira, whose husband held her legs together on the way to the hospital to give birth so that she would not hemorrhage:

Perhaps because of this story it seemed to me that the gloom spreading out from Aunt Moira had a gynecological odor, like that of the fuzzy, rubberized bandages on her legs. She was a woman I would recognize now as a likely sufferer from varicose veins, hemorrhoids, a dropped womb, cysted ovaries, inflammations, discharges, lumps and stones in various places, one of those heavy, cautiously moving, wrecked survivors of the female life, with stories to tell. [p. 34]

There is in all of Munro's writing a fascination with the grisly and the bizarre. In *Lives of Girls and Women* there is a whole gallery of grotesque characters that make up the town of Jubilee: Bella Phippen, the librarian, lame in one leg from polio and "deaf as a stone," her dentist brother, a known child molester, the schoolteacher Miss Farris who throws herself into the Wawanash River, and the Sherriffs, one of the town's oldest families, who number an alcoholic son, a suicidal daughter, and another son who spends much of his time at the local asylum. The comedy arises when these grisly details are played off against the strict conventions of a middle-class puritan town. It becomes the comedy of gossip and outraged proprieties. A good example is Aunt Moira's account of her life in nearby Porterfield, where there are two beer parlors on the main street:

From behind her darkened front windows she had watched men hooting like savages, had seen a car spin sideways and crash into a telephone pole, crushing the steering wheel into the driver's heart; she had seen two men dragging a girl who was drunk and couldn't stand up, and the girl was urinating on the street, in her clothes. She had scraped drunks' vomit off her painted fence. All this was no more than she expected. [p. 34]

Munro enriches these accounts by using the idiom of the country; for example, when we are told that the drunks were "hooting like savages," the author conveys to us the outrage and delight of the observers of the scene. "Heirs of the Living Body," perhaps more than any other section of the book, best fills the function of regionalist fiction in preserving a way of life that must finally disappear.

All the remaining sections of the novel are structured in a similar way: two very different views of life are juxtaposed, and Del struggles to separate illusion from reality.[6] In the third sec-

---

[6] In a slightly different vein, Helen Hoy, in "'Dull, Simple, Amazing, and Unfathomable': Paradox and Double Vision in Alice Munro's Fiction," *Studies in Canadian Literature* 5 (Spring 1980): 100–115, argues that for Munro reality is both prosaic and marvelous, that taking one view by itself leads to illusions about life.

tion, "Princess Ida," Del's mother tells the story of her unhappy childhood, a bleak story of rural poverty, a fat, sadistic brother, a mother who was a religious fanatic, spending all her money on Bibles. But a visit from Del's uncle presents this childhood in a very different light. The uncle is not a cruel fat person, but a generous, kind-hearted American who remembers his mother as a saintly woman who died while still very young. His memory of the mother focuses specifically on a butterfly that emerges from its cocoon in the house on Easter Sunday. Del's mother's negative memories are countered throughout this section with images of rebirth: the butterfly, Easter Sunday, the flooding of the Wawanash River connected with the mention of Egyptian gods and the uncle's wife who is curiously named Nile. Del also has a strongly negative view of her mother, but implicit in this section is the birth of understanding: "I myself was not so different from my mother, but I concealed it, knowing what dangers there were" (p. 68).

In "Age of Faith" Del struggles with the conflict between her mother's atheism and her own instinct for some kind of religious faith. In "Changes and Ceremonies" there is romance when the school puts on an operetta and Del falls in love with Frank Wales, the boy who sings the lead, but these feelings must be readjusted when the teacher who stages the operetta commits suicide without explanation and Frank Wales proves a very ordinary youth, becoming a delivery boy for the local dry cleaners instead of going on to high school. In "Lives of Girls and Women" Del's adolescent dreams of romantic love must again be readjusted to accommodate the physical realities and psychological perversities of sex. She daydreams of a passionate romance with the local radio announcer, Mr. Chamberlain, but when he takes her out for a drive in the country, he proves to be an exhibitionist whose only desire is to masturbate in front of the girl.

In "Baptizing" Del has reached the point where she must decide what kind of life she will have, what role, what occupation. Because she does well at school, her first choice is a university education, possible if she can win a scholarship. She shares this aspiration with Jerry Storey, the bright boy in her class, although she feels no romantic or physical attraction to him. Then suddenly Del is caught up in the opposite life. At a religious revival meeting she meets Garnet French, a worker in a lumber yard, and enters an intensely passionate physical relationship with him, with the prospect of becoming his wife and living the rest of her life in Jubilee. The real impact of this choice comes when they are swimming in the river and Garnet asks her to be baptized in his church. When she refuses, he tries to force her assent by holding her under the water. Abruptly she realizes that her whole person is being submerged, suffocated by this relationship, and she finds herself "fighting for my life." She realizes that her love affair with Garnet has been largely an illusion, playing a role. In the meantime she has failed to win a scholarship, so at the end of this section she has abandoned the roles of both scholar and lover.

Del's education ends here; her future, or real life, as she puts it, remains undecided. In an epilogue the question of illusion and reality and role playing is focused in the question of art in relation to life. Del conceives in her mind a Gothic novel set in Jubilee concerning the members of the Sherriff family and all their tragedies. A significant figure in her novel is an evil-looking photographer who takes pictures which are frightening because they somehow make people look older and reveal hidden things in their personalities. Here Alice Munro has created a metaphor for her own kind of art—a documentary realism which reveals something of the mystery of existence. Del visits the one surviving member of the Sherriff family, the son Bobby who spends much of his time at the asylum. She is surprised by the ordinariness of the house and the man as they share a piece of cake. But before she leaves, he stands on his toes for a moment like a dancer and smiles knowingly at the girl. This little gesture amidst all the ordinariness of life becomes a key to the future artist's vision, best expressed when she writes, "People's lives, in Jubilee as elsewhere, were dull, simple, amazing and unfathomable—deep caves paved with kitchen linoleum" (p. 210).

Who Do You Think You Are? is also an autobiographical novel. The focus here falls, not on a girl growing up, although that is part of the narrative, but on a woman's married life, her love affairs, divorce, and career. Munro's vision of human experience here is much darker, more sordid, tempered perhaps by the disaffections of middle age. Much of this book concerns the heroine as a married woman living in British Columbia. Although Munro is an astute observer of human behavior, her descriptions of life in British Columbia do not have the same depth or resonance as her fiction set in Ontario. But there is also a weakness in the early Ontario section of the book where the heroine's mother dies and she is raised from infancy by a stepmother. Munro's fiction depends so heavily on a quasi-documentary transcription of reality that the heroine's childhood with a stepmother seems contrived, lacking in the emotional exactness that characterizes the best of Munro's work. Alice Munro's father did eventually remarry after his wife's death, when the author was herself a grown woman, and it is those later scenes in *Who Do You Think You Are?* when the heroine returns to Ontario which are artistically the most authentic and effective.

The most powerful subject in Alice Munro's fiction is her mother. This figure, who is central in several short stories and in *Lives of Girls and Women*, is a source of tremendous guilt and confusion for Munro's narrator. Bizarre, unpredictable, outrageous, yet pathetic, the mother brings shame and anxiety to the young girl growing up in a conformity-minded community. Her aggressive, virginal nature is at the crux of "Walker Brothers Cowboy," a story about the narrator's genial father, a man loved and appreciated by the other women in the district. The mother appears in her most favorable light in *Lives of Girls and Women*, where she is seen as the victim of a rural, male-dominated society. In Jubilee she plays the role of the feminist writing letters to the paper signed, "Princess Ida," a reference to Tennyson's poem "The Princess" in which the royal heroine founds a college for the education and emancipation of women. She wants Del to have a university education and makes the prophetic speech about the status of women in society someday changing. But this woman is at the same time intellectually limited, emotionally unstable, and when she becomes ill, she becomes hostile towards others, paranoid, and self-pitying. An early story, "The Peace of Utrecht," deals with the mother's long illness and death. The narrator, a grown woman with two children, returns home to Ontario after the funeral and hears from her sister and elderly aunts about her mother's last illness, her endless demands for attention, her theatrical escape from the hospital in winter wearing only bathrobe and slippers. The narrator's revulsion and guilt are brought out sharply when one of the aunts tries to give her the mother's clothes that have been carefully patched and mended for further use.

In *Something I've Been Meaning to Tell You* there are two stories about the mother and others in the family in which the author lets fall the mask of storyteller and questions the authenticity of what she is writing and its capacity to exorcise her guilty feelings. "Winter Wind" describes the girl's prolonged stay in town with her very correct paternal grandmother and aunt during a winter blizzard. As in "Heirs of the Living Body" there is the disturbing contrast and antagonism between her father's family and her unconventional mother. There is order and calm at her grandmother's house, and for a time the girl enjoys its comforts— good food, ironed sheets, jasmine soap—so unlike home, where there are always washing and ironing to be done, dishes to be scrubbed, clothes that need mending. But eventually she feels stifled by the meticulous order and the intricate courtesies at her grandmother's: "I would give it all up for the moment in order to drop my coat where I chose, leave the room without having to say where I was going, read with my feet in the oven, if I like." She reflects on the details of her grandmother's life (her tomboyish appearance in an old photograph, the story of her jilted lover) and realizes perhaps why her grandmother feels hostile towards her mother, curiously threatened by her—because the latter has never repressed her feelings, never made herself live according to society's standards. But then the narrator asks herself how much can she ever know about the emotions of others:

I think as I put this down, how am I to know what I claim to know? I have used these people before. I have tricked them out and altered them and shaped them any way at all to suit my purposes. I am not doing that now, I am being as careful as I can, but I stop and wonder, I feel compunction. [p. 161]

The terrible confusion the narrator feels about her family, especially her mother, is most poignantly rendered in "The Ottawa Valley," the memory of a visit she and her mother make to the latter's relatives and childhood home in the Ottawa Valley. The mother enjoys visiting with her cousins and her brother and his family, telling old jokes and reliving some of the good times they once had together. But the first stages of her palsy are in evidence, and the narrator is frightened by the prospect of having to look after an invalid mother some day. Looking back on this time of her life, the narrator is made remorseful when she recalls how her mother sacrificed a safety pin to hold together her underwear and in so doing had to walk into the local church with her own slip showing. The scene takes place in the graveyard outside the church and quietly foreshadows the mother's death. The narrator concludes the story by once again speaking directly to the reader about the failure of art to clarify or set right the past that haunts her:

The problem, the only problem, is my mother. And she is the one of course I am trying to get; it is to reach her that this whole journey has been undertaken. With what purpose? To mark her off, to describe, to illumine, to celebrate, to get *rid* of, her; and it did not work. . . . I could go on, and on, applying what skills I have, using what tricks I know, and it would always be the same. [p. 197]

The mother has the haunting, tragic dimensions of the mother figure in Faulkner's novels and in the plays of Eugene O'Neill and Tennessee Williams. These two stories, which probe the emotional wellsprings of the author's imagination, represent the essence of Alice Munro's art.

Selected Writings

Dance of the Happy Shades. Toronto: Ryerson, 1968. Reprint, with a foreword by Hugh Garner (Toronto: McGraw-Hill Ryerson, 1973).

Lives of Girls and Women. Toronto: McGraw-Hill Ryerson, 1971. Reprint, Signet Book (New York: New American Library, 1974).

Something I've Been Meaning to Tell You. Toronto: McGraw-Hill Ryerson, 1974. Reprint, Signet Book (New York: New American Library, 1975).

Who Do You Think You Are? Toronto: Macmillan, 1978. Reprint, Signet Book (New York: New American Library, 1979).

The Moons of Jupiter. Toronto: Macmillan, 1982.

Conclusion

The reader may be surprised that this study of Canadian literature concludes with an essentially old-fashioned writer. Munro's
themes are the ego-centered, familiar ones of initiation and romantic love, her techniques those of pre–World War II realists
such as Eudora Welty, James Agee, Frank O'Connor. Where, it
might be asked, are the more experimental writers, the avant-
garde? Such writers appeared later in Canada than in the United
States and to date have received little critical or popular recognition. The reason for this is partly nationalistic, because experimental writers have found their models and sources of inspiration
outside the country. In fiction, for example, Robert Kroetsch has
followed the way of John Barth and Thomas Pynchon and written
novels which are intellectual and self-reflexive in the postmodern
manner. Kroetsch writes about vital but sexually troubled young
men whose quest for self-knowledge and creativity are bound
up with the complexities of storytelling. Kroetsch, an Albertan,
moved into this mode of fiction when he began work as an English professor at the State University of New York, Binghamton.

Canadian poetry since the 1960s has been dominated by two
sharply diverging movements. In Vancouver there appeared a
group of young writers including Frank Davey, George Bowering,
Fred Wah, and Lionel Kearns, who were sympathetic to the poets
associated with North Carolina's Black Mountain College. For a
few years they published a poetry newsletter, *Tish*, whose ana-
grammatical title flaunted their playful contempt for the traditional conventions of both poetry and polite society. These poets
have been seriously concerned with the idea of the poem as a unit
of energy wherein form and content simultaneously determine
each other. They are also concerned in their work to find a speaking voice that will establish, without the distortion of rhyme,

meter, alliteration, and so forth, their relationship to the particularities of the concrete world around them. These poets were greatly encouraged by two American writers living in Vancouver, Warren Tallman and Robin Blaser. The center of avant-garde poetry has shifted from Vancouver to Toronto and the Coach House Press; the latter has published such United States writers as Robert Creeley and Allen Ginsberg as well as experimental Canadians including Victor Coleman and sound poet B. P. Nichol.

The other strong current in Canadian poetry grew out of a resurgent Canadian nationalism, which was frequently articulated as a despair over Canada's subservience to United States culture and technology. The center of the movement was the House of Anansi Press, founded in Toronto in 1967 and home for patriotic voices such as Margaret Atwood, Dennis Lee, and Dave Godfrey. As a poet, Atwood has expressed her nationalism obliquely in *The Journals of Susanna Moodie* (1970) and *Power Politics* (1971), two collections in which the female narrator, like the spirit of the country, is being victimized by forces beyond her control—the wilderness in the first book, male sexism in the second. The most sustained voice for a political renaissance in Canada is that of Dennis Lee, whose *Civil Elegies*, first published in 1967 and revised in 1972, is a central document in the nationalism of the period. In this sequence of poems Lee focuses on the failure of the country's white inhabitants to establish an intimate relationship with the land itself and the nation's ensuing lack of moral purpose. The narrator of the poems is a powerless figure despairing over the void around him, what Lee calls "the kingdom of absence." He cites Canada's failure to protest the American war in Vietnam and the pollution of the continental environment as symptoms of the national malaise.

In fiction Margaret Atwood's *Surfacing* takes a similar stance. The heroine of the novel is on a search for her father, who is missing in the wilderness of northern Quebec. As time passes, she becomes increasingly alienated from her companions, who remain very much tourists restless to leave. The search for the missing parent in the book is an allegorical quest for Canadian identity to be found in the landscape itself, and those who are not committed to that search are labeled "Americans." The main thrust of Canadian writing in the sixties and seventies, then, as articulated in a sustained dialogue among its authors, was the quest for new forms of expression against the demand for nationalist content.

In giving an account of Canadian literature there is the related matter of whether to include writers who were born and grew up outside Canada, writers whose residence and work have nonetheless associated them with the country. This phenomenon is sometimes referred to as literature in Canada as distinct from Canadian literature. The most obvious instance is that of Malcolm Lowry, who lived sporadically in British Columbia between 1939 and 1954 and wrote *Under the Volcano* (1947) there. In the mind of the novel's drunken protagonist, Geoffrey Firmin, there are references to British Columbia, but the book is set in Mexico, and the protagonist's inferno of self-exorcism is inseparably bound up with the heat and dryness of that setting. Lowry, however, did write some fiction set exclusively in British Columbia, including an unfinished novel, *October Ferry to Gabriola*, published posthumously in 1970. His most artistically polished piece of writing with a Canadian setting is "The Forest Path to the Spring," published in the posthumous collection of stories and sketches *Hear Us O Lord from Heaven Thy Dwelling Place* (1961). "Forest Path" is a purely descriptive account of a familiar walk through the rain forest near the writer's cabin, but like Grove's rides it becomes, as W. H. New has suggested, "a celebration of life and man's relationship with natural life cycles."[1] Lowry, born in England, never took out Canadian citizenship.

Citizenship, on the other hand, rather than extended residency has been central to Brian Moore's association with Canadian literature. Born in Belfast, Moore emigrated to Canada in 1948 when he was twenty-seven years old, lived for a few years in Montreal, then left for the United States. His chief contribution to Canadian literature is *The Luck of Ginger Coffey* (1960), a novel about a self-deluding Irishman who has come to Montreal but cannot find a job which is commensurate with his romantic

---

[1] W. H. New, "Fiction," in *Literary History of Canada* (Toronto: University of Toronto Press, 1976), 3:275.

dream of success in the New World. Moore looks at Canadian urban life with the fresh and sharply focused eyes of an outsider.

In the 1960s the number of writers in Canada was greatly augmented by the immigration of many poets and novelists from England and the United States. Most of these writers associated themselves with Canadian universities, as students or lecturers. This move to Canada repeated an old pattern of immigration: the British came, tentatively, seeking better economic opportunities while retaining their cultural ties to Britain; Americans came seeking a political haven in protest to their country's Southeast Asia policies. For some of these writers such as Joyce Carol Oates, living in Canada has almost no significance to their work in either setting or point of view. For others such as Jane Rule or Audrey Thomas, Canadian experience has gradually become central to their vision of life, although in cultural identity it is probably significant that Rule's best fiction, the title story in *Theme for Diverse Instruments* (1975), and Thomas's most widely applauded book, *Songs My Mother Taught Me* (1973), are both concerned with life in America. Although he was born in the United States and did not come to Canada to teach until he was in his late twenties, Clark Blaise can claim affiliation with the country through his parents, who were French and English Canadians. In *A North American Education* (1973) Blaise explores the dilemma of cultural identity; the young hero in these stories lives in various parts of the United States as a child and eventually moves to Montreal to work as a college teacher, but in none of these places does he feel at home. British writers must similarly come to terms with their sense of displacement. The narrator of David Watmough's *No More into the Garden* (1978) lives a good life as a teacher and writer in Vancouver, but is always haunted, as the book's title suggests, by a sense of exile from his native Cornwall. Similarly, the fictions of John Metcalf and John Mills, though often set in the Canadian academic world these authors know well and satirize with anarchic humor, are informed by memories of growing up in England, which remains a final frame of reference for their work. These writers, however, all make a significant contribution to the mosaic of Canadian literature.

The slow acceptance of experimental and immigrant writing

into the mainstream of Canadian literature goes deeper than the nationalist cause. Literatures, like civilizations, evolve through different stages in relation to the experiences of a people in a particular place and social context. While Canadians share a continent and many aspects of life with the United States, the country and its literature have developed more slowly. Canadian writers such as Laurence, Munro, Purdy, and Atwood in the early 1980s were still engaged in giving a realistic account of growing up and living in Canada, the kind of national literary task that was more or less completed in the United States by the 1930s when Cather's picture of the Midwest, Faulkner's of the South, and Steinbeck's of California were added to the long familiar ones of life in New England and New York. Many of Canada's writers are still engaged in creating a literary map of the country, revealing in imaginative language what Canada looks like, what it means to grow up in and be part of a specific region. While this remains a central concern in Canadian literature, interest in the work of writers whose inspiration comes from outside the country will lag behind. The best of this work will eventually come to have its place in the tradition of Canadian literature, just as the writings of women, blacks, and other minority groups have found a significant place in the once white, male-dominated tradition of literature of the United States.

Canadian literature in fact will never be homogenous, for it is a literature written in two different languages, although in the literatures of English Canada and Quebec there are parallel thematic concerns with the wilderness, colonialism (English Canada's dominion over Quebec) and repressive religion—Calvinism and Jansenism, respectively. A comprehensive account of French-Canadian writing until roughly 1955 can be found in George Tougas's *History of French-Canadian Literature* (translated by Alta Lind Cook [Toronto: Ryerson Press, 1966]). A simplified history focusing on the novel is Jeannette Urbas's *From Thirty Acres to Modern Times: The Story of French-Canadian Literature* (Toronto: McGraw-Hill Ryerson, 1976). No native Indian or Inuit writer has yet shaped the materials of his cultural traditions into a significant body of artistic works. Indian writers (Pauline Johnson remains the best known) have invariably adapted their materials to the white sensibility to achieve acceptance and popularity and have tempered their cultural authenticity. Pauline Johnson's poems and legends are sadly the work of a colorful but sentimental Victorian, not the writings of a Mohawk singer. Several collections of Indian stories have been published; but as an oral narrative tradition transformed into a written European language, even the best compositions of Canada's native peoples involve complex problems of sources and translation. There is no introduction or guide yet to the collections of Indian myths and legends that includes all the regions of the country.

Canadian literature has developed slowly because of the country's harsh and extended pioneer conditions, its small population, and particularly because of its long-standing colonial status. The situation in the nineteenth century is well put by the Reverend E. H. Dewart, one of the first anthologizers of Canadian writing:

There is probably no country in the world, making equal pretensions to intelligence and progress, where the claims of native literature are so little felt. . . . Our mental wants are supplied by the brain of the Mother country, under circumstances that utterly preclude competition. . . . Book-sellers, too, because they make sure sales and large profits on British and American works, which have already obtained popularity, seldom take the trouble to judge of a Canadian book on its merits, or use their efforts to promote its sale.[2]

The problem for Canadian authors was not simply a matter of small markets and lack of promotion but also the state of copyright laws. An American publisher could reprint any book published in Canada without compensation to the author or original publisher. At the same time, the small Canadian market was flooded with cheap pirated editions of British books published in the United States. The Imperial Copyright Act of 1842 forbade the reprinting of British books in the colonies, but allowed American imports so that a profitable publishing industry in Canada was almost impossible in the nineteenth century.[3]

[2] E. H. Dewart, introduction to *Selections from Canadian Poets* (Montreal: Lovell, 1864), pp. ix–ixx.

[3] See H. Pearson Gundy, "Literary Publishing," in *Literary History of Canada* (Toronto: University of Toronto Press, 1976), 1:188–202.

The Imperial Copyright Act of 1842 was finally superseded by a 1911 act which enabled Canada to formulate its own copyright laws. Presses such as Copp, Clark, established in 1869, and Ryerson, established in 1829, which had been sustained by special functions (Ryerson was originally the Methodist Book and Publishing House), were now more able to compete and profit in the publishing of imaginative literature. McClelland and Stewart, which was to become the most important Canadian publishing house, was established in 1906. Canadian authors still felt the necessity of getting accepted in London or New York first, but the 1920s nonetheless saw a great expansion in Canadian publishing.

The first significant efforts to establish Canadian literature as a field for critical study also occurred in the twenties with the appearance of five histories, most notably Archibald MacMechan's *Headwaters of Canadian Literature* (1924) and Lionel Stevenson's *Appraisals of Canadian Literature* (1926), and the publishing of monographs such as Lorne Pierce's Makers of Canadian Literature series. Lorne Pierce, editor of the Ryerson Press for nearly forty years, deserves special mention in any overview of Canadian literary history for the prodigious output from his press of anthologies, poetry collections, monographs, pamphlets, and biographies, all of which are dedicated to the advancement of Canadian literature and culture. Pierce's work was romantic and nationalistic in spirit, but in spite of its excesses it laid the foundations for subsequent critical studies of Canadian writing.

A different attitude emerged in the thirties, which demanded that Canadian literature be judged by international standards. In poetry it found those standards in the modernist verse of T. S. Eliot and the later Yeats, whose works are characterized by classical and metaphysical ideals. This cosmopolitan critical spirit, first voiced in articles written by Douglas Bush, A. J. M. Smith, and F. R. Scott for the *Canadian Forum* in the late twenties, was firmly consolidated by 1943 with the publication that year of E. K. Brown's *On Canadian Poetry* and the first edition of Smith's anthology, *Book of Canadian Poetry*. Both Brown and Smith had become professors of English in distinguished American universities and wrote with great authority on the literature of their native country. Their views prevailed in the forties and fifties, although they were challenged by John Sutherland in the preface to his anthology, *Other Canadians* (1947). There he argued that Smith's cosmopolitanism was another form of colonialism wherein Canadian poetry was once again subjected to English standards. He argued for a North American rather than English orientation and for greater social realism.

In the sixties and seventies, study of Canadian literature has taken its direction from the thematic and mythopoetic criticism of Northrop Frye. His views on Canadian literature have been set forth in the annual surveys of Canadian poetry that he wrote for the *University of Toronto Quarterly*, in the conclusion to the *Literary History of Canada*, and in other essays and reviews gathered together in *The Bush Garden* (1971). Books inspired in part by Frye's critical tenets include D. G. Jones's *Butterfly on Rock* (1970), Margaret Atwood's *Survival* (1972), and John Moss's *Patterns of Isolation* (1974).

The seventies are likely to be viewed as a Golden Age for Canadian literature, for they were a period when creativity and critical enthusiasm reached their highest levels in the country's cultural history. The flourishing of literary activity was rooted in a period of relative affluence for the publishing industry and in the widespread demand in education for Canadian studies. With the prosperity of the late sixties, publishing houses began expanding their lists of fiction and poetry, taking risks with a large number of new authors. Small presses such as House of Anansi, Oberon, New Press, Borealis, and many others were founded with the assistance of government grants, furthering the chances of publication for the aspiring young writer. There were many aspirants, and some produced work of very high quality.

In part the literary bonanza of the seventies can be traced back to the vital stimulus provided to the Canadian publishing industry by the founding of the Canada Council in 1957. Government financial support allowed small Canadian publishers to survive in competition with the giant multinational corporations. From the small presses came some of the most important, seminal works of the decade: House of Anansi, for example, published Atwood's *Survival* and *Power Politics* and Frye's *The Bush Garden*; Coach House Press published the early books of poetry by Michael Ondaatje. In addition the Canada Council has sponsored the growth of Canadian literature through individual writer's grants and a writer-in-residence program at universities across the country.

The increased sophistication and self-awareness of large numbers of Canadians created a substantial interest in books about Canada. Interviews with the country's writers began to appear regularly in popular magazines, and the country's highest literary prize, the Governor General's Award, began to attract public interest. Informed reviews and opinions by William French and Ken Adachi in the Toronto newspapers and *Books in Canada*, a monthly magazine of articles and reviews, also did much to stimulate a general interest in the country's literature. But the core market for Canadian literature was centered in the universities and colleges where writers frequently read from their works and where nationalist feelings ran high. McClelland and Stewart responded by increasing the number of annual additions to their New Canadian Library, a series initiated in 1957 under the general editorship of Malcolm Ross to make Canadian writings available in paperback. Macmillan similarly expanded its Laurentian Library of Canadian paperbacks. A spate of monographs on individual authors issued from the presses, and several highly specialized studies were published to guide the reader through the newly discovered territory of Canadian literature. In addition to Atwood's *Survival* and the other studies influenced by Frye, there appeared books like Frank Davey's *From There to Here* (1974), a critical reference guide to the more experimental aspects of Canadian writing since 1960, and Robin Mathews's *Canadian Literature: Surrender or Revolution* (1978), a nationalistic and socialist view of literature in relation to politics. The high interest in Canadian literature in universities and colleges also created a scholarly demand for supplementary texts. The letters, memoirs, and minor works of writers like Lampman, Isabella Crawford, and Grove began to appear from university presses, with much competition among universities to acquire the papers of Canadian writers for their libraries. By the late 1970s a considerable apparatus was established for the study of Canadian literature.

With recessionary economics in the early eighties, the publishing industry in Canada has been hard pressed to become self-supporting. Government grants have been reduced, and some of the small presses have ceased operations. Large houses have been affected by the recession as well. Macmillan of Canada has been sold to Gage, primarily a textbook company. McClelland and Stewart has been issuing their best-selling authors, such as Laurence, Richler, and Atwood, in a joint American-Canadian paperback series, Bantam-Seal. McGill-Queens University Press, the country's second largest university press, has retained an editorial office, but the printing and distribution of books with the McGill-Queens imprint is done by the only Canadian academic press of any size, University of Toronto Press.

The eighties, however, has seen a growing interest in Canadian writing outside of the country. University courses in Canadian literature are being given in parts of Europe and the United States, and Canadian authors are now being included in anthologies of world literature. Although the economics of size will likely continue to hinder the publishing of new Canadian authors, international publishing will promote the best authors and expose them to a larger intellectual and financial market. One hopes the writers will remain distinctively Canadian while speaking with an equal voice in the international literary forum. Whatever the future for Canadian literature, it is nonetheless certain that the period during which flourished the talents of Margaret Laurence, Robertson Davies, Al Purdy, Alice Munro, Richard B. Wright, and Michael Ondaatje will be known, as Wright Morris has said of the American twenties, as that huge season.

APPENDIX A

Guide to Other Canadian Writers

Milton Acorn (b. 1923). Native to Prince Edward Island, Acorn has described himself as "a carpenter, a socialist and a poet." In the sixties he read his work in coffee houses across the country and helped to found underground newspapers in the larger cities. His poetry in such collections as *In Love and Anger* (1956) and *I've Tasted My Blood* (1970) is marked by idealism and compassion for people.

Margaret Atwood (b. 1939). The most prominent figure in Canadian literature during the 1970s, Atwood is the author of a controversial book on Canadian literature titled *Survival* and several novels and collections of poems with a feminist slant, including *Power Politics, Surfacing,* and *Life before Man.*

Fred Bodsworth (b. 1918). Works like Bodsworth's *The Last of the Curlews* (1963) and *The Sparrow's Fall* (1967) are distinguished by their sharp understanding of animal behavior and belong to a significant tradition of animal stories in Canada.

George Bowering (b. 1935). As a student at the University of British Columbia, Bowering was one of the editors of *Tish*, a poetry magazine influenced by poets associated with North Carolina's Black Mountain College. In such collections as *The Gangs of Kosmos* and *Rocky Mountain Foot* (both 1969) Bowering has established himself as one of the significant postmodern poets in Canada concerned with the kinetics of perception and the poem as a unit of energy.

Frances Brooke (1724–89). An English writer who lived in Quebec for five years, Mrs. Brooke is the author of *The History of Emily Montague* (1769), a sentimental romance in the epistolary form that uses the Canadian landscape as the basis for a sensational plot. It was the first novel written in North America.

Morley Callaghan (b. 1903). Because of a friendship with Hemingway, Callaghan has enjoyed an international reputation; certainly his memoir *That Summer in Paris* (1963) is one of the best accounts of the twenties expatriates. The purpose of his fiction, however, is very different from Hemingway's. His best novels, *Such Is My Beloved* (1934), *They Shall Inherit the Earth* (1935), and *More Joy in Heaven* (1937) are Christian parables about man's urgent need for secure moral values in a turbulent world.

Bliss Carman (1861–1929). The most Romantic and the least disciplined of the Confederation poets, Carman is best known for a handful of highly musical poems, most of which are found in his first two collections, *Low Tide on Grand Pré* (1893) and *Songs of Vagabondia* (1894).

Emily Carr (1871–1945). One of Canada's foremost painters, British Columbia's Emily Carr was also a writer whose sketches and journals give her a small but permanent place in the country's literature. *Klee Wyck* (1941) is a series of tales and sketches about the West Coast Indians, *Growing Pains* (1946) her autobiography.

Philip Child (1898–1978). Novelist, poet, and teacher, Child was one of the gentle humanists of Canadian letters. His best work is a World War I novel titled *God's Sparrows* (1936).

Fred Cogswell (b. 1917). New Brunswick teacher, translator, and editor of *The Fiddlehead* (one of the finest and most durable little magazines in Canada), Cogswell is the author of several volumes of verse which celebrate the stoic virtues of life in a harsh country with a compassion and irony reminiscent of E. A. Robinson. His first collection, *The Stunted Strong* (1954), is one of his best.

Leonard Cohen (b. 1934). A popular Montreal songwriter and novelist in the sixties, Cohen is known for the erotic idealism that characterizes such poetry collections as *The Spice-Box of Earth* (1961) and *The Energy of Slaves* (1972) and the novel *Beautiful Losers* (1966).

Ralph Connor (1860–1937). Connor was the pseudonym for Charles Wilson Gordon, a Presbyterian minister whose novels of muscular Christianity on the western frontier—*Black Rock* (1898), *Sky Pilot* (1899), and others—gained enormous international sales. His Glengarry novels, of greater literary merit, describe the Ontario lumber settlements Connor knew as a child. The *Man from Glengarry* (1901) and *Glengarry School Days* (1902) are still widely read.

Isabella Valancy Crawford (1850?–87). Little is known about this writer, who lived in poverty in Toronto and published only one book of poems, *Old Spookses' Pass, Malcolm's Katie, and Other Poems* (1884). Northrop Frye, however, has identified Crawford as Canada's first myth-making poet, and it is on that level that her best narrative poems such as "Gisli, the Chieftain" and "Malcolm's Katie" should be read.

Mazo de la Roche (1879–1961). This Ontario novelist won international audiences with *Jalna* (1927) and sequel volumes about the Whiteoak family. These books are high-quality escapist entertainment; they are also faithful to a quaint Canadian ideal of preserving an ancestral British way of life in the colonies.

James De Mille (1833–80). This Maritime author and classics professor is remembered for a utopian adventure story, *A Strange Manuscript Found in a Copper Cylinder* (1888). The novel is set in a South Polar land of cannibals who worship darkness, poverty, and death and constitutes a satire on the extremes of human behavior.

Sara Jeannette Duncan (1861–1922). The only Canadian practitioner of social realism in the manner of W. D. Howells, Duncan is remembered for *The Imperialist* (1904), an examination of the society and politics of a small Ontario town in the nineteenth century.

David Freeman (b. 1944). In *Creeps* and *Battering Ram*, produced in the seventies, this Toronto dramatist examines the plight of the handicapped in modern society.

David French (b. 1939). In such plays as *Leaving Home* and *Of the Fields, Lately*, this Toronto-based dramatist deals with the theme of "love unsatisfied" in a family of Newfoundland expatriates.

Mavis Gallant (b. 1922). An expatriate Montreal writer who lives in France, Gallant has been a frequent contributor of fiction to the *New Yorker* and is the author of such story collections as *My Heart Is Broken* (1964) and *Tales from the Fifteenth District* (1979). The short novel *Green Water, Green Sky* (1959) is a classic study of emotional alienation.

Hugh Garner (1913–80). Urban realism characterizes the fiction of Garner, who writes about his native area of Toronto in *Cabbagetown* (1950) and *Silence on the Shore* (1962). He is most highly praised as a short story writer and can be seen at his best in *The Yellow Sweater and Other Stories* (1952).

John Glassco (1909–81). The translator of major French-Canadian works, including *The Journal of Saint-Denys-Garneau*, Quebec author Glassco is also known for his *Memoirs of Montparnasse* (1970), a vivid account of a three-month visit to Paris during the 1920s. His *Selected Poems* (1971) won the Governor General's Literary Award.

Oliver Goldsmith (1794–1864). Grandnephew and namesake of the British poet, this New Brunswick writer published *The Rising Village* (1825), an optimistic reply to his uncle's famous poem. Pioneer life is described as rude but full of promise.

Ralph Gustafson (b. 1909). Gustafson is highly regarded as a poet, anthologist, and critic. The editor of *The Penguin Book of Canadian Verse* (1958), Gustafson has published his own work in *The Golden Chalice* (1935), *Rivers among Rocks* (1960), and *Fire on Stone* (1974).

Charles Yale Harrison (1898–1954). This author's novel, *Generals Die in Bed* (1930), is frequently described as the best novel in English to come out of the First World War. The harrowing eyewitness account of combat is presented in documentary fashion, without sentiment and only indirectly with moral judgment.

Samuel Hearne (1745–1792). One of Canada's most famous explorers, Hearne wrote an account of his eighteen-month journey across the Barren Lands, traveling with a band of Chipeweyan Indians in search of copper for the Hudson's Bay Company. This record of extraordinary hardships and privations was published posthumously in London as *A Journey from Prince of Wales Fort in Hudson's Bay to the Northern Ocean* (1795).

Charles Heavysege (1816–1876). An obscure, English-born cabinetmaker, Heavysege, living in Montreal, wrote neo-Elizabethan closet dramas on biblical themes. *Saul* (1857) and *Jephtha's Daughter* (1865) are his most accomplished works.

Hugh Hood (b. 1928). Hood is engaged in a projected twelve-volume fictional study of life in Canada in the twentieth century, titled *The New Age*. His short stories have been published in such collections as *Flying a Red Kite* (1962).

Anna Brownell Jameson (1794–1860). This fashionable English author came to Canada to arrange a settlement with her estranged husband, the attorney general of Upper Canada, and subsequently published an account of her visit, *Winter Studies and Summer Rambles* (1838), an interesting book of travel and observations from a feminist point of view.

D. G. Jones (b. 1929). The author of several collections of verse, including *The Sun is Axeman* (1961) and *Phrases from Orpheus* (1967), Jones is a lyric poet whose frequently mythologized subjects explore contemporary themes of communication and isolation.

William Kirby (1817–1906). Kirby's *The Golden Dog* (1877), set in preconquest Quebec, is the most popular historical romance written in Canada. Kirby lived in Niagara, but the ancien régime of Quebec for him best exemplified an ideal conservative Canadian way of life.

Raymond Knister (1899–1932). Ontario writer Knister died before his talent had matured, but his novel *White Narcissus* (1929) and a handful of short stories suggest that his painter-poet's style would have eventually given his work distinction.

Robert Kroetsch (b. 1927). Alberta-born novelist and university professor, Kroetsch has lived and worked in the United States and has been influenced there by the writers of postmodern fiction. The fragmented, self-referring mythic structures of this kind of novel can be found in *Gone Indian* (1973) and *Badlands* (1976). An earlier, exuberant novel titled *The Studhorse Man* (1969) remains a popular favorite.

Patrick Lane (b. 1939). A manual laborer and inveterate traveler, British Columbia poet Lane has published several collections, including *Mountain Oysters* (1971) and *Albino Pheasants* (1977). All his poems are characterized by a compassionate yet realistic view of the crude, often violent aspects of life and reveal his identification with the lower working class.

Stephen Leacock (1869–1944). English-born comic essayist, Leacock achieved an international reputation with a steady output of little humor books. His best known work, *Sunshine Sketches of a Little Town* (1912) is a satirical portrait of Orillia, Ontario, and a small classic of sentimental humor.

Dennis Lee (b. 1939). In *Civil Elegies* (1967) this Ontario poet writes about Canada's lack of national identity and moral purpose. Lee was one of the founders of Toronto's distinguished small press, House of Anansi.

Rosanna Leprohon (1829–1879). An English-Canadian heiress who married into an old French-Canadian family, Mrs. Leprohon wrote novels about aristocratic eighteenth-century Montreal. *Antoinette de Mirecourt* (1864) is a romantic parable about the evolution of a bicultural society in Canada.

Dorothy Livesay (b. 1909). Livesay has established a fine balance between writing personal, lyrical verse in the Imagist vein and narrative poetry of social commitment. Her works include *Green Pitcher* (1928), *Day and Night* (1944), *The Unquiet Bed* (1967), and *Ice Age* (1975). Her poetry is sometimes feminist and political but always reflects a great zest for living.

Malcolm Lowry (1909–1957). Because he lived sporadically in Vancouver from 1939 until 1954, English-born Lowry is sometimes identified as a Canadian author. *Under the Volcano* (1947), Lowry's masterpiece, takes place in Mexico, but many of the short stories contained in *Hear Us O Lord from Heaven Thy Dwelling Place* (1961) are set in British Columbia.

Thomas McCulloch (1776–1843). A Scottish Presbyterian minister in Pictou, Nova Scotia, McCulloch wrote a series of fictional letters for the *Acadian Recorder* (1821–22) attacking the thriftlessness and dissipation of the local citizenry. These satirical sketches were published posthumously in 1860 as *The Stepsure Letters*.

Hugh MacLennan (b. 1907). In *Barometer Rising* (1941) and *Two Solitudes* (1945) this classics and English professor at McGill University has written the first serious Canadian novels to take the national identity as their subject. The relationship of father and son is more central to subsequent novels such as *Each Man's Son* (1951).

Eli Mandel (b. 1922). In his early poems, under the influence of Northrop Frye, Mandel translates personal filial anxieties into the minotaur myth, but in later pieces found in *An Idiot Joy* (1967) he throws off traditional masks and becomes more openly the modern poet in search of himself as a man.

W. O. Mitchell (b. 1914). In *Who Has Seen the Wind* (1947) this western novelist from Saskatchewan has written one of the country's finest books about growing up on the prairie.

Lucy Maude Montgomery (1874–1942). Born and raised in Prince Edward Island, Montgomery is the author of *Anne of Green Gables* (1908), a regional idyll that has become a children's classic.

Farley Mowat (b. 1921). This peripatetic wilderness writer is best known for *Never Cry Wolf* (1963), a study of two doomed Arctic wolves, and *A Whale for the Killing* (1972), the story of a giant fin whale trapped in a pond along the Newfoundland coast, where it is tormented to death by sportsmen in power boats.

John Newlove (b. 1938). In his poems Newlove becomes a twentieth century everyman whose weaknesses are mercilessly exposed and whose cynicism and despair implicate the whole of society. His books include *Moving in Alone* (1965), *Black Night Window* (1968), and *Lies* (1972).

Alden Nowlan (b. 1933). In collections such as *Bread, Wine, and Salt* (1967) this Maritime poet writes with brutal honesty and deep feeling about his unhappy childhood and about the poverty of his environment.

Howard O'Hagan (1902–1982). One of the most evocative novels written in the west is O'Hagan's *Tay John* (1939), the story of a half-breed that goes back to the myths and legends of the Indians of the Yellowhead region of the Rockies.

Michael Ondaatje (b. 1943). Born in Ceylon, Ondaatje came to Canada in 1962, where he began early to publish such distinguished collections of poetry as *Dainty Monsters* (1967) and *Rat Jelly* (1973). His work is characterized by the ordinary illuminated by the exotic, especially the violent and fantastic.

Martha Ostenso (1900–1963). Of Scandinavian descent, Ostenso is known chiefly as a minor American novelist, but *Wild Geese* (1925), her first and most successful fiction, is set in Manitoba, where she lived from 1915 to 1921. *Wild Geese* is an early example of western realism.

P. K. Page (b. 1917). English-born poet and painter, Page has written poems of social protest, but her best pieces focus on individual alienation and disillusionment. *The Metal and the Flower* (1954) and *Cry Ararat!* (1967) are two collections of her carefully crafted poems.

James Reaney (b. 1926). Poet, short story writer, and playwright, Reaney has been particularly interested in the creative imagination of the child and the repressed adolescent. His plays include *The Kildeer*, *The Easter Egg*, and a distinguished trilogy about the Donnelleys, a nineteenth-century Irish family who lived in Reaney's southwestern Ontario.

John Richardson (1796–1852). Born on the Niagara frontier and a soldier in the War of 1812, Major Richardson wrote a lively historical romance titled *Wacousta* (1832) about an earlier frontier battle, Pontiac's siege of Detroit in 1763.

Mordecai Richler (b. 1931). One of the most persistent critics of Canadian society, Richler writes novels that effectively combine satire and autobiography. Montreal Jewish life is the subject of his exuberant masterpiece, *The Apprenticeship of Duddy Kravitz* (1959).

Gwen Pharis Ringwood (b. 1910). Beginning in the late 1930s, this western playwright wrote ten realistic plays, including *Still Stands the House* and *Dark Harvest*, which are set in rural Alberta and focus on strained family relations during the depression.

Charles G. D. Roberts (1860–1943). With the publication of over sixty books and a literary career that took him to New York and London, Roberts enjoyed an international reputation as a poet and novelist which culminated with his being knighted in 1935. However, only a few descriptive landscape poems and a handful of animal stories are read with interest today. *In Divers Tones* (1886) and *Songs of the Common Day* (1893) contain his best verse.

W. W. E. Ross (1894–1966). In *Laconics* (1930) Ross reduced poems to their essentials, their bare bones, in the manner of the Imagists. His work was later honored in a collection titled *Experiment* (1956), published by a group of younger poets.

George Ryga (b. 1932). Considered one of the most successful dramatists in English Canada, this Alberta author of Ukrainian background, writes with compassion of minority peoples and society's oppressed. His masterpiece, *The Ecstasy of Rita Joe*, examines the plight of Indians who leave the reserve to live in the city.

Laura Goodman Salverson (1890–1970). The daughter of Icelandic immigrants, Salverson wrote idealistic novels about pioneering in northern Manitoba. Although *The Viking Heart* (1923) is her most popular book, her autobiography, *Confessions of an Immigrant's Daughter* (1939), is worthy of attention for its realistic account of pioneer life.

Duncan Campbell Scott (1862–1947). With Ottawa's Department of Indian Affairs for more than fifty years, Scott was a Victorian poet whose best verse was inspired by his work with the Indians and his direct experience of the northern wilderness. One of the Confederation poets, Scott published his first book, *The*

Magic House and Other Poems, in 1893 and brought out a major collection titled *Poems* in 1923.

F. R. Scott (b. 1899). A distinguished professor of constitutional law at McGill University, Scott was also one of the poets who brought the forces of modernism to bear on Canadian writing. His Imagist landscape poems, his satires, and poems embodying his social idealism can be found in such collections as *Overture* (1945), *The Eye of the Needle* (1957), and *Selected Poems* (1966).

Robert Service (1874–1958). Originally from England, Service was the troubadour of the Yukon gold rush days, best remembered for such pieces as "The Shooting of Dan McGrew" and "The Cremation of Sam McGee," published in *Songs of a Sourdough* (1907).

A. J. M. Smith (1902–1980). Poet, teacher, critic, anthologizer, Smith was the leader of the young Montreal poets in the late twenties who challenged literary nationalism and argued for the cosmopolitan values of the modernist movement. His early Imagist poem, "The Lonely Land," is probably anthologized more than any other Canadian poem. His collections include *News From the Phoenix* (1943) and *A Sort of Ecstasy* (1954).

Raymond Souster (b. 1921). In this Toronto poet's verse there is a quiet but genuine pity for the victims of social inequalities. In such collections as *The Colour of the Times* (1962) and *Lost and Found* (1968) Souster, like William Carlos Williams, is concerned with actualities rather than life's mythic or symbolic dimensions.

R. J. C. Stead (1880–1959). A prairie realist, Stead is known for *Grain* (1926), a novel which describes the life of an unexceptional farm boy who does not dream of a better, more fulfilling life elsewhere but is needlessly driven from the farm by social pressures.

Catharine Parr Traill (1802–1899). Unlike her sister Susanna Moodie, Traill approached emigration and pioneering as an adventure and gave an optimistic account of her experience in letters to her mother, published as *The Backwoods of Canada*

(1836), and to other prospective emigrants in *The Canadian Settler's Guide* (1855).

Miriam Waddington (b. 1917). The nature of love, especially the joys and frustrations of sexual love, are Waddington's chief theme in such poetry collections as *The Season's Lovers* (1958) and *Say Yes* (1969). Her first collection, *Green World* (1945), however, is concerned with the evils and ugliness of industrial society.

Sheila Watson (b. 1919). Watson is the author of *The Double Hook* (1959), the story of a mountain family written in an experimental, poetic style wherein perception is action.

Phyllis Webb (b. 1927). In such collections as *The Sea Is Also a Garden* (1962), *Naked Poems* (1965), and *Wilson's Bowl* (1980) this British Columbia poet writes in a meticulously crafted style about pain, loss, and death and is also self-consciously preoccupied with language as the medium of presenting these experiences.

Rudy Wiebe (b. 1934). This Alberta novelist writes about Mennonite society in *Peace Shall Destroy Many* (1962) and about the disappearance of the Indian way of life in *The Temptations of Big Bear* (1973).

Adele Wiseman (b. 1928). A member of a Ukrainian-Jewish family in Winnipeg, Wiseman is the author of *The Sacrifice* (1956), one of the most successful novels about the immigrant experience in Canada.

Richard B. Wright (b. 1937). With the satirist's keen eye for pretension and hypocrisy, Ontario novelist Wright has written novels, including *The Weekend Man* (1971) and *In the Middle of a Life* (1973), which expose the threadbare values of contemporary urban life. Beneath the comic surface of Wright's books there is a mordant, all-pervasive nihilism.

The Governor General's Awards

The Governor General's Literary Awards were instituted in 1936 by the Canadian Authors' Association to honor the accomplishments of distinguished English-Canadian writers. In 1959 the Canada Council assumed responsibility for the awards, and a French-language section was added. There have always been three basic categories: fiction, nonfiction, and poetry / drama. In 1981 poetry and drama were given separate categories. Initially the winners received a medal, but that was changed to a specially bound copy of the author's winning book. After the Canada Council took over, a cash prize was given as well.

Fiction

1936
Bertrand Booker
Think of the Earth

1937
Laura Goodman Salverson
The Dark Weaver

1938
Gwethalyn Graham
The Swiss Sonata

1939
Franklin D. McDowell
The Champlain Road

1940
Philippe Panneton (Ringuet)
Thirty Acres (translation)

1941
Alan Sullivan
Three Came to Ville Marie

1942
G. Herbert Sallans
Little Man

1943
Thomas H. Raddall
The Pied Piper of Dipper Creek

1944
Gwethalyn Graham
Earth and High Heaven

1945
Hugh MacLennan
Two Solitudes

1946
Winifred Bambrick
Continental Review

1947
Gabrielle Roy
The Tin Flute (translation)

1948
Hugh MacLennan
The Precipice

1949
Philip Child
Mr. Ames against Time

1950
Germaine Guèvremont
The Outlander (translation)

1951
Morley Callaghan
The Loved and the Lost

1952
David Walker
The Pillar

1953
David Walker
Digby

1954
Igor Gouzenko
The Fall of a Titan

1955
Lionel Shapiro
The Sixth of June

1956
Adele Wiseman
The Sacrifice

1957
Gabrielle Roy
Street of Riches (translation)

1958
Colin McDougall
Execution

1959
Hugh MacLennan
The Watch That Ends the Night

1960
Brian Moore
The Luck of Ginger Coffey

1961
Malcolm Lowry
Hear Us O Lord from Heaven Thy Dwelling Place

1962
Kildare Dobbs
Running to Paradise

1963
Hugh Garner
Hugh Garner's Best Stories

1964
Douglas LePan
The Deserter

1965
No award

1966
Margaret Laurence
A Jest of God

1967
No award

1968
Alice Munro
Dance of the Happy Shades
Mordecai Richler
Cocksure

1969
Robert Kroetsch
The Studhorse Man

1970
David Godfrey
The New Ancestors

1971
Mordecai Richler
St. Urbain's Horseman

1972
Robertson Davies
The Manticore

1973
Rudy Wiebe
The Temptations of Big Bear

1974
Margaret Laurence
The Diviners

1975
Brian Moore
The Great Victorian Collection

1976
Marian Engel
Bear

1977
Timothy Findley
The Wars

1978
Alice Munro
Who Do You Think You Are?

1979
Jack Hodgins
The Resurrection of Joseph Bourne

1980
George Bowering
Burning Water

1981
Mavis Gallant
Home Truths

1982
Guy Vanderhaeghe
Man Descending

Poetry / Drama

1936
No award

1937
E. J. Pratt
The Fable of the Goats

1938
Kenneth Leslie
By Stubborn Stars

1939
Arthur S. Bourinot
Under the Sun

1940
E. J. Pratt
Brebeuf and His Brethren

1941
Anne Marriott
Calling Adventurers

1942
Earle Birney
David and Other Poems

1943
A. J. M. Smith
News of the Phoenix

1944
Dorothy Livesay
Day and Night

1945
Earle Birney
Now Is Time

1946
Robert Finch
Poems

1947
Dorothy Livesay
Poems for People

1948
A. M. Klein
*The Rocking Chair and
Other Poems*

1949
James Reaney
The Red Heart

1950
James Wreford Watson
Of Time and the Lover

1951
Charles Bruce
The Mulgrave Road

1952
E. J. Pratt
Towards the Last Spike

1953
Douglas LePan
The Net and the Sword

1954
P. K. Page
The Metal and the Flower

1955
Wilfred Watson
Friday's Child

1956
Robert A. D. Ford
A Window on the North

1957
Jay Macpherson
The Boatman

1958
James Reaney
A Suit of Nettles

1959
Irving Layton
Red Carpet for the Sun

1960
Margaret Avison
Winter Sun

1961
Robert Finch
Acis in Oxford

1962
James Reaney
The Killdeer and Other Plays
Twelve Letters to a Small Town

1963
No award

1964
Raymond Souster
The Colour of the Times

1965
Al Purdy
The Cariboo Horses

1966
Margaret Atwood
The Circle Game

1967
Eli Mandel
An Idiot Joy
Alden Nowlan
Bread, Wine, and Salt

1968
Leonard Cohen
Selected Poems, 1956–68

1969
George Bowering
Rocky Mountain Foot
The Gangs of Kosmos
Gwendolyn MacEwen
The Shadow-Maker

1970
B. P. Nichol
Still Water
Beach Head
The True Eventual Story of

Billy the Kid
*The Cosmic Chef: An Evening
of Concrete*
Michael Ondaatje
*The Collected Works of Billy
the Kid*

1971
John Glassco
Selected Poems

1972
Dennis Lee
Civil Elegies and Other Poems
John Newlove
Lies

1973
Miriam Mandel
Lions at Her Face

1974
Ralph Gustafson
Fire on Stone

1975
Milton Acorn
The Island Means Minago

1976
Joe Rosenblatt
Top Soil

1977
D. G. Jones
*Under the Thunder the Flowers
Light up the Earth*

1978
Patrick Lane
Poems New and Selected

1979
Michael Ondaatje
*There's a Trick with a Knife I'm
Learning to Do*

1980
Stephen Scobie
McAlmon's Chinese Opera

1981
F. R. Scott
Collected Poems
Sharon Pollock
Blood Relations and Other Plays

1982
John Gray
Billy Bishop Goes to War [drama]
Phyllis Webb
The Vision Tree [poetry]

Selected Bibliography

Important works on individual authors are cited in the footnotes for each essay. The titles listed below are more general books of Canadian literary criticism, including histories, thematic studies, and interviews with individual authors.

Atwood, Margaret. *Survival: A Thematic Guide to Canadian Literature*. Toronto: Anansi, 1972.

Brown, E. K. *On Canadian Poetry*. 1943. Rev. ed. Ottawa: Tecumseh Press, 1973.

Cameron, Donald. *Conversations with Canadian Novelists*. Toronto: Macmillan, 1972.

Frye, Northrop. *The Bush Garden: Essays on the Canadian Imagination*. Toronto: Anansi, 1971.

Gibson, Graeme. *Eleven Canadian Novelists*. Toronto: Anansi, 1973.

Harrison, Dick. *Unnamed Country: The Struggle for a Canadian Prairie Fiction*. Edmonton: University of Alberta Press, 1977.

Jones, D. G. *Butterfly on Rock: A Study of Themes and Images in Canadian Literature*. Toronto: University of Toronto Press, 1970.

Klinck, Carl, ed. *Literary History of Canada*. New ed. 3 vols. Toronto: University of Toronto Press, 1976.

MacMechan, Archibald M. *Headwaters of Canadian Literature*. Toronto: McClelland and Stewart, 1924.

Mandel, Eli, ed. *Contexts of Canadian Criticism*. Chicago: University of Chicago Press, 1971.

Marshall, Tom. *Harsh and Lovely Land: The Major Canadian Poets and the Making of a Canadian Tradition*. Vancouver: University of British Columbia Press, 1979.

McCourt, Edward. *The Canadian West in Fiction*. 1949. Rev. ed. Toronto: McGraw-Hill Ryerson, 1970.

Moss, John. *Patterns of Isolation in English Canadian Fiction*. Toronto: McClelland and Stewart, 1974.

———. *A Reader's Guide to the Canadian Novel*. Toronto: McClelland and Stewart, 1981.

————. *Sex and Violence in the Canadian Novel: The Ancestral Present*. Toronto: McClelland and Stewart, 1977.

New, William H. *Articulating West: Essays on Purpose and Form in Modern Canadian Literature*. Toronto: New Press, 1972.

Northey, Margot. *The Haunted Wilderness: The Gothic and Grotesque in Canadian Fiction*. Toronto: University of Toronto Press, 1976.

Pacey, Desmond. *Creative Writing in Canada: A Short History of English-Canadian Literature*. Toronto: McGraw-Hill Ryerson, 1961.

————. *Ten Canadian Poets: A Group of Biographical and Critical Essays*. Toronto: Ryerson, 1968.

Ricou, Laurence. *Vertical Man / Horizontal World: Man and Landscape in Canadian Prairie Fiction*. Vancouver: University of British Columbia, 1973.

Staines, David, ed. *The Canadian Imagination: Dimensions of a Literary Culture*. Cambridge, Mass.: Harvard University Press, 1977.

Stephens, Donald G., ed. *Writers of the Prairies*. Vancouver: University of British Columbia Press, 1973.

Story, Norah. *The Oxford Companion to Canadian History and Literature*. Toronto: Oxford University Press, 1967.

Waterston, Elizabeth. *Survey: A Short History of Canadian Literature*. Toronto: Methuen, 1973.

Wilson, Edmund. *O Canada: An American's Notes on Canadian Culture*. New York: Farrar, Straus & Giroux, 1965.

Woodcock, George. *Odysseus Ever Returning: Essays on Canadian Writers and Writing*. Toronto: McClelland and Stewart, 1970.

Index

Major discussions of authors appear on the pages shown in italic.